Materializing Queer Desire

MATERIALIZING QUEER DESIRE

Oscar Wilde to Andy Warhol

ELISA GLICK

SUNY
PRESS

Published by
State University of New York Press, Albany

Printed in the United States of America

For information, contact State University of New York Press, Albany, NY
www.sunypress.edu

Production, Robert Puchalik
Marketing, Michael Campochiaro

Library of Congress Cataloging-in-Publication Data

Glick, Elisa.
Materializing queer desire : Oscar Wilde to Andy Warhol / Elisa Glick.
p. cm.
Includes bibliographical references and index.
ISBN 978-1-4384-2725-6 (alk. paper)
ISBN 978-1-4384-2726-3 (pbk. : alk. paper)
1. Homosexuality and literature. 2. Dandyism in literature. 3. Queer theory. I. Title.
PN56.H57G56 2009
809'.933352664—dc22

2008047580

10 9 8 7 6 5 4 3 2 1

In memory of my grandmother,

Mary Feld

Contents

ILLUSTRATIONS

Acknowledgments

This book had its origins in my dissertation, "Modern Love: Queer Subjects and the Contradictions of Modernity," which I wrote at Brown University under the direction and guidance of Ellen Rooney, Neil Lazarus, Nancy Armstrong, and Carolyn Dean. I am indebted to each and every one of them for their intellectual generosity, inspiration, and insights, which made it possible for me to write this project at its earliest and most crucial stage.

I am grateful to the many friends, colleagues, and mentors who helped me in various ways with this book, including Sam Bullington, Rebecca Dingo, Kevin Floyd, Rosemary Hennessy, Sharon Holland, James Holstun, Valerie Kaussen, Jonathan Katz, Jackie Litt, Janet Lyon, Ellie Ragland, Robert Scholes, and Jeffrey J. Williams. My wonderful friends Mark Meyers, Gautam Premnath, and Kasturi Ray were a tremendous help to me at various stages of this project's development; my work benefited greatly from their comments, encouragement, and readings. I owe a very special debt to Laurie Mintz, whose generosity and wisdom have forever changed my life and work.

For their assistance with research, permissions, or illustrations, I thank John W. Smith, former archivist at the Andy Warhol Museum; Geralyn Huxley and Greg Pierce of the Andy Warhol Museum; Anne Barker of the University of Missouri Library; Carmen Beck of Lincoln University Library; Owen Pillion; Penny Smith-Parris; Jessica Jennrich; and Mark Lehman. Extra special thanks to Greg Burchard of the Andy Warhol Museum.

I am grateful to the following for their kind permission to reproduce these illustrations: © The Andy Warhol Foundation for the Visual Arts/ARS, New York: Figures 6.1, 6.2, 6.3, 6.4, 6.6, 6.7; the Andy Warhol Museum: Figure 6.5; Adam Wallacavage: Figure A.1; Sarah Kate Watson: Figure A.2.

An earlier version of chapter 1 appeared in *Cultural Critique* 48 (Spring 2001): 129–63. Chapter 4 first appeared as "Harlem's Queer Dandy: African American Modernism and the Artifice of Blackness" in *Modern Fiction Studies* 49.3 (Fall 2003) [Special Issue: Racechange and the Fictions of Identity]: 414–42.

I am grateful to my terrific editor, Larin McLaughlin, for believing in this project and providing me with invaluable assistance through the various stages of its development. I wish to thank the anonymous readers at SUNY Press, who each helped me to sharpen and more clearly articulate my argument. On the production side, I would like to express my appreciation to Kelli W. LeRoux, Robert Puchalik, and my copyeditor, Rosemary Wellner, for their excellent work readying this book for publication.

Finally, I extend a heartfelt thank you to my wonderful mother, who has taught me much more than she realizes. I could not have written this book without the faith, love, and unflagging support of my partner, Carolyn Sullivan, who helped me through the process every step of the way with patience and good humor—even when I was in short supply of both. My dearest thanks and deepest love go to her. This book is dedicated to the memory of my beloved grandmother, Mary Feld. I miss you. The gift of your love has meant more than I could ever express.

Introduction

What is the relationship between homosexuality, cultural modernism, and modernity? How does the queer subject come to occupy such a central and, in many respects, contradictory place in the modern world? What role does capitalism play in the development of modern gay and lesbian identities? This book takes up these questions by using the figure of the dandy to propose a theory of how and why gay and lesbian subjects became heroes of modern life.[1] My analysis focuses on six icons of modernism: the nineteenth-century, Wildean dandy; the fin-de-siècle decadent Sapphist; the "mannish" lesbian dandy; the queer, black dandy of the Harlem Renaissance; the gutter dandy or queer junkie in cold war America; and the Warholian "Pop" dandy. Oscar Wilde and Andy Warhol are bookends for my project because both use tropes of dandyism to show how the "secret" of the commodity produces (in different ways, in different times, and on different levels) modern gay identity as a dialectical contradiction between the "seen" and the "unseen"—what Michel Foucault has famously described as "the open secret."

But how, I ask, did homosexuality and secrecy become entangled in the first place? How has queer identity come to be defined as a paradox of visibility? When I first posed these questions it seemed logical to turn to the late nineteenth-century medicalization of homosexuality, which ushered in an era of new visibility for marginalized and "perverse" sexualities. For the story of the invention of the homosexual is usually told within the context of the rise of late nineteenth-century sexology. In Foucault's well-known formulation in *The History of Sexuality*, the religious category of "sodomite" was transformed into the medical and psychiatric category of "homosexual" by sexologists such as Richard von Krafft-Ebing and Havelock Ellis. What had once been an immoral act that any sinner might indulge in was transformed in 1868 into an abnormal identity characterized by a congenital "hermaphrodism of the soul." As Foucault famously puts it, "the homosexual was now a species" (43). But why did doctors define a norm through sexuality at this particular historical moment? Foucault himself asks but never answers a crucial question: was the creation of the homosexual and other perverse sexual types "motivated by one basic concern: to ensure population, to reproduce labor capacity, to perpetuate the form of social relations: in short, to constitute a sexuality that is economically useful and politically conservative?" (36–37).

This book responds to Foucault's question by demonstrating that theories of sexuality and theories of the commodity have been mutually invested since the late nineteenth century. Rather than seeing the medical and psychiatric invention of the homosexual and the new boom in production and consumption as discrete events, this study theorizes the emergence of gay/lesbian identity—particularly the dandy's aestheticized cultivation of enjoyment—in relation to capitalism's increasing investment in producing and regulating desire and pleasure.[2] Historians and theorists of sexuality have demonstrated that two seemingly paradoxical developments—the destabilization of gender boundaries and reification of sexuality into the narrow and oppositional hetero/homo binary—were overdetermined by political, economic, and social shifts distinctive to the late nineteenth century (Birken; Chauncey; Dean *Sexuality*; D'Emilio; D'Emilio and Freedman; Hennessy; Katz). These shifts were primarily but not exclusively grounded in the contradictions of capitalist production, which sought both to produce desire and control the "unruly" possibilities it engendered (Hennessy 102). I therefore regard the gay subject as emerging out of the specifically modern, capitalist contradiction between the public world of production and industry and the private world of consumption and pleasure. Although recent scholarship has argued that the rise of consumer culture (or the "consumer revolution") can be traced to the eighteenth century or even earlier, the widespread distribution of "consumer goods" does not single-handedly facilitate the production of uniquely modern types of consuming and desiring subjects.[3] The late nineteenth-century reorganization of social life around consumerism made the commodity and its contradictions the focal point of a new world order, engendering a distinctly modern epistemology of the subject. It is not until 1870 that the rise of mass markets, mass media, and advertising "displaced unmet needs into new desires," creating an apparent contradiction between rationalization and reification and modernity's disruptive and unlimited expansion of desire (Hennessy 99). Furthermore, the historical opposition between production and consumption took on a new significance with the advent of industrialism and mass consumption, which both consolidated and extended capitalism's fundamental division between appearance and essence.[4]

The well-known formulation of homosexuality as an "open secret"—a paradoxical synthesis of invisibility and visibility—links the logic of the queer to the logic of the commodity, making gay and lesbian identity a privileged emblem for capitalism's contradiction between hidden, inner relations and the visibility of outward appearances. In his theory of commodity fetishism, Karl Marx famously describes this split between what appears to be and what really is as the "secret" of the commodity-form; in other words, the commodity's "mysterious" character is the result of a system of exchange that mystifies social relations, so that relations between people take the form of relations between things. Marx locates the historically specific experience of alienation in this social reality, in which commodities control the producers instead of being controlled by them. Building on Marx's work, Georg Lukács argues that the two aspects of commodity fetishism I have just described—the essential objectification of human relations and the appearance of the independence of the world of things—penetrate all forms of subjectivity and daily life under capitalism. Lukács's analysis enables us to see that the diverse ideological effects of the commodity's universal dominance—or, as Fredric Jameson puts it, the "strategies of containment" capitalism necessitates—"can be unmasked only by confrontation with the ideal of totality which they at once imply and repress" (*Political Unconscious* 53).[5] As my study seeks to demonstrate, the commodity's drive to dominate the culture of modernity—which engenders the phenomenon of reification—is still the "specific problem for our age, the age of modern capitalism" (Lukács 84).

There is an unfortunate tendency in contemporary theory and politics to be suspicious of or even hostile to any focus on social totality, as though acknowledging the existence of a constitutive, determining structure (however complexly theorized) inevitably erases or subsumes difference, particularity, and asymmetry. But social totalities always exist in and through their connections with multiple complexes; they are not undifferentiated wholes (Mészáros 65). Recognizing the centrality of the logic of commodification in modern social life is not equivalent to conceptualizing capitalism as monolithic or fetishizing economics as mechanistically all-determining. In fact, the Marxist concept of dialectics famously critiques the economic determinism of political economy by positing that the totality of capitalist society can only be grasped in specific and complex mediations (or interconnections) that are always changing.[6] Building on this dialectical approach, I seek to open up a space for thinking about the connectedness of concepts and categories that are usually divorced. My goal is to theorize the multiple and complex interconnections between seemingly separate spheres of modern life, particularly the social world and the realm of personal life or "lifestyle." The dandy's heroic modernism interests me because it is not simply a glorification of lifestyle—a retreat from politics and history into a separate, personal realm of art and beauty—but rather an attempt to challenge these sedimented distinctions. Throughout this study, I pay attention to the intricate ways in which culture, the aesthetic, and the erotic are mediated by commodity relations in modern society. By examining the ongoing process of interaction between queer identity and the commodity-form, I offer a rethinking of those models of modernity that separate the aesthetic/erotic from the economic, and models that render the first set of terms epiphenomenal.

My effort to capture the complex interrelation of culture and society draws upon a major insight of the Frankfurt school: culture must be regarded as a site of social production that is neither epiphenomenal nor fully autonomous (Jay 54). Following this line of thinking—which seeks to bridge social divisions—I do not characterize modern capitalist society as inauthentic or reductively repressive, nor do I regard modernity fatalistically.[7] At various points in this study, I demonstrate the positive possibilities for queer cultural and artistic production to revalue the erotic and reconfigure categories like "reification," "blackness," and "commodity aesthetics." Nevertheless, my project is not to show how gay and lesbian people subvert or otherwise challenge the exigencies of capitalist oppression. Although queerness is not represented here as only or primarily a disruptive force in modern culture, I do not theorize gay and lesbian identities or queer artistic production as simply effects of capitalist reification, where the latter is conceptualized in empirical rather than dialectical terms. To the contrary, my readings of artists such as Renée Vivien, William S. Burroughs, and Andy Warhol demonstrate that queer aesthetics can and do offer a *promesse de bonheur* in a society that commodifies desire and subordinates freedom and happiness in the name of progress.[8] This is not an utopian claim since, as Herbert Marcuse argues, the contradiction between freedom and oppression constitutes a "dialectic of liberation" at the heart of capitalism: "the apparently inseparable unity—inseparable for the system—of productivity and destruction, of satisfaction of needs and repression, of liberty within a system of servitude" ("Liberation" 280). My argument is that dandies and other queer heroes of modern life are iconic because they mobilize capitalism's simultaneous capacities for reification and liberation.

Although the *concept* of the "modern" is, as Terry Eagleton has put it, "a kind of permanent ontological possibility" that disrupts historical periodization, I use this term in the more specific sense of the modernizing project that thinkers such as Max Weber, Theodor Adorno, and Max Horkheimer have associated with the history and tradition of the Enlightenment (63). I do not believe any account or definition of "modernity" can be understood apart from the development and imperatives of capital accumulation. While it is important to recognize the analytical and sociohistorical differences between modernity and capitalism, this study will provide evidence for the ways in which these social formations are fundamentally linked. I follow Adorno and Horkheimer in viewing capitalism as—to borrow Peter Wagner's succinct formulation—"a one-dimensional elaboration of the Enlightenment promise, and thus the particular version of modernity that has become dominant" (4). Because the dialectical approach of the Frankfurt school is crucial to the theory of modernity I have been elaborating, I resist the tendency of some theorists to separate "good" and "bad" aspects of modernity. (The most famous articulation of such a separation is no doubt Habermas's "Modernity—An Incomplete Project.") My goal instead is to illuminate capitalism's fundamental and profound contradictions, which makes modernity both a simultaneously destructive and creative force, producing the paradoxical experience of modern life as repressive and progressive.

To say that capitalism and modernity are interrelated forms of social experience is not to deny that there are important reasons for maintaining the analytical distinction between these categories as well as their cultural and ideological expressions. In what follows, I do not subsume capitalism under modernity (as modernization theories tend to), nor do I subsume modernity under capitalism. While some Marxist accounts have found the latter move rather too tempting, I would argue against it. I do so not because this perspective collapses the temporal and historical specificities of these categories and so "naturalizes" capitalism, as Ellen Meiksins Wood claims, but rather because certain features of modernity—such as the rise of the modern nation-state—cannot be assimilated to capitalism, as Wood herself persuasively demonstrates. The central contradictions with which this study is concerned—appearance/essence and public/private—are actualized through particular social relations that bring into focus their manifest connections. At the same time, it is crucial to note that the contradiction between appearance and essence is produced by the capitalist mode of production, whereas the public/private split more properly belongs to the social processes of modernity, since the division of the modern world into pubic and private spheres is characteristic of the modern nation-state. The dual function of these contradictions directs our attention to my argument about homosexuality and modernity; as we shall see, the queer dandy becomes a privileged emblem of the modern by incorporating contradictions that are specific to the internal relations of both capitalism and modernity.

This understanding of queer identity enables me to address the structural basis for a key problem overlooked in the recent efflorescence of lesbian and gay studies: the simultaneous positioning of the queer subject as a privileged emblem of the modern and as a dissident in revolt against modern society. Although both lesbian and gay identities are located at the opposite poles of modernity by a wide range of theorists, cultural critics, and historians, I know of no other study that remarks upon or attempts to account for the contradictory notions of gay subjectivity that proliferate in modern culture. The figures of the lesbian and the male homosexual are depicted as, on the one hand, distinctly modern subversions of sex and gender norms and, on the other, as subjects who stand in opposition to the industrialization and commodification of modern life. My study aims to bring these opposing models of queer identity together by showing them to be inextricably bound up with each other, and inextricably bound up with the histories of capitalism and social modernity. I see gay identity itself as paradigmatic of a new and distinctly modern form of consciousness that is constructed around the public/private binary. This divided and contradictory form of subjectivity emerged in relation to the modern (particularly European) nation-state and was ultimately intensified by capitalist forces, which further estranged the "personal" from the "social" and "political." As Oscar Wilde's *The Picture of Dorian Gray* demonstrates, the queer dandy in particular is a privileged emblem for this twofold subject who is radically split between public and private. By demonstrating the interrelation of rationalization (the public world of production, market imperatives, and work) and erotics (the private world of feelings, consumption, and pleasure) in gay and lesbian identities, my study constructs a materialist account of modern queer consciousness that challenges and revises tendencies to oppose "private" eroticism and the systems of value that govern "public" interests.

My claim about the paradigmatic and contradictory place of the queer subject in modern culture is indebted to Eve Kosofsky Sedgwick's influential argument for the centrality of "the epistemology of the closet" in modern Western culture. According to Sedgwick, the figures of "the closet" and "coming out"—both uniquely indicative for homophobia in a way that is distinct from other oppressions (*Epistemology of the Closet* 75)—are the most recognizable emblems for the nexus of visibility and secrecy that makes queer identity indispensable to modern cultural organization:

> I want to argue that a lot of the energy of attention and demarcation that has swirled around issues of homosexuality since the end of the nineteenth century, in Europe and the United States, has been impelled by the distinctively indicative relation of homosexuality to wider mappings of secrecy and disclosure, and of the private and public, that were and are critically problematical for the gender, sexual, and economic structures of the heterosexist culture at large. (*Epistemology of the Closet* 71)

Sedgwick persuasively demonstrates how the pervasive, "epistemologically charged" (72) oppositions of secrecy/disclosure and public/private have a gay (particularly male) specificity. Although her work provides evidence for the importance of queerness in the construction of modern subjectivity, she does not address the context of capital and, like Foucault, she deliberately avoids positing causes for the institution of modern sexual identities (*Epistemology of the Closet*

9). Nevertheless, Sedgwick's analysis helps us to see how gay identity emerged as the embodiment of capitalist modernity's constitutive contradictions (public/private, work/play, appearance/essence), and thus became the twentieth century's most contested and yet symptomatic form of modern subjectivity.

By using the figure of the dandy to address the modern constitution of gay and lesbian subjectivities, I do not aspire to encapsulate the entirety of gay people's experiences of modernity in this project. My more specific goal is to illuminate various dialectical images of homosexuality that picture the dandy as a queer hero of modern life. I have chosen to focus my project on dandyism because it directly engages the issues that are at the conceptual center of the book—visibility, commodification, modernity, decadence, and desire—embodying a relation to capitalism that is at once rebellious and complicit. The figure of the dandy also attains a unique stature because of his centrality in accounts of modernity and homosexuality. "The last spark of heroism amid decadence," dandyism and its contradictions have defined modern gay identity since the turn of the century (Baudelaire, *Painter of Modern Life* 28–29). This is not to say that the dandy always has been gay or thought to have been gay. For Beau Brummell and the Regency dandies of the early nineteenth century, for example, there was not a clear-cut association of effeminate dandyism and same-sex desire. But, as Alan Sinfield and Ed Cohen have convincingly argued, after Oscar Wilde's trial in 1895, the effeminate dandy was linked to the homosexual in the public imagination. My study of modern dandyism begins at this moment, after which it became impossible not to think of the dandy as queer. Demonstrating the power of this cultural logic, lesbian artists—such as Natalie Barney, Romaine Brooks, Radclyffe Hall, and Renée Vivien—drew upon the traditions of dandyism and decadent aestheticism "as part of a desire to make a newly emerging lesbian identity publicly visible" (Elliott and Wallace 19).

The dandy for me is not a frozen or unchanging figure. Paying attention to questions of historical specificity and variation, I am particularly interested in highlighting the ways in which queer dandyism and capitalism have changed over time. I wish to emphasize that registering such distinctions is always, in my view, a method of mediation in and of itself. Throughout this study, I treat sexuality and the commodity-form as internally related phenomena that take different forms within the same historical and temporal process. While I strive to attend to the complexity and differentiation between and among forms of dandyism and queer desire, my goal is to articulate certain historical and theoretical consistencies through which queer dandyism's specific contradictions have been realized. I do so in an effort to grasp the consolidations and continuities of identity-political formations—not to deny difference, but to defetishize it. From this perspective, my criticism deliberately strives to materialize an apparently paradoxical theory of modern gay identity:

I offer a historicizing narrative about queer dandyism that is not grounded in a continuum of historical progress but rather in sedimented images—what Walter Benjamin has famously conceptualized as "dialectics at a standstill."[9] This means that, at certain moments in my argument, I take the risk of deprivileging contradiction's more dynamic elements in order to capture a nonnarrative dialectic that inhabits unique constellations of images.

In my effort to illuminate dialectical images of the dandy, my study combines British, French, and American literary texts, cultural history, visual culture, and critical theory from the fin de siècle to the present. I steer away from organizing my argument and readings around discrete disciplinary objects; instead, I present readers with a juxtaposition of forms, genres, traditions, and discourses that reflects my interdisciplinary approach to the study of culture. In large measure, this move is authorized by well-recognized work in modernist studies that has demonstrated the affiliations between various forms of artistic and literary modernisms as transnational phenomena. This is not to reinforce traditional accounts of modernism as the aesthetic production of a cosmopolitan, international avant-garde, since the tension between nationalism and internationalism, or the local and the global, is one fundamental feature of both modernism and modernity. Nor do I discount the complex role of national cultures and politics in the production and reception of modernist works. In fact, I am especially fascinated by distinctively American forms of cultural modernism that appear in the twentieth century—such as the Harlem Renaissance and the Beat movement—and how these movements redirect modernism's Eurocentered slant by resisting the hegemony of European avant-garde aesthetics. While my analysis focuses on aesthetic modernism, I hope the afterword's engagement with the "new dandyism" in contemporary popular culture will encourage readers to think about modernism and mass culture in dialectical terms. My interest in the tropes of dandyism is not only or simply historical, but also theoretical and political. I therefore ask readers to be mindful of the implicit interplay of past, present, and future that gives rise to the dialectical images I examine here. For it is the pressures and possibilities of the present that are contained within the last century's modern queer icons.

Conceptualizing the logic of the queer in relation to the structural contradictions of capitalism helps us to understand the intersections and affiliations between modes of cultural critique that are too often segregated in contemporary theory and politics. By investigating the connections between theories of gay/lesbian identity and theories of commodity culture, this book aims to challenge the critical commonplace that opposes class and queerness as forms of social theory and political struggle. The widening of the rift between Marxism and other elements of the left in recent years has positioned queer and Marxist theories as at best unrelated, at worst antagonistic, forms of social critique. Queer theorists, committed to a fundamentally postmodernist politics of difference and the destabilization of overarching narratives, have been suspicious of Marxism's emphasis on the determining force of class and its privileging of the economic over the erotic. In their view, this framework inevitably subordinates queer politics to the project of class struggle. Underscoring the importance of a social totality, Marxists, meanwhile, have criticized queer theorists' inattentiveness to the material determinations and social inequalities that shape all identity formations—including sexual identities—under global capitalism, making pleasure and sexual agency more available to some than others.

However, recent work by authors such as Eric O. Clarke, Kevin Floyd, Rosemary Hennessy, Matthew Tinkcom, and Amy Villarejo suggest that a distinctly queer brand of Marxism may be taking root in contemporary criticism.[10] This emergent body of criticism shares with the sociologist Henning Bech a conception of gay identity as fundamentally dialectical. In his work *When Men Meet: Homosexuality and Modernity* (Danish edition, 1987; English translation, 1997), Bech argues persuasively for the distinctive relationship between urban modernity and homosexuality, emphasizing the fundamentally dialectical character of gay identity. Although he does not link his theory of "absent homosexuality" to the commodity-form, my own analysis of queer identity as a dialectical contradiction has much in common with his view of homosexuality as a dialectic between presence and absence (Bech 38, 81). While my project draws upon Bech's insights, its more specific goal is to account for the contradictions that shape queer subjectivity.

While this book provides an argument for a materialist conception of sexuality, it does not survey scholarship that falls under the rubric of Marxist or materialist queer studies. Nor do I offer an introduction to the history of dandyism or to the various intellectual, artistic, and bohemian versions of dandyism that have dared to take beauty, pleasure, and refinement seriously since the nineteenth century. Instead, I work *within* a materialist framework to make a theoretical argument about the role of queer dandies in cultural modernism and constructions of modern subjectivity. I am invested in a dialectical method that approaches forms of cultural production immanently (from within) in order to expose what they leave unsaid: their inconsistencies, interconnections, and contradictions. This means that I strive to examine my objects of analysis on their own terms, while simultaneously linking the logic of aporias governing a particular text to the social relations that shape it. My goal is not to reconcile culture to society in any simple or reductive way, but rather to expose the complexities and irreconcilabilities of an individual work of art. I therefore heed Adorno's admonition for the cultural critic: "A successful work, according to immanent criticism, is not one which resolves objective contradictions in a spurious harmony, but one which expresses the idea of harmony negatively by embodying the contradictions, pure and uncompromised, in its innermost structure" (*Prisms* 32). This is, I believe, a crucial argument to make in light of certain dematerializing trends in queer studies, which present gay and lesbian identities as fluid and heterogeneous but also ultimately enigmatic and unknowable. By linking contradiction and nonidentity to the logic of capital, we are able to account for the dialectic that defines gay and lesbian subject formation: the queer as both in revolt against modernity and as a privileged emblem of the modern.

This analysis is based on the argument that gay male and lesbian identity formations are mutually constitutive. Since the 1970s, scholarship about gay and lesbian identities, cultures, and communities has seldom investigated or elaborated the cross-gender ties that the critical and pedagogical framework of "gay and lesbian studies" clearly seems to suggest. There are, of course, historical and political reasons for the divide between gay and lesbian criticisms and its persistence in contemporary queer studies. Gay male theories have often subsumed gender under sexuality, failing to account for—or sometimes even to acknowledge—the specific struggles facing lesbians. Conversely, lesbian theories, which emerged in relation to the politics of lesbian-feminism, have tended to privilege gender over sexuality and focused on developing lesbian studies as a separate, women-centered practice. My point here is not to disavow the complexity of these critical knowledges, or the connections between them. For example, in the academy, the institutionalization of gay and lesbian/queer studies has in many respects emerged out of women's and gender studies, suggesting a structural link between these fields. Nevertheless, gay male and lesbian discourses have overwhelmingly failed to consider such mutual investments as they relate to the process of identity formation and definition. In the field of literary criticism, the conceptualization of separate gay male and lesbian literary traditions is, I would argue, symptomatic of this division. Only in researching this project did I discover (quite unexpectedly) the fertile connections between lesbian and gay male engagements with tropes of dandyism and decadence.

Wary of contemporary queer theory's tendency to bypass material contextualization, including the gendered context of commodity relations, I distinguish between constructions of same-sex desire that are primarily male and those that are primarily female at various points in this study. In so doing, I make an effort to analyze the specificity of gay male and lesbian identities and experiences. For example, I am especially interested in demonstrating how a lesbian modernist such as Renée Vivien both inhabits and subverts the traditions of dandyism and decadence, linking artifice to nature in order to conceptualize lesbian desire outside the bounds of masculine authority and bourgeois society. At the same time, I am committed to examining the cross-gender connections between male homosexuality and lesbianism as forms of personal, social, and political identification. By studying such subjectivities together, we can, I contend, better see the inner contradictions and dynamics that give rise to modern gay and lesbian identities. It is for this reason that the title of my work refers to "queer" identities and desires, despite the theoretical, historical, and political difficulties this term presents. Since this project begins in the late nineteenth century, we must confront another problem with no established solutions: how to name the homosexual at a time when, in Alan Sinfield's memorable phrase, the love that dare not speak its name "hardly *had* a name" (3). By the end of the nineteenth century, "homosexual" had been adopted by both sexologists and homosexuals themselves (Weeks 102), and "queer" had become a slang word for homosexual (Showalter 112). Despite its different meanings over the last century, I use "queer" to define a distinctly modern formation of same-sex identification and desire that is characteristic of both the late nineteenth century and twentieth century. "Gay," of course, has its origins in the post-Stonewall movement for gay and lesbian liberation, and is, strictly speaking, anachronistic in a late nineteenth or early twentieth-century context. However, I employ this term synonymously with "homosexual," "lesbian," and "queer" because it has increasingly been applied as an "overarching label" by scholars (Sedgwick, *Epistemology of the Closet* 17).

I begin my study with Oscar Wilde's inaugural figuration of what I call the "dialectics of dandyism." This chapter seeks to rethink the pervasive definition of dandyism as a sincere and studied effort to be, as Wilde himself might put it, as superficial and artificial as possible. Associated with the "feminization" of modern culture, this notion of dandyism as a devotion to surface presents the dandy as a privileged figure in the development of modern cultural forms precisely because the dandified aesthete's cultivation of beauty, style, and pleasure embraces the erotics and aesthetics of the commodity. However, I argue that the stereotypical image of the dandy as the embodiment of style over substance—a preoccupation with artifice that seeks to liberate form from content—fails to account for the dialectical character of gay male dandyism as Wilde theorizes it in *The Picture of Dorian Gray* (1891). Building on a wide range of histories and cultural criticism that present the late nineteenth-century dandy as the premier model of modern gay subjectivity, I use Marx's theory of the "secret" of the commodity to illuminate the "secret" of gay identity as Oscar Wilde presents it in *The Picture of Dorian Gray*. In this way, I offer an alternative to the prevalent notion that dandies like Wilde's Dorian Gray privilege style over substance, and appearance over essence. Arguing instead for a dialectical conception of gay male identity, I show how Wilde defines the dandy as an unremitting struggle between visible appearance and concealed reality. As I demonstrate, this ongoing dialectic is the "secret" of that distinctly modern form of split subjectivity we now call gay.

In chapter 2, I take up the work of the expatriate English poet Renée Vivien in order to examine the fin-de-siècle figure of the decadent Sapphist or "perverse" lesbian, an icon of modernism who has much in common with the dandy. Vivien's immersion in the decadent movement provides a clear link between the aestheticism of the homosexual dandy and the artificiality of the perverse lesbian. Vivien's poetry interests me because of its complex contradictions, which present an apparently paradoxical reworking of the Baudelairean "flower of evil" through a utopian politics of Sapphic revival. Whereas her decadent work defines the lesbian as a spectacle of artifice and perversity, her work that invokes Sappho and ancient Lesbos uses bright images of female freedom to move toward a more affirmative conception of lesbian desire. Departing from the critical propensity to separate these opposing poetics, I demonstrate that while Vivien's decadent poetry critiques the world in ruins that is bourgeois society, this nightmarish vision always coalesces with her utopian vision of Lesbos as the location of an authentic and liberated female sexuality. An unlikely synthesis of the decadent movement's fantasy image of the ultramodern, artificial lesbian and a naturalized and heroic vision of Sapphism, Vivien's decadent Sapphist is a shimmering, negative embodiment of the utopian possibility contained within a modern world in decline.

Extending my argument about the lesbian as an icon of modernism, chapter 3 looks at our most enduring stereotype of lesbian identity, the "mannish lesbian." Signaling an apparent break from the decadence of the nineteenth-century dandy and the lesbian *fleur du mal*, Radclyffe Hall's *The Well of Loneliness* (1928) frames masculine lesbian identity as a repudiation of decadence and femininity; nevertheless, in seeking to fashion the mannish lesbian as the apotheosis of bourgeois respectability, Hall draws upon the figuration of the leisured, dandified aesthete. Yet because she grounds her work on new medical definitions of homosexuality as "sexual inversion," she articulates a conception of queer dandyism that manifests its essential contradictions in a new way. Unlike the Wildean dandy, for example, who seeks to dispense with the body and nature, Hall's lesbian dandy is defined primarily in relation to these categories. For precisely this reason, many literary and cultural critics have argued that Hall's novel seeks to naturalize same-sex love in order to gain social acceptance for homosexuals and lesbians. However, the trope of sexual inversion does not erase the oppositions I have been defining as constitutive of modern gay and lesbian identities, primarily appearance/essence, production/consumption, and artifice/nature. As we shall see, Hall's account of the mannish lesbian as "a fact in nature" actually produces this new subject as the very embodiment of modernity's contradictions.

Chapter 4 turns to a less prominent modernist icon, the queer black dandy who circulates in the literary and artistic production of the Harlem Renaissance. One of my central claims is that the African American dandy's revision of nineteenth-century, European models of dandyism and decadence serves a strategic purpose; by appropriating the self-consciously decadent aesthetic of the Wildean dandy, Renaissance writers and artists such as Wallace Thurman and Richard Bruce Nugent critique the cult of authenticity surrounding the cultural construction of blackness. In the visual art of Nugent and Thurman's *Infants of the Spring* (1932), the queer figure of the black dandy protests against the commodification of black identity that dominated the so-called Negro craze of the 1920s. In so doing, he disrupts both the fetishizing of the primitive that propels "Harlemania" and the nostalgia for African origins that infuses the New Negro movement. The queer black dandy's rebellion against the culture of capitalism gives birth to a new aesthetic that combines the naturalized simplicity and vigor of primitivism with the artifice of decadence—making legible a distinctly African American incarnation of the new forms of desire, identity, and community emerging in modern, urban culture.

Chapter 5 seeks to account for the paradox of visibility at the heart of a new postwar logic that links homosexuality and addiction in the figure of the queer junkie. This paradox makes William Burroughs's form of gutter dandyism a privileged emblem for the contradictions that define gay and lesbian identity in cold war America. An incarnation of the open secret, queer identity during this period is an object of surveillance that eludes containment, making it both hypervisible and invisible. My goal is to show how this contradictory logic of visibility is embedded in the logic of capital—specifically, the imperatives of postwar Fordism and the crisis of masculinity it eventuated. Like other outlaw masculinities of the Beat movement, Burroughs's gutter dandy reinforces and mobilizes postwar anxieties about feminization; he is in rebellion against the penetration of male subjectivity by the commodity-form even as he is represented as a perverse, feminized subject in the gender ideology of the cold war consensus. This figure inhabits a contradiction between the reification and dehumanization of everyday life and modernity's promise of liberation (through an aesthetics of perception and transgressive eroticism). Moreover, the opposition between invisibility and hypervisibility that defines this Burroughsian icon is an extension of the appearance/essence split that, as I have earlier argued, is at once paradigmatic of the queer and the commodity. The twin imperatives of secrecy and disclosure acquire a new form in cold war America due to the porousness and instability of the boundaries between public and private in postwar society. In the cold war culture of surveillance and containment, the secret takes on a more undefined and paranoid form, making queer identity hypervisible in its imperceptibility. As we shall see, this produces a new dialectic in the figure of the gutter dandy.

Continuing and extending my focus on postwar masculinity, my final chapter analyzes the artistic production and dandified persona of Andy Warhol by examining the artist's engagement with questions of desire, aesthetics, and commodification. It draws on a wide range of materials from the 1950s, 1960s, and 1970s including Warhol's films, writings, collections, commercial art, Pop paintings, and private and public drawings. My argument situates the artist's work within both gay subcultural styles and the reorganization of masculinity that was one aspect of American society's shift to Fordist models of mass production and consumption. I take up this project by focusing on Warhol's two stylistic strategies for addressing the different but related problems of masculine identity and artmaking in commodity culture: "camp" and a sensibility I call "outlaw masculinity." I show how these aesthetic strategies challenge the increasing penetration of capital into American society while also embracing the liberatory potential of a queer commodity aesthetics. Celebrating an improbable form of dandyism grounded in the Pop sensibility, Warhol proposes new queer relation to the commodity-form that combines the rationalizing force of the economic with the libidinal energy of the sensuous/aesthetic.

At the core of this project is my belief that queer cultural production has much to tell us about the contradictions of capitalist modernity and what it means to be modern. By focusing on queer dandyism and its changing relation to the sphere of the commodity, my project aims to trace the themes of dandyism and decadence as they travel across time and place and register differences in region, gender, class, and race. Because I see these themes as especially salient to both gay male and lesbian identity formations, all my subsequent chapters build on the opening argument I make about the nineteenth-century gay male dandy. Nevertheless, although I frame figures as disparate as Radclyffe Hall's mannish lesbian and William S. Burroughs's queer junkie in terms of the thematics of dandyism and decadence, I do not theorize any of these twentieth-century figures as mere extensions of that earlier model of dandyism. I am most interested in the ways in which the central contradictions of dandyism are transformed by the successors of the Wildean dandy. In all my readings, I strive to pay attention to the new and various forms that modern queer consciousness takes. Simultaneously, I emphasize that the contradictions embodied in queer subjectivity at any particular historical moment are never discontinuous from those that shaped earlier models of sexual regulation, reification, and resistance.

1

THE DIALECTICS OF DANDYISM

Modern gay identity is pervaded by the trope of the secret. Building on the work of Michel Foucault and D. A. Miller, the literary and cultural critic Eve Sedgwick has argued that gay identity is fundamentally shaped by the dualism of secrecy and disclosure, but since "telling" is both prohibited and required, queer identity is always an internal contradiction between opacity and transparency, at once hidden and revealed.[1] It is this double bind between secrecy and disclosure that Sedgwick refers to when, arguing for the enduring centrality of the epistemology of the closet for gay people and culture, she points to the way that homosexual identity has been "distinctly constituted *as* secrecy" from its inception (73).

But how do we account for this conjunction of homosexuality and secrecy? How has the queer come to be defined as a contradiction between the "seen" and the "unseen"—a disjunction between the visibility of outward appearances and the invisibility of inner relations? I hope to answer these questions by providing a theory of how the dandy emerges out of the structural contradictions of capitalism—in particular, the opposition between outward appearance and inner essence. A wide range of historians and cultural critics have placed the dandy at the center of debates about the history of the homosexual in the West, the history of modern culture, and the role of the queer in constructions of modern identity. While they have agreed on the centrality of the dandy in gay and lesbian history—presenting him as the premier model of modern gay subjectivity—scholars have disagreed on the meaning of dandyism itself.[2] With this in mind, I will discuss two of the most influential models of dandyism, which both view the dandy as a privileged figure in the development of modern cultural forms.

The first model of dandyism, formulated by Susan Sontag in her influential essay "Notes on 'Camp,'" associates homosexual aestheticism with the "unmistakably modern" (275) project of "seeing the world as an aesthetic phenomenon," which is to say "in terms of artifice, of stylization" (277). If Sontag's essay is still seen as "groundbreaking" and "seminal" by contemporary cultural critics (Bergman, "Strategic Camp" 92; Ross 62), this is in part because her model of homosexual aestheticism persists as a central motif of gay masculinity. Of course, Sontag's model takes a new and different form in, for instance, the muscular aesthetic of contemporary gay male culture, in which the stylization and aestheticization of the self take a decidedly corporeal turn. Nonetheless, I would argue that the contemporary vogue for the gym body—which is at least in part propelled by the notion, to quote the novelist Andrew Holleran, that homosexuals "*are* their looks . . . *are* their bodies" (72)—also represents the newest face of homosexual aestheticism and so demonstrates its ongoing relevance for gay male subject formation. To be sure, this model of homosexuality as a cultivation of surface is most famously linked to the dandy and his embodiment of style over substance. As the cultural critic Michael Bronski puts it, "dandyism was an exercise in perfecting the externals"; as a result, the dandy for Bronski is "all style and no content" (*Cultural Clash* 57). This reading of dandyism as a preoccupation with surface tends to conceive of gay identity solely or primarily in terms of artifice, aesthetics, commodity fetishism, and style. Associated with the "feminization" of modern culture, the dandy comes to represent a retreat from politics and history into art and/or commodity culture.[3]

I want to distinguish this model of dandyism as style from a second model that views dandyism as political rebellion. Although many of the best contemporary critics join the two models (think, for example, of Rita Felski or Alan Sinfield), there are strong reasons for maintaining a historical separation between them.[4] As Ellen Moers indicates in her landmark study, *The Dandy: Brummell to Beerbohm*, it is not until the late nineteenth century that the popularization of Baudelaire's and Barbey d'Aurevilly's works remakes dandyism into an intellectual and antibourgeois pose. The reworked notion of dandyism as a protest against modern industrial capitalism has become the foundation for contemporary queer studies' "take" on the aristocratic turn-of-the-century gay male stereotype, as well as the foundation for queer theory's promotion of a contemporary "politics of style." For critics like Jonathan Dollimore, who have extended the Baudelairean model, gay style is not seen as an abandonment of politics, but rather the site of political engagement. For instance, Dollimore views "dissident" aesthetic and cultural practices such as early modern cross-dressing, Oscar Wilde's "transgressive aesthetic," and the camp sensibility of postmodern gay culture as controversial and subversive because they function "as a style, and even more as a politics" of resistance (318). In this paradigm, dandyism becomes one instance of what Barbey d'Aurevilly calls "the revolt of the individual against the established order" (33)—a revolt against heterosexual norms, materialism, industriousness, and utilitarianism.

The two models I have just described locate dandyism at the opposite poles of modernity, simultaneously positioning the queer subject as a privileged emblem of the modern and as a dissident in revolt against modern society. In the first account, the dandy embraces the erotics and aesthetics of the commodity, celebrating the cultivation of beauty, pleasure, and style. In the second account, the dandy protests against the commodification of modern life, the drive toward production, and the elevation of instrumental reason. This chapter aims to bring these two models together in a new way by showing their underlying connections with each other and with the logic of the commodity relation. In so doing, I seek to theorize gay identity in and through the development of capitalist social formations. By showing how the dandy straddles the contradictions of capitalist modernity in Oscar Wilde's *The Picture of Dorian Gray* (1891), I offer a symptomatic reading of the novel that will provide a context for understanding how the gay male subject came to combine appearance and essence in the first place.

The question of essentialism has been debated at length in feminist theory, gay/lesbian studies, and queer theory; I will not, therefore, rehearse those arguments here.[5] Nevertheless, it is worth noting that the familiar constructionism/essentialism opposition that structured those debates was often incorrectly defined, since social constructionists typically treated any and all uses of "essence" as a form of biological reductionism. Clearly, women, queers, racial and ethnic minorities, and other subordinated social groups know all too well the material effects of such reifying notions of essence. For precisely this reason, I want to emphasize that my work does not conceptualize essence as natural, unified, immutable, or universal. Despite social constructionists' suggestions to the contrary, it is possible to theorize essentialism in radically historical and material terms; in fact, only idealist social theory abstracts essence from social processes. As Herbert Marcuse argues, essence can only be conceptualized in relation to a specific appearance, and this relation "originates in history and changes in history" (*Negations* 74). Following Marcuse, I deploy the concept of essence as a dynamic and complex historical formation that (like the forms of appearance to which it is opposed) emerges in the context of a particular set of social relations—here, the social relations of modern industrial capitalism.[6]

At once a study of the commodity and a study of the queer, this chapter seeks to demonstrate that the link between homosexuality and secrecy is overdetermined by the public/private binary that characterizes capitalist modernity. Gay identity is itself paradigmatic of a new form of consciousness that capitalist social relations engender, embodied most recognizably in the bourgeois subject: a radically split, contradictory subjectivity that is constructed around the opposition between public and private, outside and inside.[7] This "splitting of man into his *public* and his *private* self," which Marx also calls the contradiction between the *citoyen* (citizen of the state) and the *bourgeois* (member of civil society) is itself produced by the contradiction between the political state and civil society that was engendered by the rise of the modern European nation-state—a contradiction that was consolidated under modern industrial capitalism (Marx, "On the Jewish Question" 222).[8] In short, to discover the "secret" of gay identity, we must trace the unfolding of the internal contradictions of capitalism.

Explaining the mystical nature of the production and exchange of commodities under capitalism, Norman Geras states that "because the forms taken by capitalist social relations, their modes of appearance, are historically specific ones, they are puzzling forms, they contain a secret" (73). Geras's use of the term "secret" can be traced directly to Marx, who, in his theory of commodity fetishism, explains that the "secret" of the commodity-form, its "mysterious" character, is the result of a system of exchange that mystifies social relations, so that relations between people take the form of relations between things. As Marx puts it in *Capital*:

> the labour of the private individual manifests itself in an element of the total labour of society only through the relations which the act of exchange establishes between the products, and through their mediation, between the producers. To the producers, therefore, the social relations between their private labours appear as what they are, i.e., they do not appear as direct social relations between persons in their work, but rather as material relations between persons and social relations between things. (165–66)

Marx makes it clear that while the distinction between what appears to be and what really is functions as a smoke screen for capital, the split between appearance and essence is not imaginary. Instead, Marx draws a crucial distinction between two levels of reality: the forms of appearance and the hidden or secret relations of those forms.[9] In this way, Marx argues for the necessity and objectivity of the "illusion," since the appearance of social relations as relations between things is never simply false. We must therefore abandon what Lukács calls "an inflexible confrontation of true and false" in order to comprehend capitalism's contradictions as *real* illusions (86). The "magic" of capitalist production is that social life really does take material shape in certain external appearances that conceal their inner, essential relations; in other words, capitalism organizes reality into a new division between form and content—more specifically, a division between the forms of value and their social content.[10]

A privileged emblem for the contradictions of capitalism, the queer is perhaps the quintessential embodiment of the split between appearance and essence I have been describing. In making this argument, I do not mean to suggest that queerness is a metaphor for, or is analogous to, the commodity-form. Because they are internally related, the logic of the queer dandy *is* the logic of the commodity. Indeed, the paradox of homosexuality as the "open secret" perfectly represents the way the gay male dandy installs a logic particular to the commodity form and its contradictions. In Wilde's *The Picture of Dorian Gray*, the artist Basil Hallward expresses this sense of homosexuality as both known and unknowable—the double bind of gay identity—when he declares, "I have grown to love secrecy. It seems to be the one thing that can make modern life mysterious or marvelous to us. The commonest thing is delightful if one only hides it" (7). This now familiar comment on the pleasure of secrecy identifies the homosexual as one who, in the words of D. A. Miller, "secretes" his subjectivity; in this way, the queer is "radically inaccessible to the culture that would otherwise entirely determine him" (195–96). This reading of gay identity represents the queer as an unsolvable mystery. Enigmatic and veiled, the homosexual can then easily be assimilated to the position of cultural outsider. As Alan Sinfield puts it, "the secret keeps a topic like homosexuality in the private sphere, but under surveillance, allowing it to hover on the edge of public visibility" (9). By way of the secret, cultural critics have tended to conceptualize queerness as an underground identity—a mode of subjectivity that is constituted as personal and private and therefore outside the public sphere. In contrast, I hope to demonstrate that, by constituting his hero in the dialectical relation between public and private, Wilde reveals the former as the appearance of privatization that conceals the essentially social character of queerness. The secret, then, needs to be understood as the mystification of a historically specific social reality. I believe we recognize Dorian as gay not because of his effeminacy and aestheticism, or even because of the "strange rumours about his mode of life" (111), but because he exists in the space between capitalist modernity's dialectical contradictions.

At the beginning of the novel, Basil Hallward shows Lord Henry Wotton a painting he is working on, a "full-length portrait of a young man of extraordinary personal beauty," who is, of course, Dorian Gray (5). In telling Lord Henry about Dorian, Basil emphasizes that Dorian's "fascinating" personality has come to dominate his life and art (9). Strangely, although the portrait represents his effort to inaugurate "an entirely new manner in art," Hallward tells Wotton that he will never exhibit it. As Basil explains it, this is

> because, without intending it, I have put into it some expression of all this curious artistic idolatry, of which, of course, I have never cared to speak to him [Dorian]. He knows nothing about it. He shall never know anything

> about it. But the world might guess it; and I will not bare my soul to their shallow, prying eyes. My heart shall never be put under their microscope. There is too much of myself in the thing, Harry—too much of myself! (13)

Declaring that his love for Dorian must remain secret, Basil here exemplifies the love that dare not speak its name. But we must remember that the "secret" of the portrait exceeds Basil's unspeakable desire for Dorian, since the portrait eventually becomes the emblem of (and medium for) Dorian's double identity. Although the portrait functions as a sign for the homosexual as eternally beautiful youth, Wilde does not define gay identity solely through this image. Finally, queerness in the text inheres not in the image of Dorian Gray, but in the networks of secrecy that constitute this image. Wilde makes it clear that the portrait does not exhibit a single secret; rather, it is the site for a circulation of secrecy in which all three characters—Basil, Dorian, and Lord Henry—are implicated.

On several different levels, Hallward's portrait of Gray instantiates the appearance/essence split that is paradigmatic of the queer. Instituting the logic of the commodity, the portrait is a "mysterious" form because its outward appearance conceals its inner essence. As Basil's remarks reveal, the portrait contains a hidden meaning that is not immediately visible but can be uncovered through mediating or "microscopic" analysis. This is why Dorian increasingly secretes the portrait, first putting up a screen in front of it and then finally moving it to a dusty, unused room on the top floor of his house, a room to which only he holds the key. Despite this sense of the portrait as a dangerous mirror or magnifying glass, which may disclose the inner, private self, Basil and Dorian have reoccurring discussions about whether there is a buried content delineated in the portrait's form—whether there is, in fact, really something (else) to see. When Basil briefly considers exhibiting the portrait, he tells Dorian, "it seemed to me that I had been foolish in imagining that I had seen anything in it, more than that you were extremely good-looking and that I could paint" (101). Constituted as a mode of secrecy, and therefore haunted by invisibility, homosexuality risks becoming a disappearing act. Although Wilde is fascinated by the way identity can dissolve into a vanishing point, queerness does not disappear in *The Picture of Dorian Gray*. Wilde materializes homosexual identity in fundamentally modern terms—as something ephemeral, variable, and elusive. It is my contention that the ambiguity about whether queer desire is "there" or not is itself an effect of the mystifying appearance of gay identity as I have been describing it. It is, in other words, inherent to the dialectical contradictions that shape the gay subject.

I have said that, on several levels, the portrait exemplifies a distinctly queer split between appearance and essence. Until now, I have shown the way the portrait itself instantiates this split. Understood as a phenomenal form whose buried, essential relations manifest a meaning that is always complex, enigmatic, and resistant to interpretation, the portrait *is* the queer. Read this way, we can see how the portrait itself reproduces the division between appearance and essence that Wilde represents in the magical relationship between Dorian and his portrait. It is this relation between portrait and subject—the portrait as hidden essence and Dorian as external appearance—to which I will now turn my attention. This mystical relationship develops when, after first seeing the finished portrait, Gray makes a very famous wish—a wish that seems to rearrange the relation between form and content:

> How sad it is! I shall grow old, and horrible, and dreadful. But this picture will remain always young. It will never be older than this particular day of June. . . . If it were only the other way! If it were I who was to be always young, and the picture that was to grow old! For that—for that—I would give everything! Yes, there is nothing in the whole world I would not give! I would give my soul for that! (25–26)

At first glance, it may be tempting to read Dorian's fatal wish simply in relation to a homosexual aesthetic that privileges youth and beauty, as the critic Alan Sinfield has done. Pointing out the novel's correlation of corruption with loss of youth and beauty, Sinfield states that "the ageing process is made to represent moral degeneracy; then, as now, this is a proposition that seems unethical in mainstream culture but which answers to a fantasy in gay male subculture" (103–4). Although I would want to complicate the notion that Wilde's figuration of virtue as beauty is unique to gay male subcultures, I agree with Sinfield that Dorian's desire to reconcile external appearance and inner essence has a gay specificity. However, this gay specificity is, in my opinion, resolutely grounded in the social relations of modern industrial capitalism.

By now, it is a critical commonplace to assert that Wilde's novel, like Robert Louis Stevenson's *Dr. Jekyll and Mr. Hyde*, represents subjectivity as fundamentally split. Best encapsulated in the Victorian cliché of the "divided self," Wilde's depiction of Dorian Gray as a combination of warring forces uses the vocabulary of the mind-body split in order to address the problem of regulating desire in modern culture. Classical philosophy's duality of thought and being (characteristic of Kant, for example) takes on a new significance when read in the context of contradictions historically specific to capitalist modernity, contradictions I have been defining primarily through the antithesis of essence and appearance. According to Georg Lukács, the duality of thought and existence is an antinomy of bourgeois thought because it is characteristic of the reification that permeates every aspect of capitalist society.[11] Wilde's novel is a meditation on the process of reification as it relates to the "war" between the desiring, consumer-subject and the rational, producer-subject in the wake of a consumer revolution that had reorganized late-Victorian social life around the universal dominance of the commodity-form (I will return to this topic in the next section). As Wilde puts it, "Soul and body, body and soul—how mysterious they were! There was animalism in the soul, and the body had its moments of spirituality. . . . Who could say where the fleshly impulse ceased, or the psychical impulse began? How shallow were the arbitrary definitions of ordinary psychologists!" (52–53).

Deconstructing the Cartesian opposition between mind and body, Wilde takes pleasure in challenging the mastery of the rational, Enlightenment subject (who is also the subject of "ordinary" psychology) by asserting the interpenetration of "thought" and "passion." But even as it challenges the bourgeois antithesis of thought and existence, Wilde's treatment of the mind-body split conceptualizes a particularly middle-class experience of self-alienation. Indeed, the struggle between soul and body in Dorian Gray becomes a sign for the cultural problem of the bourgeois subject as radically split and self-contradictory. Lukács describes this splitting up of the subject as a "doubling of personality," which in bourgeois consciousness assumes a "rigidly twofold form." Dorian, as we shall see, is the victim of such a rigidly twofold and therefore "unmanageable" dialectic (Lukács 165–66).

Interestingly enough, Hallward and Wotton see no evidence of this struggle in their friend. In fact, for both Basil and Lord Henry, Dorian astounds because he seems to *undo* the opposition between the body and the soul, exteriors and interiors. Wotton observes that "with his beautiful face, and his beautiful soul, he [Dorian] was a thing to wonder at" (52). The ideal of masculinity that Basil and Henry see embodied in Gray is characteristic of the Enlightenment's concept of transparency, which glorified "a body that told no lies and kept no secrets" (Hunt, *Family Romance* 97). Persisting into the nineteenth and twentieth centuries, this Enlightenment ideal of manhood joins body and soul by effacing the distinction between public and private selves.[12] Hallward worships Dorian not simply because he is a "beautiful creature" (7), but because he represents a mythic ideal of unified being that is itself the definition of manly beauty in modern culture: "Unconsciously he defines for me the lines of a fresh school, a school that is to have in it all the passion of the romantic spirit, all the perfection of the spirit that is Greek. The harmony of soul and body—how much that is! We in our madness have separated the two, and have invented a realism that is vulgar, an ideality that is void" (13). *We in our madness have separated the two.* Basil's ideal of transparency, a fusion of outward appearance and inner essence, employs a distinctly middle-class concept of virtue to define a new, modern notion of masculine beauty. I say Basil's ideal, but this notion of a "harmony of soul and body" is equally fascinating to Lord Henry and Dorian, so much so that the latter makes a "mad" wish to unite what had been separate. When he looks into the portrait and declares that he wishes it could grow old instead of him, Dorian seeks to become an embodiment of Wotton's dictum: "To be good is to be in harmony with one's self" (69). Gray hopes to merge appearance and essence, displacing the dialectic and rewriting the relation between form and content. In other words, he entertains the fantasy of producing in himself the fiction of a secretless self—a self that refuses the distinction between public and private. Wilde's point, of course, is that this unity between identity and the conditions of its production is precisely what Dorian lacks. Nevertheless, to Hallward and Wotton—both of whom are captivated by Gray's "beautiful face, and his beautiful soul" (52)—it is also precisely what Dorian seems most to possess.

"The harmony of soul and body" that Gray exhibits at the level of visibility is, in fact, a defining feature of the mystifying appearance of gay identity as Wilde presents it. This apparent unity between outside and inside masks the division on which gay identity is actually based. Expressing the commodity's contradictions, gay identity takes material shape in a phenomenal form that conceals its real relations. This is not to say that the forms of gay identity are illusory or in some sense false, but rather that they wear a disguise.[13] Certainly, the association of gay subjectivity with secrecy, masking, and doubleness reflects this legacy. As I have already stated, in his treatment of the portrait as "the most magical of mirrors" (93), Wilde presents gay identity as a contradiction between what appears to be and what is. We have seen that both Basil and Dorian worry that the portrait functions as a revelatory mirror or magnifying glass, which divulges the truth of their desires. But the portrait, as a sign for the mystifying appearance of gay identity, does not reflect identity but deflects it, divides it. The portrait as "magical mirror" is not an image of transparency, of identity revealed, but more important an image of doubling, of identity split open. Emblematic of a set of mystifying social contradictions, Dorian Gray is the incarnation of a distinctly queer form of subjectivity that inhabits (rather than resolves or exorcizes) capitalism's double binds. However, if the queer is defined by this dualistic construction of identity, this sense of the opposition between appearance and essence, it is nevertheless crucial to remember that Dorian's story is most of all a doomed effort to transcend these dualisms. In the end, Wilde defines the gay male dandy as the one who endlessly seeks to unite his divided subjectivity but who can never do so.

CONTRADICTIONS OF THE COLLECTION

Wilde describes Dorian's collection in vibrant detail in chapter 11, which has been called "a textbook psychology of fin-de-siècle economic man" by the eminent Wilde scholar Regenia Gagnier ("Is Market Society the *Fin* of History?" 302). Like Jean des Esseintes, the decadent hero of J. K. Huysmans's *Against*

Nature (*À Rebours*; 1884), Gray collects in order to satisfy his "passion for sensations." Dorian dedicates himself to acquiring a wide range of luxurious commodities that appeal to the senses—first exotic perfumes from the East, then rare musical instruments, then exquisite jewels, and finally embroideries, tapestries, and ecclesiastical vestments. Collecting with a fervor that nears obsession, Dorian devotes himself to the aesthetics of the series. For example, when he becomes interested in embroideries, Wilde notes that "for a whole year, he sought to accumulate the most exquisite specimens that he could find of textile and embroidered work" (121). Like other late nineteenth-century dandies, Dorian's consumption aims to rise above the vulgarity of commodity culture, just as his dandyism aims to rise above the immediate materialities of dress and exterior elegance. As Wilde explains,

> in his inmost heart he desired to be something more than a mere *arbiter elegantiarum*, to be consulted on the wearing of a jewel, or the knotting of a necktie, or the conduct of a cane. He sought to elaborate some new scheme of life that would have its reasoned philosophy and its ordered principles, and find in the spiritualizing of the senses its highest realization. (113)

Wilde depicts Dorian's seemingly endless appetite for exotic, luxury objects as the exterior manifestation of his inner intellectual and artistic superiority—setting up a continuity between appearance and essence that will eventually be exposed as an ideological fiction. Gray's "spiritualizing of the senses" can be understood in the context of the novel's extended inquiry into the dangers of repression and the positive value of pleasure. This debate is summed up in an especially famous aphorism by Lord Henry, who declares that "the only way to get rid of a temptation is to yield to it" (19). Wotton's notion of desire as discharge reflects a consumerist ideology that is the foundation of his philosophy of "new Hedonism." But, as new Hedonism's "visible symbol" (23), Dorian raises the question of whether or not desire can ever be fulfilled, or disposed of, in the way that Wotton suggests. Like the cigarette, which is "the perfect type of a perfect pleasure" because "it leaves one unsatisfied" (71), the culture of commodity production engenders desires that are fundamentally insatiable. As Jean Baudrillard argues, the sphere of value is haunted by a fundamental "ambivalence" that takes the form of lack or "deficit," constructing desire under capitalism as an impossible demand. This "refusal of fulfillment"—which Baudrillard theorizes as a complex fascination with lack and negativity—is linked to capitalism's phantasmatic promise of satisfaction in an endlessly renewing dialectic (*For a Critique* 207). As we shall see, Dorian is governed by this very dialectic of desire as his voracious appetites inevitably outstrip his demand for fulfillment and he is launched toward self-dispossession by "mad hungers that grew more ravenous as he fed them" (113).

But if Dorian's commodity fetishism is propelled by insatiable hungers that drive him to ceaselessly "search for sensations" (115), it must also be understood as a "strategy of distinction" that aims to confer aesthetic and social superiority through separation and distancing (Bourdieu 56, 66). Collecting objects from different places, nations, and historical periods, Dorian yearns to transcend the limitations of everyday consumption. Resisting bourgeois or mass styles of consumption, his elitist consumption looks back to the traditional aristocracy for inspiration, shunning that which is merely merchandise—the "unrefined" consumption of an increasingly massified society—and instead valuing objects that are unique, handmade, and rare. In this respect, Gray implicitly repudiates the mechanical reproduction at the heart of the consumer revolution, privileging the imperfections and detail of hand labor over the uniformity of the machine. In *The Theory of the Leisure Class*, Thorstein Veblen suggests that this facet of conspicuous consumption, or "honorific" consumption, is fundamentally an effort to discriminate not between commodities, but between classes: "The objection to machine producers is often formulated as an objection to the commonness of such goods. What is common is within the (pecuniary) reach of many people. Its consumption is therefore not honorific, since it does not serve the purpose of a favourable invidious comparison with other consumers" (160–61). As Veblen indicates, gentlemen of taste distinguish themselves from the bourgeoisie and the working class when they insist on consuming originals, not copies. Collecting objects that are distinguished by their uniqueness and rarity, Dorian elevates his taste above that of the "undiscerning" masses in the way that Veblen describes, while simultaneously creating an aestheticized style of consumption that aims to transcend market imperatives.

Dorian's acquisition of luxuries and curios not only seeks to affirm his "aristocratic" distinction, but also aims to build a self-created world by aestheticizing experience itself. Gray yearns not so much for the enjoyment provided by an individual object, but for the aesthetic pleasure provided by its reconstitution as part of his collection. In this way, his accumulation of rare and beautiful objects seeks to create a separate world that is an alternative to the sterility and uniformity of the mass market. Wilde illustrates this in the following excerpt, in which he describes the dandy as a nighttime traveler in the dreamworld of commodity culture:[14]

> Out of the unreal shadows of the night comes back to us the real life that we had known. We have to resume it where we had left off, and there steals over us a terrible sense of the necessity for the continuance of energy in the same wearisome round of stereotyped habits, or a wild longing, it may be, that our eyelids might open some morning upon a world that had been refashioned anew in the darkness for our pleasure, a world in which things would have

> fresh shapes and colours, and be changed, or have other secrets, a world in which the past would have little or no place, or survive, at any rate, in no conscious form of obligation or regret, the remembrance even of joy having its bitterness, and the memories of pleasure their pain.
>
> It was the creation of such worlds as these that seemed to Dorian Gray to be the true object, or amongst the true objects, of life. (115)

Like des Esseintes, Dorian hopes to create a fantasy world that will transport him beyond ordinary reality and to a place where the past is banished, where illusion triumphs over reality, and where commodities take on the "fresh shapes and colours" of a revitalized world of objects. Dorian's "wild longing" to refashion the world for his own pleasure—via objects that produce authentic pleasure and beauty—is a wholesale embracing of the ideology that sustains modern consumer society, which, as Baudrillard asserts, requires individuals to complete themselves in and through commodities.[15] In this respect, Gray should remind us of Walter Benjamin's portrait of the collector who has an exceptional intimacy with the objects he possesses; as Benjamin explains in the essay "Unpacking My Library," the collector's acquisitions do not "come alive in him, it is he who lives in them" (*Illuminations* 67). Like Benjamin's vision of the collector who "disappear[s] inside" his collection (67), Dorian seeks to lose himself in the seductive world of objects. And yet he also shares the dandy's desire to "shake off" the rationalization and commodification of modern culture, hoping to transcend the "wearisome round" of the everyday—the ugliness and vulgarity of his own time and place. Consequently, Dorian is in the contradictory position of seeking to escape the reification of bourgeois society by dissolving his desires into the very dreamworld from which he hopes to awaken.

Both enchanted and threatened by the commodity dreamworld that engulfs him, Dorian Gray's ambivalent desire for objects is actually a repudiation of value that strives to free the commodity from its mundane existence in the system of exchange. As Benjamin argues, the collector seeks to "[strip] things of their commodity character by means of his possession of them" (*Charles Baudelaire* 168).[16] Hoping to liberate objects from their identities as commodities, Dorian shares the collector's impulse to create a separate sphere in which enjoyment is unmediated by the circuit of exchange value. As a result, he makes unnecessary things his only necessities and yearns to usher in a new order that would overturn the supposed primacy of needs. In this way, his collection exposes the very concept of needs as ideological, itself a product of the commodity relations that manufacture it.[17] At the same time—and this point should be emphasized—Dorian's effort to fashion a world in which "things [are] free from the bondage of being useful" inadvertently repeats the logic of exchange value, which is the apotheosis of the commodity because it renders objects useless (Benjamin, *Charles Baudelaire* 169). As Wilde reveals, the objects Gray acquires—jewels, musical instruments, perfumes, embroideries, tapestries, and other luxurious "treasures"—are detached from needs and use value because their "function" is strictly aesthetic (Wilde 122). But, as part of the collection, these objects are abstracted from their use value even more, since, as Baudrillard puts it, in the collected object "only the *idea is consumed*"; in other words, such collected, ornamental objects are emblematic of a process of commodification that transforms things into "culturized" signs that displace function and utility (*Selected Writings* 24, 32). Finally, the contexts of production and labor are effaced as Dorian places his possessions in artificial isolation, seeking a world purified of mediation and fetishizing the abstraction and formality that the system of commodity production confers upon objects.

And subjects, for Dorian is himself the most dazzling objet d'art in his collection. As embodied in the exquisitely fascinating personality of Dorian Gray, Wilde's dandy occupies the elite company of those who seek to "make themselves perfect by the worship of beauty" (113). In this way, Gray hopes to circumvent the contradictions of commodity culture by practicing, as Lord Henry puts it, "the great aristocratic art of doing absolutely nothing" (30). Like the objects in his collection, he aestheticizes himself in an attempt to outstrip "the bondage of being useful." We may trace this conception of dandyism back to Barbey d'Aurevilly, who declared that the dandy "does not work; he exists" (264), and Baudelaire, for whom dandyism was a "cult of the self" characterized by "first and foremost the burning need to create for oneself a personal originality" (27). In his development of a personal originality, Gray frequently adopts "certain modes of thought," briefly "abandon[ing] himself to their subtle influences," and then he locates the object of his intellectual curiosity elsewhere (115). Through this "continued forward flight" in which desire becomes its own object, Dorian rejects the drive toward specialization characteristic of capitalism's division of labor, fashioning himself as an artist-in-life whose art leaves no material product (Baudrillard, *Selected Writings* 45). Favoring individuality over uniformity, Wilde's dandy is romanticism's swan song; he resists productivity in order to fashion himself into a protest against the ugliness and instrumentality of modern industrial capitalism. As Lord Henry tells Dorian, "You are the type of what the age is searching for, and what it is afraid it has found. I am so glad that you have never done anything, never carved a statue, or painted a picture, or produced anything outside of yourself! Life has been your art!" (187). In turning himself into a work of art, Dorian Gray embodies one of the central contradictions of dandyism: aspiring to an aesthetic sensibility that would rise above the commodification of modern life, he challenges forms of bourgeois self-presentation that erase originality, while simultaneously cultivating a stylistic individuality—a "sense of distinction"—that is grounded in the social dynamics of class privilege.[18]

REMEMBRANCE OF THINGS PAST

Dorian's collection seeks not only to transcend the commodification of modern life, but also to salvage wholeness from the ruins of history. The acquisition of luxurious and rare objects from other eras manifests a fetishistic impulse (the desire to make whole what is lacking) that aims both to repair history and, as Bourdieu argues in the following passage, to conquer time: "to possess things from the past . . . is to master time, through all those things whose common feature is that they can only be acquired in the course of time, by means of time, against time, that is, by inheritance or through dispositions which, like the taste for old things, are likewise only acquired with time and applied by those who can take their time" (71–72).

The collector, then, achieves a sense of aesthetic distinction by deploying what Bourdieu calls "a social power over time" that crystallizes history in order to master time itself (71). Paradoxically enough, Dorian's collection attempts to triumph over time by escaping its dominion through forgetfulness. As Wilde states, "for these treasures, and everything that he [Dorian] collected in his lovely house, were to be to him means of forgetfulness, modes by which he could escape, for a season, from the fear that seemed to him at times to be almost too great to be borne" (122). Susan Stewart comments on the amnesiac aspect of collection, which "seeks a form of self-enclosure which is possible because of its ahistoricism. The collection replaces history with *classification*, with order beyond the realm of temporality" (151). Since it deprivileges the past tense of history in favor of the present tense of the collector—whose organization of objects always directs us to the self who chooses and arranges those objects—the collection is an exercise in forgetting that renders time "simultaneous or synchronous within the collection's world" (Stewart 151). In this way, Dorian's collection breaks free of dynamic or diachronic time in order to escape into the stillness and eternity of those "moments of a life that is itself but a moment" (Wilde 114). The forgetfulness that Gray experiences in such moments is grounded in the contradictions of the collection, which, like the commodity itself, is split into unreconciled but interdependent components. Dorian's collection becomes a mode of transcendence or oblivion precisely because it is at once an act of personal originality, affirming the individual in the face of mass culture, and an effacing of individuality, dissolving the boundaries of the self into a new modern interiority.

This complex and contradictory impulse to forget does not obliterate the past but allows Dorian to disappear inside it. Ultimately, Gray's conspicuous consumption becomes a form of return that restages the past in the context of the collection. Astounding fashionable guests with "the wanton luxury and gorgeous splendour of his mode of life," Dorian seems to be propelled by nostalgia for the luxury and leisure of aristocratic privilege, and his collecting—although it induces an amnesiac reverie in him—is also fundamentally a quest to revisit the past, to recollect history (Wilde 123). When Huysmans's des Esseintes declares his "nostalgic yearning for another age," he perfectly captures the dandy's individualized effort to fight industrialization, rationalization, and modern "progress," even as he utilizes new forms of technology to enact his decadent rebellion against nature (181). In both Wilde and Huysmans, this backward-looking desire to escape modern mass culture is coupled with a contempt for the masses, those "vulgar mortals" who lack the refinement to appreciate the aesthetic triumph of, say, mechanical fishes or artificial wines (to cite two examples from Huysmans's novel). As Ellen Moers has asserted, dandyism and its aesthetics of taste function as a justification for a "reassertion of traditional privilege" at a time when barriers of class, rank, and birth were breaking down (130).

I wish to emphasize that the dandy's protest is neither simply a nostalgic mimicking of the past nor a wish for the reinstating of what once was. At first glance, it may seem that Dorian, for example, collects relics of an extinct European nobility (their jewelry, tapestries, and embroideries) in an effort to reconstitute the aristocratic world. But, unlike the brothers Goncourt, Edmond and Jules, who dedicated their lives to recreating the art, objects, and style of Old Regime France, Gray shares the dandy's hope of establishing a new kind of aristocracy, one based on spiritual, aesthetic, and intellectual elitism.[19] Baudelaire emphasizes this point in his classic study of modernity, *The Painter of Modern Life*: "Dandyism does not even consist, as many thoughtless people seem to believe, in an immoderate taste for the toilet and material elegance. For the perfect dandy these things are no more than symbols of his aristocratic superiority of mind" (27). Ultimately, this insistence on the intellectual and spiritual superiority of aestheticism cloaks the dandy's investment in maintaining and reinforcing his own class privilege, thus mystifying the class interests that structure his relationship to modernity. As even Baudelaire admits, dandyism requires both money and leisure: "These beings have no other calling but to cultivate the idea of beauty in their persons, to satisfy their passions, to feel and to think. They thus possess a vast abundance both of time and money, without which fantasy, reduced to a state of passing reverie, can hardly be translated into action" (27). The dandy may possess, as Baudelaire says, a "characteristic quality of opposition and revolt," but his rebellion is also bound up with the oppressive social relations in which he is entangled (28). This becomes clear if we examine another aspect of the relationship between dandyism and capitalism: Wilde's insertion of the dandy in the dialectic between the primitive and the civilized.

The Picture of Dorian Gray demonstrates that the dandy's rebellion requires the exoticism of the primitive in order to create a space outside the modern. Wilde details Dorian's study of "barbaric music" and his collection of fantastic musical instruments from "the tombs of dead nations or among the few savage tribes that have survived contact with Western civilization" (117).

In these representations, Wilde depicts Dorian as a conqueror filled with an imperialist nostalgia for the "vanishing primitive."[20] Gray is engaged not in a civilizing mission but in a conservation of savagery, staging

> concerts in which mad gypsies tore wild music from little zithers, or grave yellow-shawled Tunisians plucked at the strained strings of monstrous lutes, while grinning negroes beat monotonously upon copper drums, and, crouching upon scarlet mats, slim turbaned Indians blew through long pipes of reed or brass, and charmed, or feigned to charm, great hooded snakes and horrible horned adders. (117)

Imported as "exotic" objects by Dorian, the "savage" musicians are pictured as colonial possessions who perform a spectacle of Otherness for the dandy's pleasure. The racist ideology of primitivism that operates here is, of course, a cardinal fantasy of imperialism.[21] Dorian views people of the East and South as artifacts from an authentic, premodern past whose color and pulse stand in opposition to the rationalization and commodification of modern culture. Fascinated by the passionate elementality of these native non-Western people and their strange instruments, "things of bestial shape and with hideous voices" (118), he uses the "barbaric" musicians to turn his house into a museum, offering his guests not an imitation of the colonial world, but the colonial world itself, wondrously preserved. Despite the affinity he shares with the "noble savage," who, like the dandy, resists an increasingly intrusive urban and industrial society, Dorian distinguishes his aestheticism from that of the black and Oriental musicians who cannot rise above the brute materiality of nature and the body. As Rita Felski states, decadence performs a dual negation that critiques both modern industrial capitalism and the "nostalgic yearning for an idyll of unmediated nature."[22] Like women, who have—as Lord Henry declares—"wonderfully primitive instincts" (90), the Oriental, colonial musicians are marked as authentic and elemental so as to highlight the distinctly modern artificiality of the dandy. Because it depends on a nostalgia both elitist and imperialist, the dandy's revolt against modernity is only expressed in the most pessimistic way; replacing history with commemoration, the fantasy of the past that he seeks to construct is already hopelessly lost. It is perhaps for this reason that the dandy turns from the past to the present, ultimately losing himself in the alienation and reification of modern metropolitan life.

REIFICATION AND QUEER CONSCIOUSNESS

As I have suggested, Dorian's double or split self is characteristic of what Lukács theorizes as the "rigidly twofold form" of bourgeois consciousness. As

Lukács argues, "the proletariat social reality does not exist in this double form" because workers recognize themselves as objects of the process of production that turns them into commodities, whereas the bourgeois or capitalist mistakenly imagines himself to be the subject or supervisor of reified social relations (165). Despite the differences that mediation produces in a social reality that is immediately "the same" for everyone, reification and its effects inevitably shape all forms of consciousness, bourgeois and proletariat. The worker's subjectivity is the most extreme example of reified consciousness under capitalism, but those who cultivate the aesthetic, like collectors or dandies, also face the same problems of objectification and reification. Lukács asserts that "the specialised 'virtuoso,' the vendor of his objectified and reified faculties does not just become the [passive] observer of society; he also lapses into a contemplative attitude *vis-à-vis* the workings of his own objectified and reified faculties" (100). The reification that results from this "contemplative attitude" toward the self may be inevitable, since the dandy makes a fetish of the abstraction and formality that structures both objects and subjects of exchange. As Wilde's novel indicates, the dandy does not attempt to achieve mastery over objects as much as he seeks to share in the object pleasures he attributes to the world of commodities. He empathizes with commodities, much in the way that the flâneur does. In this way, he seeks to transcend capitalism's oppositions in order to enact a new relation between subject and object.

But the affinity the dandy feels for the inorganic world eventually transforms him. Wilde first signals this transformation when Dorian declares to Basil that he will no longer be at the mercy of his emotions. In response, Hallward exclaims, "Dorian, this is horrible! Something has changed you completely" (195). He looks the same, but Dorian is undergoing a metamorphosis into an utterly reified being, a metamorphosis that culminates in his murder of Basil. Wilde describes his protagonist in almost vampiric terms as Gray's quest for transcendence turns from the consumption of objects to the consumption of people.[23] Here, Dorian is at his most reified, resembling nothing so much as Marx's famous description of capital as dead labor that lives only by sucking living labor; as Marx explains, capital obtains its fluidity, its ability to ceaselessly change form, "by constantly sucking in living labour as its soul, vampire-like" (*Grundrisse* 646). Describing Dorian's face moments before he murders Basil, Wilde notes that "there was neither real sorrow in it nor real joy. There was simply the passion of the spectator" (135). Wilde directly links this inability to experience emotion—the well-known detachment of the dandy—to Gray's conspicuous consumption, reminding us that the quintessential spectator is the shopper, intoxicated by the shimmering spectacle of the commodity form:[24]

> I love beautiful things that one can touch and handle. Old brocades, green bronzes, lacquerworks, carved ivories, exquisite surroundings, luxury, pomp,

> there is much to be got from all these. But the artistic temperament that they create, or at any rate reveal, is still more to me. To become the spectator of one's own life, as Harry says, is to escape the suffering of life. (96–97)

Of course, Dorian is wrong. When he becomes the spectator of his own life or, as Lukács would put it, when he lapses into a contemplative attitude toward the workings of his own objectified and reified faculties, Dorian does not build a refuge from modern life. Instead, he plunges toward fragmentation as his spectatorship results in a dangerous splitting of subjectivity. In this way, he demonstrates the degree to which he has modeled himself on the structure of the commodity, or, even better, he demonstrates the degree to which the commodity has made him in its own image. Indeed, Wilde's novel suggests that the fetishism of the commodity produces a transfer of meaning, value, and vitality from people to things. While the commodities that he cherishes are powerful and creative, producing social effects in the world by shaping the characters of those who possess them, Dorian experiences a growing sense of powerlessness and objectification (a development that becomes more explicit as his saturation in sensation renders him not only unable to feel but also unable to control his own destiny). Like the city's grotesque residents, beings of objectified labor who "moved like monstrous marionettes, and made gestures like live things" (160), Dorian becomes dehumanized not only because he is alienated from the society in which he lives, but also because he is alienated from himself. Unlike these members of the working class, however, Gray believes himself to be "at home in this self-alienation" until, of course, it is too late for him to save himself (Lukács 149). In Wilde's formulation, the estrangement and reification of the gay male dandy must be viewed in the context of the social relations that are its source. Accordingly, Dorian watches "the sordid shame of the great city" because in it he recognizes the origin of his own petrified nature (159).

For Dorian, the desire to abolish the opposition of appearance and essence ultimately leads him to embrace the very aspects of modern life he would appear to despise. As I have been arguing, Gray seeks to transcend capitalism's double binds through a kind of consumption that is honorific and so spiritualized and aestheticized. In Wilde's representation of the collection, Dorian's consumption is viewed as refined and noble because it aims to refashion—or perfect—the self and the world simultaneously. Critics who have studied Huysmans's work in particular have observed that the dandy's quest for an aestheticized existence eventually leads him to retreat into the interior, where he seeks to divorce himself from the new forms of public life emerging in the modern metropolis.[25] But *The Picture of Dorian Gray* indicates that the dandy's attempt to create a private, interior space that, to quote Benjamin, would "support him in his illusions" also leads him back to the public world that both attracts and repels him (*Charles Baudelaire* 167). As we shall see, Dorian does not blur the public and the private by projecting an aestheticized domain of interiority onto the public sphere; instead, he is a testament to the more complicated interpenetration of opposites that structures the dandy's relationship to modernity. "Horribly agitated" by the dialectical nature of his existence (144), Dorian finds himself losing control of his consumption as his "method of procuring extraordinary sensations" (184) exhausts itself, and, like a drug user who moves on to a more powerful drug for a better high, he finally seeks sensory stimuli not in the pursuit of beauty, but in the pursuit of ugliness. If Dorian's collection evokes eighteenth-century associations of consumption and civilization, linking the accumulation of luxury goods to a distinctly aristocratic "civilizing process," then his attraction to the ugliness and corruption of the city no longer pretends to be a form of honorific consumption.[26] However, Gray's notorious experiences in the "dreadful houses," taverns, and opium dens of Whitechapel and London are, Wilde indicates, merely another facet of his search for sensations (132). Dorian's mysterious visits to the "vile and degraded" places of the city may, of course, be cloaked references to his homosexual double life. Nevertheless, I have been trying to show that Wilde defines Dorian as queer not by dropping hints about his "vices" and the "whispered scandals" that circulate about them (124), nor by intimating, perhaps, that his hero may be doing more than "brawling" with the "foreign sailors" he meets "in a low den in the distant parts of Whitechapel" (123); no, Wilde invokes the "secret" of Dorian's identity—his queerness—by positioning him in the dialectical relation between the public and the private. Like his collection of beautiful things, Gray's wanderings among "the foulest dens" of the city aim to submerge the self in a reverie of forgetfulness (132):

> Ugliness that had once been hateful to him because it made things real, became clear to him now for that very reason. Ugliness was the one reality. The coarse brawl, the loathsome den, the crude violence of disordered life, the very vileness of thief and outcast, were more vivid, in their intense actuality of impression, than all the gracious shapes of Art, the dreamy shadows of Song. They were what he needed for forgetfulness. In three days he would be free. (160–61)

Dorian's horrified fascination with the spectacle of the modern city embraces ugliness as a kind of hyperrealism even as it becomes a means of intoxication for him. Both the public nightmare of metropolitan brutality and the private dreamworld of the collection are narcotics, distancing him from ordinary reality and offering an illusion of an escape from the sterility and uniformity of capitalist modernity. From this perspective, Dorian's experiences in the city appear to be an extension of the collection's hermeticism—the dandy's attempt to turn the external world into another interior. However, this fascination with the ugliness of the metropolis is not simply about the appearance of privatization—it is also a paradoxical attempt to expose the totality of relations that define his social world.

Like the aestheticized interior, the city is a phantasmagoria for Dorian, but not because Wilde collapses the distinction between these two spaces. Although intoxicated by the dark currents of urban life, he is also haunted by the city's miseries and those of its inhabitants. The "dull rage" in Dorian's heart (160) as he sees the city for what it is—a place of prostitution, addiction, poverty, and crime—suggests a Baudelairean rebellion against the myth of progress and the hypocrisy of bourgeois society. If Wilde's representation of the city invokes the darkness and monstrosity of Baudelaire's Paris, it is because, like Baudelaire, Wilde seeks to lay bare the barbarism of late-Victorian capitalism: the enchanting spectacle of modern culture, Wilde tells us, cannot be separated from the repression it necessarily brings forth. Filled with fear and desire for the "intense actuality of impression" that ugliness provides, Dorian discovers that the asylum he seeks from the urban-industrial landscape is doomed. Soon, his narcotic pleasures turn to "hideous hungers," and he can no longer separate himself from the ruined world of the metropolis that draws him in, its foggy streets entrapping him "like the black web of some sprawling spider" (160). Radically split by the dialectic between public and private—which shapes the reified social processes at the heart of both the aestheticized, interior world of the collection and the alienation of the city—Dorian is a privileged emblem for the duality that defines queer consciousness.

CONCLUSION

Unlike Huysmans, who finally presents a hollowing out of the dandy, a sense of form emptied of content, Wilde offers what Benjamin would call a "dialectical image" of the dandy (*Charles Baudelaire* 171). Gray's pursuit of pleasure ends in alienation and reification, but this should not be taken to mean that Wilde carries the dandy into negation, as Ellen Moers has argued about des Esseintes. According to Wilde, the dandy's protest is not simply an attempt to liberate formal elements from the necessity and totality of content; it always has a function even when it appears to be a purely aesthetic attitude. Dorian Gray is not, as the literary critic Judith Halberstam argues, "all form and no content"—a stylized but essentially vacant being who embraces only the fleeting beauty of illusions (*Skin Shows* 58); as I have argued, Wilde does not evacuate the queer of materiality, but reconceptualizes the "essence" of gay identity as both fugitive and contingent, characteristics most often invoked as hallmarks of the modern. Nevertheless, since his identity is divided, mysterious, and masked, Dorian is always a contradiction of outward appearance and inner essence.

This is perhaps most apparent in the conclusion to the novel, when Dorian decides to free himself from his past by destroying the portrait that functions as the "mirror of his soul." However, when he picks up his knife and defiantly stabs the portrait, Gray actually murders himself. Dorian is not a casualty of morality or sentimentality, as many of Wilde's critics have asserted.[27] Wilde's novel, and its spectacular ending in particular, demonstrate the dialectical construction of modern gay identity. Dorian must die when he stabs the portrait because he can only exist in the relation between the public and the private, a relation that Wilde literalizes in the portrait and its subject. Like any turn-of-the-century dandy, Dorian plays with the divisions between public/private, production/consumption, and appearance/essence in order to dispense with them. When he ends up dispensing with himself, however, it is because he fails to recognize that to be queer is to be perpetually suspended between the contradictions of capitalism—or, to put it another way, to be queer is to be that contradiction.

In this chapter, I have sought to rethink the prevalent notion that dandies like Wilde's Dorian Gray and J. K. Huysmans's des Esseintes privilege appearance over essence. I have done so not only out of a desire to theorize queer subjectivity in and through the forms of capitalist social relations, but also out of a conviction that Wilde unwittingly conceptualizes the gay male dandy in precisely these terms. Shortly after he finishes painting Dorian's portrait, Basil Hallward declines an invitation to go to the theater with Wotton and Gray. Wilde describes the scene like this: "The painter bit his lip and walked over, cup in hand, to the picture. 'I shall stay with the real Dorian,' he said, sadly" (29). This notion that the portrait is the "real" or "original" Dorian might suggest that Wilde depicts the dandy as an empty form and assigns him to the world of appearances. By representing Gray as an aesthetic object above all else, Wilde would seem to be encoding a theory of dandyism as homosexual aestheticism; from this perspective, the dandy becomes a mere creature of the surface, as self-worshiper with a privileged relation to the world of consumption and aesthetics. But—and here is the crux of my argument—this is only half the story. We must remember that, like the capitalist social relations in which it is grounded, gay identity is a puzzling form; it contains a secret. As I have demonstrated in my discussion of Marx's theory of commodity fetishism, capitalism cannot be said to be "really" its outward appearance or its underlying essence; it is always both at once. Similarly, Wilde's theory of gay subjectivity suggests that the "real" Dorian is neither portrait nor person, appearance nor essence. He remains, finally, a spectacle of contradiction.

Rooted in a split, gay subjectivity delimits the fundamental paradox realized in the commodity form. Divided against itself, gay male identity is for

Wilde an ongoing struggle between visible appearance and concealed reality. Wilde captures this sense of the dialectics of gay male subjectivity in the final lines of the novel, which present us with a striking image of gay identity as fatally fractured:

> When they [Dorian's servants] entered, they found hanging upon the wall a splendid portrait of their master as they had last seen him, in all the wonder of his exquisite youth and beauty. Lying on the floor was a dead man, in evening dress, with a knife in his heart. He was withered, wrinkled, and loathsome of visage. It was not till they examined the rings that they recognized who it was. (193)

Making modernity visible with an almost cinematic precision, Wilde gives us a permanent picture of queerness as "the terrible pleasure of a double life" (151). In Wilde's formulation, gay identity is the site of spectacular contradictions that are inextricably linked but are nevertheless opposing and mutually exclusive; in the words of Guy Debord, they "[unite] what is separate, but [unite] it only *in its separateness*" (22). Wilde's use of the spectacle does not erase the boundary between outward appearance and inner essence, but neither does it resolve this conflict by privileging one over the other. Framing this differently, we might say that the final reversal between the portrait and its subject uses Dorian's death to foreground the questions of identity and identification that the novel addresses. The problem of recognition faced by the servants—who is the "real" Dorian Gray?—cannot be solved once and for all because the gay subject straddles the divisions between appearance/essence and public/private that capitalism consolidates and intensifies. But this should not be taken to mean that Wilde defines the queer as opaque and unknowable. On the contrary, the argument I have just presented challenges well-known interpretations of *The Picture of Dorian Gray* as a multiplicity of secrets, which tantalize readers by evoking mysteries that are never disclosed. My project has been to show that Wilde does disclose the profound antagonisms that shape the dandy into an unremitting dialectic. As I have demonstrated, this ongoing dialectic is the "secret" of that distinctly modern form of split subjectivity we now call gay.

2

THE SEDUCTIONS OF SAPPHIC DECADENCE

The late nineteenth-century decadent movement provided modern European culture with its most dangerous and irresistibly seductive image of female same-sex passion, the "perverse" lesbian. This hauntingly beautiful figure makes an unforgettable (and controversial) appearance in the work of expatriate English poet Renée Vivien, who is best known today for the contemporary Sapphic circle she created with Natalie Barney in turn-of-the-century Paris. When discussed by scholars of feminist and lesbian studies, the perverse lesbian is typically represented as a fantasy of male decadent poets—such as Baudelaire, Pierre Louÿs, and Algernon Swinburne—for whom the depraved and aestheticized lesbian was an object of fascination, identification, and condemnation. This view of the Sapphic *femme damnée* and the decadent tradition from which she emerges has, of course, had a major effect on the reception of Vivien's work. For example, because she sees decadence primarily as a masculinist and misogynistic movement, Lillian Faderman presents Vivien as a misguided and self-destructive follower of Baudelaire and Louÿs. Faderman argues that, because Vivien imbibes the decadent movement's figure of the "flower of evil," her poetry reiterates decadence's failings by privileging images of lesbian evil and exoticism.[1] Although feminist literary critics have understandably emphasized the importance of Sappho in Vivien's life and work, it was not only the legacy of the Greek poet that propelled this modern-day Sapphist to construct a lesbian poetics; for Vivien, the perverse lesbian of decadence productively extends a Sapphic tradition, contributing to the transformation of modern sexual and gender norms. As Sandra Gilbert and Susan

Gubar have asserted, Vivien "subversively insinuates . . . that the lesbian is the epitome of the decadent and that decadence is fundamentally a lesbian literary tradition" (228). Vivien's immersion in the aesthetic sensibilities of decadence and symbolism was not unique among modernist lesbian writers and painters. For example, Bridget Elliott and Jo-Ann Wallace have shown how Natalie Barney and Romaine Brooks revived decadent aesthetics to make "a newly emerging lesbian identity publicly visible" (19).[2] Because decadence linked the aestheticism of the homosexual dandy with the artificiality of the perverse lesbian, modernist lesbians were able to construct new models of lesbian subjectivity by refashioning many of the motifs of dandyism—including homosexual aestheticism, decadence, artifice, rebellion against bourgeois society, nostalgia, and protest against modernization.

Vivien's notion of Sapphic decadence offers us much more than a reiteration of the Baudelairean *fleur du mal*—the lesbian as a fiercely passionate but doomed practitioner of what the poet calls "the delicate art of vice"—"l'art délicat du vice" (Vivien, "Lucidité," *Poèmes de Renée Vivien* 1). In the poet's work, the importance of Sappho's legacy for the production of a desiring lesbian subject and feminist utopian ideal results in a new and distinctly lesbian relation to the discourse of decadent aestheticism—one that illuminates the dialectic of decadence and utopia at the heart of capitalist modernity.[3] Literary critics such as Elyse Blankley and Shari Benstock have claimed that a feminist aesthetic is evident in Vivien's unprecedented reclamation of Sappho as a poet and lesbian foremother. The revision of Sappho's life that Vivien undertook, along with her translation of Sappho's fragments, infused Vivien's own poetry as she invoked the model of Sappho's life and work to move beyond the decadent definition of lesbianism as sterile, masochistic, and doomed and toward a more positive conception of lesbian desire as creative and fertile. For example, in poems like "Douceur de mes chants . . ." ("Softness of my songs . . ."), she presents an utopian vision of Sappho's city, imagining a glorious return to the island paradise where the poet's "soul soars once more"—"Voici que mon âme a repris son essor"—among a vibrant community of women who will join her in "re-sing[ing] to an intoxicated earth/The hymn of Lesbos" (*Muse* 2, 23–24)—"Et nous redirons à la terre enivrée/L'hymne de Lesbôs" (*Poèmes de Renée Vivien* 2, 23–24).[4] Contrasting the darkness and morbidity of Vivien's decadent poetics with the bright vision of female freedom typical of her Sapphic work, critics Benstock, Blankley, and Tama Lea Engelking present the poet's decadent and Sapphic aesthetics as distinct and opposed projects. As Benstock argues, we must "separate the two contradictory poetic stances reflected in Vivien's poetry—one combining images of morbidity, exoticism, and enclosure; the other transforming these images to ones of fertility, independence, and the freedom of a liberated female body and spirit" (*Women of the Left Bank* 286).

Departing from the critical propensity to separate such "contradictory poetic stances," I argue that Vivien's reified, decadent lesbian negatively embodies the utopian potential of Sapphic beauty and pleasure contained within it. Her seemingly paradoxical model of Sapphic decadence registers the dialectical contradiction of reification and liberation that—as I argued at the outset—defines capitalist modernity. However, I wish to emphasize that this contradiction finds its own dialectic in Vivien's distinctly lesbian counterimages of artifice and nature, which express an unlikely synthesis of the decadent movement's fantasy image of the ultramodern, artificial lesbian with a naturalized and heroic vision of Sapphism. In her decadent work in particular, Vivien mourns the impossibility of achieving an emancipated, autonomous lesbian identity in a patriarchal and capitalist world. Describing men as "political adversaries" who have commodified and fragmented the female body, she exposes the humiliation, suffering, and injustices that the specifically lesbian subject must endure in a world that commodifies and degrades eroticism between women (*A Woman Appeared to Me* 8). Indeed, her writings suggest that such heterosexist oppression is inseparable from the capitalist society that produces it. From this perspective, she invigorates decadence's most subversive insights, using its negativity to mobilize a critique of the ugliness and brutality of modern life, especially for self-proclaimed Sapphists and other lovers of women.[5]

I locate in Vivien's decadent poetry what Adorno would call a negative embodiment of decadence's negativity: "In a world of brutal and oppressed life, decadence becomes the refuge of a potentially better life by renouncing its allegiance to this one and to its culture, its crudeness, and its sublimity" (*Prisms* 72). As Adorno points out, this negative dialectics of decadence is not simply an unmediated utopian yearning, but rather the image of utopian possibility that is contained within decadence's reified universe. Since artifice for Vivien fuses seduction and commodification, her decadent poetry performs a striking double move. It both participates in the decadent impulse to fetishize the female body as seductive and reified object of desire *and* critiques the social conditions that have turned the modern lesbian subject into a painted corpse. If Vivien's perverse lesbian ultimately surrenders to emptiness and reification, this is because she has become the hollow soul of the commodity itself. In this context, Vivien's decadent aesthetic performs a dual negation that critiques both modern industrial capitalism and the "nostalgic yearning for an idyll of unmediated nature."[6] However, while her decadent poetry critiques the world in ruins that is bourgeois society, this nightmarish vision always coalesces with her utopian vision of Lesbos as the location of a "natural" female sexuality. In this way, Vivien's work demonstrates that the fascination with decadence and the seemingly contradictory fascination with origins are in reality "two sides of one and the same phenomenon"—they are two opposing and mutually exclusive aspects of modernity that are nevertheless inextricably linked (Calinescu 64).

By materializing lesbian identity through the opposition of artifice and nature, Vivien does not seek to abolish the contradictions that shape the lesbian subject but instead—as Marx would put it—she "provides the form within which they have room to move" (*Capital* 198). As I hope to demonstrate, her figure of the decadent Sapphist presents lesbian identity as a privileged emblem for modernity's most recognizable contradictions—particularly decadence/utopia, modern/ancient, and ephemeral/eternal. For Vivien, lesbian love embodies "the passing moment and of all the suggestions of eternity that it contains" (Baudelaire, *Painter of Modern Life* 5)—both the epitome of modern restlessness and the flicker of infinity contained within it. Demonstrating the lesbian's privileged status as a modernist icon, the ephemeral/eternal dialectic is crucial to my argument because it offers Vivien's most affirmative articulation of the utopian potentiality she finds in the figure of the decadent Sapphist. A symbol of the artificial paradise of commodity culture that makes desire an impossible demand, lesbian passion is simultaneously an "insatiable thirst" ("la soif impérieuse") and the "full cup" of desire's satisfaction ("mon âme est une coupe pleine"), thereby making the lesbian subject the incarnation of the contradictions inherent in the logic of commodity fetishism ("La Soif impérieuse," *Poèmes de Renée Vivien* 6). Indeed, as a fetishized commodity in the sexual marketplace, Vivien's perverse lesbian exhibits the prostitution of the soul that invades modern subjectivity. But as the poem "Ainsi je parlerai . . ." ("Like This I Would Speak") reveals, it is because of her sense of hollowness and alienation that Vivien rejects the modern world and returns to the "ancient splendor" of Mytilène ("Laisse-moi retourner vers la splendeur ancienne"), preferring pagan and classical values to the modern morality that has "silenced" the "chants of Lesbos": "God, your strict law was never mine,/And I lived like a simple pagan" (*Sweet Hour* 3–4)—"Seigneur, ta stricte loi ne fut jamais la mienne,/Et je vécus ainsi qu'une simple païenne" (*Poèmes de Renée Vivien* 3–4). It would seem that she theorizes the interpenetration of modernity and antiquity very much like Baudelaire does; however, since she uses the past as means to reconstruct the future, Vivien portrays her figure of the decadent Sapphist as the negative embodiment of a longing for utopia that is both nostalgic and revolutionary.

For Vivien, the artificial, perverse lesbian of decadence becomes a new, transhistorical Sapphist who merges the ephemeral with the eternal; and yet the naturalized world of lesbian love functions very much like artificiality does for dandies and decadents—as the basis for an escape from the commodification of modern culture. Sharing the dandy's desire to "shake off" the rationalization and instrumentality of a modern, mechanized world, Vivien, Barney, and their circle sought to create a separate world that would serve as an alternative to the limitations of bourgeois society, the sterility of the mass market, and the ugliness and alienation of modern city life. As Karla Jay suggests in her discussion of Barney and Vivien's trip to the isle of Lesbos in 1904: "Barney and Vivien believed that Lesbian societies offered positive and viable alternatives to the failures of modern mass culture" (*The Amazon and the Page* 115).[7] Vivien and Barney's desire to establish a utopian colony for poets on the island of Lesbos was never realized but their effort to rebuild Lesbos in Paris flourished in the seclusion of Barney's "wild" garden, where they and their friends aspired to live in terms they imagined as both aesthetic and natural, modern and ancient. Like Barney, Vivien ultimately discovered her "ancient soul" ("âme antique") in the very epicenter of modernity, and crossed "the disparate centuries" only to recover the raptures of Mytilène in the ruined metropolis that seemed to threaten her with extinction ("En débarquant à Mytilène" ["Landing at Mytilène"], *Poèmes de Renée Vivien* 2). As my reading seeks to demonstrate, Vivien's utopian expression of Sapphic decadence is iconic precisely because it embraces such contradictions.

ARTIFICE/NATURE

Both in revolt against modernity and a privileged emblem for the modern, Vivien's lesbian subject simultaneously stands inside and outside the world of turn-of-the-century Paris. In the poet's work, the lesbian emerges as an exile or "solitary voyager" ("la voyageuse solitaire")[8] who is shipwrecked in a materialistic and unbeautiful century that disdains Sappho's daughters; as Vivien puts it, "Everywhere I go I repeat: *I do not belong here*" (*The Amazon and the Page* 108). Like the dandy who protests against the ugliness of modern life, which is for him simultaneously brutal and banal, Vivien experienced contemporary Paris as a place of despair and disintegration. The narrator of her novel, *A Woman Appeared to Me*, describes the hopelessness that ensues from her confrontation with urban industrialism: "I went out soon into the swarming streets. I was depressed by the noise and confusion. The ugliness of the city crushed me" (33). Bruised by the devastating effects of the modern metropolis, Vivien transformed her home into an aestheticized dreamworld very much like the decadent hero of J. K. Huysmans's *À Rebours* (*Against Nature*) or Oscar Wilde's *The Picture of Dorian Gray*. Behind the walls and sealed windows of her Parisian apartment, Vivien created an exotic refuge from city life where she lived a sensual and artistic existence amid her collection of Oriental, Middle Eastern, and Mediterranean objets d'art (*A Woman Appeared to Me* vii).[9]

In Vivien's decadent poetry, this hermeticism is often framed as a response to modern society's oppression of the lesbian. "Let us stay behind closed doors" ("tenons les portes closes"), she declares to her lover in the poem "Intérieur," which glorifies interior space not so much as a fantasy world but more as a fortress "far from the pavement's turbulence" ("Loin des pavés houleux"). Having retreated to this private sanctuary, Vivien hopes to escape the "hatred" and "harsh looks of others" that is the lesbian subject's destiny in a modern world governed by "the cold outlook of the street/Where each one passes with jaded, rushing feet" (*Sweet Hour* 17–18)—"l'aspect glacial de la rue/Où chacun passe, avec une hâte recrue" ("Intérieur," *Poèmes de Renée Vivien* 17–18). Like Huysmans's des Esseintes, who seeks to transport himself beyond ordinary reality without ever leaving the confines of his home, Vivien transforms the bourgeois interior into a threshold to another, more glorious, world: "My eyes on the carpet, more polished than sand,/I idly recreate the golden river-banks/Where the clarity of beautiful yesterdays still linger" (68)—"Les yeux sur le tapis plus lisse que le sable,/J'évoque indolemment les rives aux pois d'or/Où la clarté des beaux autrefois flotte encor" ("Paroles à l'Amie" ["Words to a Lover"], *Poèmes de Renée Vivien* 9–11). However, although Vivien seeks "the Impossible Palace of Dreams," she is trapped in "an inhospitable world," an inferno that echoes with "the protracted screams/Of women" (*Muse* 3–4)—"Et pendant que le cri des femmes se prolonge,/Je cherche le Palais Impossible du Songe" ("La Mauvaise Auberge" ["The Sorry Hostelry"], *Poèmes de Renée Vivien* 3–4). From this perspective, she does not see herself as a damned or "cursed woman/Who deafly courts the flames of hell" (as she believes others do), but as a victim of a Baudelairean incarnation of hell that is located in the present moment (69).[10] Stripping the belle époque of its phantasmagoria, Vivien exposes the present as bankrupt, and the modern world as a "chaotic night" ("la nuit chaotique") of pain, emptiness, and death ("Sous la Rafale" ["Under the Storm"], *Poèmes de Renée Vivien* 1).[11]

It is in this context that I seek to reframe the poet's famous "obsession" with death. Her image of the dead or dying lesbian does not simply record a funereal fascination or mimic the decadent movement's vision of lesbianism as an eroticism in decline; instead, this iconography critiques the social conditions that entomb Sappho's descendants in an urban-industrial hell governed by "vile law"—"la loi vile"—and "impure morality"—"leur morale impure" ("Paroles à l'Amie," *Poèmes de Renée Vivien* 33; 41). Vivien's lesbian subject seems to be on the verge of extinction because she has been transformed into a hollowed-out object of desire. For example, in the poem "Je pleure sur Toi . . ." ("I Cry Over You . . .") the speaker mourns over the blank eyes and "lifeless spirit" of her beloved, who has relinquished her "fluid body" ("ton corps fluide") to "a common husband" ("l'époux vulgaire"). Vivien declares, "I come to weep for you, like one mourns a death" (*Sweet Hour* 4)—"Et je viens te pleurer, comme on pleure une morte" (*Poèmes de Renée Vivien* 4). In another poem, "Le Pilori" ("The Pillory"), the lesbian speaker describes her suffering and humiliation at the hands of a violent crowd, concluding "since then/My face is like the face of one dead" (*Sweet Hour* 17–18)—"Et depuis lors/Mon visage est pareil à la face des morts" (*Poèmes de Renée Vivien* 17–18). Throughout her work, Vivien's images of death, corpses, and entombment are emblematic of the emptiness and reification that overtake the modern lesbian subject.

In offering this political reading of her decadent project, it is not my intention to minimize Vivien's fascination with gloom, darkness, and death, or deny that she is captivated by a form of melancholy beauty that she finds alluring precisely because it is in the process of disintegrating. In *A Woman Appeared to Me*, for instance, the narrator San Giovanni departs from literary decadence's extravagantly sensual and ornamental style to declare, simply: "I love you because you are so wasted and pale, because you are going to die" (16–17). Ghostly pale, motionless, and reified, Vivien's decadent image of lesbian identity exhibits what Benjamin calls "the sex appeal of the inorganic" (Benjamin, *Reflections* 153). Possessing the seductiveness particular to hollow forms, like the commodity, the lesbian subject Vivien adores often seems to drift soundlessly "from sleep into death,/From night to the tomb, from dream to silence" (*Muse* 1–2)—"Doucement tu passas du sommeil à la mort,/De la nuit à la tombe et du rêve au silence" ("Épitaphe" ["Epitaph"], *Poèmes de Renée Vivien* 1–2). But in the poem "Sommeil" ("Sleep"), the speaker watches her slumbering lover, whose sleep "terrifies" because it is "as cold and profound/As eternal sleep" (*Muse* 1–2)—"Ton sommeil m'épouvante, il est froid et profond/Ainsi que le Sommeil aux langueurs éternelles" (*Poèmes de Renée Vivien* 1–2). The poem concludes:

> Foretasting mortal sorrow, final doom,
> I do not know that your breath has not fled like the breath
> Of the flowers, without agony or rattle of death,
> Into the distant night where dawn succumbs in the gloom
> And that this bed of love is not already the tomb. (*Muse* 6–10)[12]

Vivien is fascinated by the beautiful corpse—but she is simultaneously horrified by the alarming ease with which the threat of annihilation invades modern lesbian identity. For Vivien, to be a lesbian in modern society is to be extinguished so slowly that life bleeds into death.[13]

Because the lesbian identity she theorizes is an emblem for the hollowing out of inner life that characterizes capitalist modernity, the true "death" of the lesbian subject is her incarnation as the soul of the commodity. In her decadent work, Vivien, like Baudelaire, critiques the deadening effects of modernity by seeing the corpse "from the inside" (Buck-Morss 196), as in the following passage from *A Woman Appeared to Me*, in which the narrator, San Giovanni, declares:

> I had ceased to exist. I was a soul imprisoned in a corpse. I was a formless and confused mass, without substance or boundaries. I was floating with no other sensation than shuddering nudity. A thought surfaced in this empty consciousness, a thought sharper than desire or prayer: A personality! a body! a name! Oh, to become someone. To be what I was, even though I had already forgotten who I was! (Vivien 29)

Whereas Baudelaire "experienced the death of the soul in the still-living body," Vivien inverts Baudelaire's formulation to depict the modern lesbian as a living soul trapped in a cadaver (Buck-Morss 196). An exile doomed to wander through the raging "storm" and "chaotic night" of the modern world, Vivien's San Giovanni fragments and dissolves in the reifying currents of modern life ("Sous la Rafale," *Poèmes de Renée Vivien* 1, 22). Like the commodity itself, Vivien's lesbian subject is here depicted as "a roving soul in search of a body"[14]—possessing the "unanchored empathetic capacity" (Bernheimer 73) that Benjamin describes as the very essence of the commodity-soul; as Marx puts it, "A born leveller and cynic, it is always ready to exchange not only soul, but body, with each and every other commodity, be it more repulsive than Maritornes herself" (*Capital* 179). This "holy prostitution of the soul" is not valorized by Vivien (as Baudelaire does) but, instead, becomes a mark of the lesbian's degradation in a commodified world.

Like the dandy whose aestheticism aspires to rise above commodity society, Vivien's lesbian subject takes refuge in the realm of art. In the poem "Sur la Place publique" ("In the Public Square"), the poet describes a harpist who uses her music and singing to drown out "the greedy bargaining" and jeers that surround her in the public square ("Mais, dans l'enivrement de ma propre musique,/Je ne percevais point la rumeur du marché"). Elated by her own music, she seems to transcend the chaos of the market, experiencing a crystalline moment when "the noise of the town ceased." However, feeling mocked and bruised by the hopelessness of her situation, she discovers that "The harp shattered right in my hands in the night" (*Sweet Hour* 32)—"La harpe se brisa sous mes mains, dans la nuit" (*Poèmes de Renée Vivien* 36). The violence and darkness of this image hint at something that Vivien says more directly in another poem of the same collection. "The city powerful and harsh" ("la cité forte et rude") may be drowned out for a moment or an hour, but, ultimately, only death provides a release for "exiles" like Vivien, who savor the "repose" and "appeasement" of silence and darkness: "Slow death gently effaced the noise and the light . . ./I came to know the August face of night"—"La mort lente effaçait la lumière et le bruit . . ./Je connus le visage auguste de la nuit" ("Nous nous sommes assises" ["We Were Seated"], *Poèmes de Renée Vivien* 28–29). This sense of death as redemptive is even expressed in a poem like "Départ" ("Departure"), which contains some of Vivien's bleakest imagery: "Darkness comes to drown your hair of asphodele light./The bats beat, bruising their wings, against my door" (*Muse* 6–7). The poem concludes, "For the sea and death, at last, restore me tonight" (*Muse* 10).[15] Death becomes restorative for Vivien because she sees the modern world as empty and dead, and the ancient past as "more alive" and "more resonant" than the present.[16] Her decadent and Sapphic poetics intersect in this contradictory moment, in which the ancient lesbian of Mytilène and the decadent lesbian of modern day Paris are both imagined in the vocabulary of redemption.

Of course, Vivien's attempt to redeem lesbian identity is typically linked to her fascination with the "beautiful yesterdays" of Sappho's Lesbos. As a wide range of scholars have attested, Vivien was certainly not the only lesbian of her day to fall under Lesbos's "silvery" spell ("Sappho Enchants the Sirens," *The Woman and the Wolf* 93).[17] For Vivien, as for other members of Paris's artistic and literary lesbian community, Sappho's legacy was a refuge in a "cheerless and more barren age" (Doolittle 68). As the poet H.D. puts it in her essay, "The Wise Sappho": "She is the island of artistic perfection where the lover of ancient beauty (shipwrecked in the modern world) may yet find foothold and take breath and gain courage for new adventures and dream of yet unexplored continents and realms of future artistic achievement" (67). Sappho's descendants may have been adrift in the modern world, as H.D. implies, but lesbian society nonetheless took root in Paris, perhaps most famously in 1909 (the year that Vivien died) when Natalie Barney established her celebrated Left Bank salon.[18] In the years prior to Barney's Académie des Femmes, Vivien read her poetry beneath the Temple à l'Amitié in Barney's wooded garden, reviving the "long-vanished harmonies" of ancient Lesbos among a contemporary Sapphic circle that Barney was then beginning to create ("Sappho Enchants the Sirens," *The Woman and the Wolf* 94). There, in the heart of Paris, women such as Colette, the ex-Marquise de Belboeuf, Sarah Bernhardt, and Dolly Wilde wore Greek robes and participated in "pagan rituals" and "theatricals" that celebrated love and friendship between women (48; Weiss 101–3). For Barney and Vivien, who believed that "certain among us have conserved the rites/Of this shining Lesbos golden as an altar" ("Certaines d'entre nous ont conservé les rites/De ce brûlant Lesbos doré comme un autel"), these dramatic efforts to re-create Lesbos in Paris were indeed evidence that, as Vivien puts it, "Sappho lives again and reigns in our quivering bodies" (*Sweet Hour* 41)—"Psappha revit et règne en nos corps frémissants" ("Psappha revit" ["Sappho Lives Again"], *Poèmes de Renée Vivien* 13–14; 41).

The importance of Sappho's work in Vivien's poetry should not be interpreted as an uncomplicated form of nostalgia—a mimicking of the past that solely seeks to revive "faded joys" ("Où donc irai-je? . . ." ["Where Then Will I Go? . . ."], *Poèmes de Renée Vivien* 10). Vivien may have been "trying, as do all the nostalgic . . . [to] revive for an hour the grace of a vanished era" (*A*

Woman Appeared to Me 9), but what is most interesting about her project is that she looks back to the past in order to move dialectically forward, liberating the utopian potential of lesbian desire that is latent within the culture of decadence.[19] In one poem inspired by Sappho's fragment "Someone, I believe, will remember us in the future," Vivien becomes the "someone" who remembers Sappho and her lover Atthis and, in turn, tells her own "Atthis" that "Future beings will not forget us"—"Les êtres futurs ne nous oublieront pas" ("Dans les lendemains . . ." ["On tomorrows . . ."], *Poèmes de Renée Vivien* 2). Vivien's search for historical continuity in the face of the ephemerality of the present ultimately leads her to link past, present, and future; while she welcomes Sappho into the present, finding in her work a dazzling immediacy that transcends "tears of returning"—"les larmes des retours" ("Douceur de mes chants . . ." ["Softness of my songs . . ."], *Poèmes de Renée Vivien* 6)—she simultaneously places herself in the past of "future evenings," when she imagines that beautiful young women who do not know her poems will turn their "irresolute steps towards the future"—"Tournant vers l'avenir vos pas irrésolus" ("Par les Soirs futurs" ["In the Future Evenings"], *Poèmes de Renée Vivien* 10). Even more important, Vivien's incorporation of Sappho's lyrics into her own poems[20] creates a montage of past and present that puts into formal terms the thematic I want to emphasize: uniting the archaic and the modern in a dialectical image, Vivien illuminates the transformative potential of the present moment in order to construct an alternative future. Because it simultaneously embodies impulses toward the past and the future, her wish to redeem the ur-past of the Sapphist is as revolutionary as it is reactionary. Vivien is indeed fascinated by an idealized and naturalized vision of female freedom, but it is by way of this utopian imagery that her Sapphic poetics perform a remarkable negative embodiment of decadence, "telescoping the past through the present" as a way of unlocking an emancipatory future of lesbian passion and possibility.[21] Although she always holds out Mytilène, that glorious female city, as an emblem of the lesbian community she dreams of rebuilding, Vivien never allows us to forget that she longs for Lesbos from the negativity of her own time and place, where the modern day Sapphist has become a painted corpse, prostituted by commodity society's reified desire.

SO BLONDE, SO PALE

I do not anymore wish to see
The world except through the veil
Of your hair, so blonde, so pale,
For my soul is weary of my destiny.
("Chanson," *Muse* 1–4)

J'ai l'âme lasse du destin
Et je ne veux plus voir le monde
Qu'à travers le voile divin
De tes pâles cheveux de blonde.
("Chanson," *Poèmes de Renée Vivien* 1–4)

Vivien's protest against the commodification of the female body is evident in her appropriation and revision of the image of the prostitute. For Vivien's predecessor Baudelaire, the prostitute was a complex and seductive symbol of both feminine vice and "the special beauty of evil" that haunts inauthentic and commercialized love (*Painter of Modern Life* 38).[22] Although she shares Baudelaire's ambivalent attraction to the artifice of the courtesan, Vivien uses the image of the prostitute to condemn not the depravity of female sexuality but the form that it takes under capitalism—most specifically, the commodification and degradation of lesbian eroticism. As Elyse Blankley has noted, Vivien's Sapphic revival is an attempt to reimagine lesbian desire apart from the Parisian brothel—a context that dominates the representation of lesbianism in the poetry of both Baudelaire and Pierre Louÿs. In Baudelaire and Louÿs's version of shared female eroticism, lesbian lovers with "hollow eyes" ("les filles aux yeux creux") perform acts of "sterile voluptuousness" ("stérile volupté") for a voyeuristic male customer.[23] In the poem "Le Dédain de Psappha" ("The Disdain of Sappho"), though, Vivien implies that such conditions will not rob her of her faith in the power and beauty of love between women: "You will never know how to tarnish the devotion/Of my passion for the beauty of women" (*Muse* 5–6)—"Vous ne saurez point ternir la piété/De ma passion pour la beauté des femmes" (*Poèmes de Renée Vivien* 5–6). But Vivien's work also demonstrates the impossibility of disengaging from a world that "disdains" lesbian love and its pleasures, a world that reduces the practices once honored on Lesbos to "vices" and demotes Sappho's descendants to whores.

The connection between lesbianism and prostitution in France has been firmly established by scholars of modern culture.[24] In *Women for Hire: Prostitution and Sexuality in France after 1850*, Alain Corbin suggests that this link dates back to Parent-Duchâtelet's influential work *De la prostitution dans la ville de Paris*, which not only describes lesbians as the lowest category of courtesans but also advocates regulation to impede the "spread" of homosexuality among prostitutes (Corbin 7–8, 12). The obsessive attempt to contain prostitutes' deviant sexuality persisted as late as 1887 when, as Lillian Faderman reports, "lesbianism among prostitutes was apparently so widespread that some attempt was made through the Municipal Council of Paris to halt it" (*Surpassing the Love of Men* 282). By the late nineteenth century, representations of lesbians and prostitutes were so inextricably linked that it is often impossible to distinguish between them.[25] In *Nana*, for example, Emile Zola's well-known novel about a Parisian courtesan, the figure of the prostitute is a decomposing object of desire—at once carnivorous and seductive—whose degeneracy is marked by her bisexuality and lesbianism. This predatory image of the lesbian prostitute is closely related to pornographic representations of *femmes vicieuses* [perverse women], "women with lesbian tendencies who would prostitute themselves for money, ruin men with their desire for luxuries and, in the end, destroy men's virility, if they were not victimized first" (Hunt, *The Invention of Pornography* 339). A ubiquitous and threatening emblem of the fantastical extremes of gendered identity at the fin de siècle, *femmes vicieuses* and *femmes damnées* were objects of a powerful male fascination that sought both to contain and fetishize the image of the omnivorous whore. By the turn of the century, "pleasure guides" to Paris used lesbian sex to advertise the exoticism of Paris' bordellos, presenting the lesbian couple as "the crowning jewel of a Parisian brothel" (Blankley 49). Because she symbolized the erosion of bourgeois social order, the lesbian became a precious commodity, objectified by the emerging circuit of exchange value.

In the poem "Sonnet," Vivien demonstrates the way in which the "sapphist/whore connection" (to borrow Blankley's term) causes relationships between women to be haunted by the figure of the prostitute. Pale, cold, and motionless, the object of the poet's desire is an incarnation of the prostitute. The poem describes a world in which lesbian love has been emptied of its power and glory:

> Your strange hair, cold light,
> Has pale glows and blond dullness;
> Your gaze has the blue of ether and waves;
> Your gown has the chill of the breeze and the woods.
> (*Muse* 1–4)

Here, we can see the way in which the lesbian, like the prostitute, takes on the dull but seductive glimmer of the commodity. Drained of warmth, anesthetized, and possessing "the sex appeal of the inorganic" (Benjamin, *Reflections* 153)—as represented by the deceptive glimmer of her strange hair—Vivien's lesbian is an utterly reified being who inhabits a desert where "the night air spreads the dust from many worlds" ("l'air nocturne répand la poussière des mondes"). The poem continues:

> The moon grazed you with a slanted glow . . .
> It was terrible, like prophetic lightning
> Revealing the hideous below your beauty.

I saw—as one sees a flower fade—
On your mouth, like summer auroras,
The withered smile of an old whore.
(*Muse* 9–14)[26]

By focusing on the moment of revelation when the whore becomes visible beneath the enticing image of the poet's beloved, Vivien emphasizes the way in which the lesbian and the prostitute are ineluctably bound up with each other; or, to put it another way, she emphasizes the way in which lesbian experience is overdetermined by the commodification of women's sexuality in the marketplace. Certainly, Vivien's image of the prostitute is a morbid emblem of degeneration, recalling the famous nineteenth-century French dandies, the brothers Goncourt, and their description of the Parisian *grande cocotte*, La Païva: "a figure that, underneath the appearance of a courtesan still young enough for her profession, is one hundred years old and takes on at times the undefinable terror of a painted corpse."[27] This notion of the prostitute as painted corpse is characteristic of Baudelaire's work as well, and informs Vivien's portrayal of the ancient whore as a symbol of the dark underside of modern life—"a perfect image of the savagery that lurks in the midst of civilization" (Baudelaire, *Painter of Modern Life* 16). Fashioned in the image of the prostitute, then, Vivien's lesbian must be simultaneously beautiful and hideous, both the glimmering object of desire and the withered victim of a violent and decaying world.

It is this notion of modern lesbian identity as the combination of dialectical oppositions that, I believe, has been so misunderstood by Vivien's readers. Once we recognize that, for Vivien, lesbian identity is itself a contradiction, we can begin to make sense of the contradictions in her poetry, linking the decadent vision of the lesbian-as-prostitute to the glorification of virginity that characterizes her Mytilène poems. In these poems inspired by Sappho, Vivien extols the wonders of being "Pale from solitude, drunk with chastity!"—"Pâle de solitude, ivre de chasteté!" ("Velléité" ["Velleity"], *Poèmes de Renée Vivien* 8) and declares that she will "remain virgin as the serene snow"—"Je demeurerai vierge comme la neige/Sereine" ("Je demeurerai . . . ," *Poèmes de Renée Vivien* 1). Introduced with Sappho's fragment "I shall always be virgin," her poem "Je demeurerai . . ." challenges the cultural meaning of female chastity:

As breath of the north and river of rain,
I shall flee imprint and soiling stain.
The grasp that strangles, the kiss that infects
        And wounds I shall shun.
(*Muse* 4–7)[28]

Vivien does not celebrate sexual purity, but a defiant refusal to submit to male degradation. Similarly, in the poem "Ainsi qu'une pomme . . ." ("As an Apple . . ."), she incorporates fragments of Sappho into her work to protest against the objectification of the female body and celebrate an autonomous female sexuality. When she declares that "You shine forth, mocking the vain cupidity/Of the covetous passerby"(*Muse* 7–8)—"Tu t'épanouis, raillant les convoitises/Vaines des passants" (*Poèmes de Renée Vivien* 7–8)—she seems to offer a response to Baudelaire's famous sonnet "A une passante" ("To a Passer-by") about a beautiful, female passer-by whom the poet desires after seeing her briefly in the street.[29] Vivien's figure of the lesbian-as-virgin attains a statuesque inaccessibility as she rewrites Baudelaire's image of the female passer-by and offers a vision of the lesbian body removed from the street and the circulation of the marketplace: "You keep the fruit of your body beautiful/And inaccessible" (*Muse* 11–12)—"Tu gardes, ô vierge inaccessible et belle,/Le fruit de ton corps" (*Poèmes de Renée Vivien* 11–12). By glorifying this "chaste" and unreachable Sapphic lesbian, Vivien's Mytilène poems would seem unreconcilable with her decadent vision of the lesbian as prostitute. However, as I have been arguing, Vivien's decadent and Sapphic poetics are opposed extremes, but they are simultaneously "two inseparable moments, which belong to and mutually condition each other" (Marx, *Capital* 140). Clearly, the female body cannot be protected from the brutality of patriarchy and capitalism in Vivien's darker, decadent poems—it is not splendidly unavailable as it is in the Sapphic poems. And yet the perverse, decadent lesbian is an emblem of the ephemeral who is also inaccessible and out of reach like the virginal, Sapphic lesbian; indeed, the Sapphic lesbian's island paradise on Lesbos is the very embodiment of the decadent lesbian's vision of isolation as freedom.

If much of her explicitly feminist work evokes the past of Lesbos, this is because Vivien sees the modern world as a treacherous and "inhospitable" place that echoes with "the protracted screams of women" ("La Mauvaise Auberge" ["The Sorry Hostelry"], *Poèmes de Renée Vivien* 3–4). Her stress on artificial beauty ultimately challenges the decadent tradition's aesthetic view of lesbian identity, since it is by way of this metaphor that Vivien protests against the modern social formations that have imprisoned women and commodified the female body. At the same time, the veiling and masking of a femininity not found in nature are part of the perverse lesbian's power to captivate her "prey," and so have a dark, seductive appeal in Vivien's work. From this perspective, Vivien's construction of the lesbian's artificiality demonstrates an affiliation with decadent nineteenth-century images of lesbian eroticism, as well as an affiliation with the dandies of Baudelaire and Huysmans. Like Baudelaire's "flowers of evil" or Huysmans's des Esseintes, her decadent Sapphist is a twilight creature who privileges the artificial over the natural, languorously pointing to the exhaustion of beauty in a ruined world. Yet, if she uses the trope of the artificial to aestheticize lesbian identity much as her nineteenth-century predecessors did, she simultaneously embarks upon a remarkable departure from decadence's aesthetic philosophy. Unlike Huysmans's des Esseintes, who seeks to live a completely artificial existence, or Baudelaire, who celebrates the "sublime deformation of Nature," Vivien does not fetishize artifice as transcendence of nature and corporeality; instead, she yokes it primarily to the seductions and deceptions of the market (Baudelaire, *Painter of Modern Life* 33).

In the poem "Sonnet" (reproduced in full next), the familiar rhetoric of the alluring artfulness of female beauty is transformed in the course of the poem as Vivien simultaneously invokes in the fetishistic ideology of female beauty—which follows, as Baudrillard has pointed out, the fetishistic logic of the commodity—and critiques its effects (Baudrillard 94–95). Here, lesbian artifice becomes an emblem for bourgeois society's fusion of seduction and commodification:

> The pomp of jewels, the vanity of curled tresses
> Mix the polish of art with your perverse charm.
> Even the gardenias which winter cannot harm
> Die in your hands of your impure caresses.
>
> Your delicately delineated mouth expresses
> The artifice, the inflections of poetry.
> Your breasts blossom in pale luxury
> Under the cleverly half-open folds of your dresses.
>
> The reflection of sapphires darkens in the somber night
> Of your eyes. Your undulous body that troubles my sight
> Makes a gleaming furrow of gold in the middle of the night.
>
> When you pass, holding a subtle smile for me,
> Blonde pastel surcharged with gems and perfumery,
> I dream of the splendor of your body naked and free.
> ("Sonnet," *Muse*)[30]

"Your delicately delineated mouth expresses/The artifice, the inflections of poetry." This image of artifice as written on and in the details of the lesbian body should remind us that Vivien follows Baudelaire by conceptualizing the lesbian as the aesthetic par excellence. However, while the dandy and male decadent employ artifice to effect a glorious transcendence of nature, for the decadent Sapphist the trope of the artificial is both celebrated and condemned.

Invoking commodity culture's nexus of femininity, luxury, and artifice, Vivien uses the model of the courtesan to depict the lesbian as an elaborately decorated erotic object—painted, costumed, and bejeweled. Although herself a captive, this captivatingly sensual object of desire is also a desiring subject who remains fundamentally untouchable and inaccessible (much like the virginal subject of "Ainsi qu'une pomme . . ."). She teases passers-by with the sight of "the cleverly half-open folds of [her] dresses" and her lingering, "subtle smile," which seduces and beckons like the alluring face of the commodity itself. The reader may recognize in her gleaming, "subtle smile" for the speaker another, darker smile—the vestigial image of "the withered smile of an old whore" ("Sonnet"14). A polished gem glowing before the drapery of the nighttime world, the decadent Sapphist's "undulous body" seems to break free of its constraints, making "a gleaming furrow of gold in the middle of the night."

Vivien subverts the aesthetic or ornamental view of lesbian identity by infusing the modern Sapphist with a materiality and agency that are absent from the work of male decadent poets such as Baudelaire. Since the lesbian was a symbolic object of desire and damnation for these poets, the decadent tradition had "no attitude towards her in real life" (Benjamin, *Charles Baudelaire* 93). Vivien's interest in the social experience of the lesbian subject, however, complicates her treatment of artificiality considerably. Condemning the artificial world of the bourgeoisie that disguises women's social and economic reality, she demonstrates that the appearance of luxury and leisure is a mystification—it conceals the fact that, as she puts it in the poem "Lucidity": "Your soul has become withered, your body has been abused" (*Muse* 13)—"Et ton âme est flétrie et ton corps est usé" ("Lucidité," *Poèmes de Renée Vivien* 13). In the final line of "Sonnet," Vivien invokes the utopianism of her Sapphic poems as she privileges nature over artifice, envisioning the liberation of the female body from its fetishization as ornament and object ("I dream of the splendor of your body naked and free"—"Je songe à la splendeur de ton corps libre et nu"). Indeed, the poem's movement from the rhetoric of decadence to the rhetoric of nature and liberation not only demonstrates the political importance of decadence in Vivien's project, but also illuminates the poet's dialectical vision, in which the decadent and utopian aspects of the modern lesbian subject are endlessly renewed.

CONSTANT CRAVING

Vivien's decadent poetry depicts love between women as a "burning desire," an ecstatic but torturous form of pleasure that is the sublime realization of a new economy of desire. Like Baudelaire who describes lesbians as doomed beings with "slakeless thirsts"—"soifs inassouvies"—("Femmes damnées," *Les Fleurs du mal* 27) and "hungering hearts"—"cœurs ambitieux"—("Lesbos," *Les Fleurs du mal* 27), Vivien defines the lesbian as an ardent sufferer: "Oh! the eternal hunger, the eternal thirst/And the eternal regret!"—"Ah! l'éternelle faim et la soif éternelle/Et l'éternel regret!" ("Ta forme est un éclair . . ." ["Your Form Is a Gleam . . ."], *Poèmes de Renée Vivien* 7–8). In her decadent work, this aspect of lesbian love is not condemned as a mark of sterility (as in Baudelaire's poetry), but instead is celebrated as a subversive form of desire that defers fulfillment and so wrenches pleasure from its typical goal. Vivien's effort to challenge nineteenth-century decadent definitions of lesbian love as sterile, evil, and doomed is most readily apparent in her Sapphic poetics. In her poems that invoke Sappho and Lesbos, she reimagines shared female eroticism as a transcendent communion that replaces "the torments of Eros" ("les tourments de l'Érôs") with mutual pleasure and contentment ("Douceur de mes chants . . ." 22). In the poem "Veillée heureuse" ("Happy Vigil"), for example, the enraptured speaker watches over her sleeping lover, whose childlike, "perfect visage" ("visage parfait") is a fitting symbol of a love innocent, pure, and—above all—fulfilled; as she buoyantly declares, "my heart is peaceful and satisfied"—"mon cœur est doux et satisfait" (*Poèmes de Renée Vivien* 9, 12). For Vivien, however, the Sapphist is always caught between competing constructions of lesbian identity. In her novel, *A Woman Appeared to Me*, the decadent conception of lesbianism as torturous passion and the redemptive conception of lesbianism as peaceful satisfaction are embodied in the figures of Vally the Perverse and Eva the Redeemer, who represent the opposing faces of female same-sex desire between which the narrator is hopelessly ensnared. When Vivien presents Sapphic sexuality as both an eternal ache and a dreamworld of enfolding comfort—both an emblem of desire and its phantasmatic satisfaction—she situates the lesbian "between the two walls of the impossible" (Lacan 167), defining the modern lesbian subject as one who yearns endlessly for fulfillment but who is nevertheless haunted by her own refusal to fulfill her "savage desire"—"Désir farouche" ("Départ," *Poèmes de Renée Vivien* 4).

Of course, the notion that women are fundamentally insatiable has a long history, taking on a particular force in the fin de siècle's misogynistic representations of devouring femininity, which locate the lesbian among deviant women, like prostitutes, whose voracious desire is an emblem of their revolt against bourgeois society.[31] Carolyn Dean notes that, in lesbians, sexual inversion "reiterated received ideas about the power and insatiability of female desire" (*The Frail Social Body* 183). Dean's claim that lesbian identity needs to be examined in the context of hegemonic constructions of femininity should remind us that this gendered frame of reference is at work for Vivien as it was for Baudelaire before her, defining the figure of the perverse lesbian as hyperfeminine in her sexual insatiability. However, Vivien's dialectic of lesbian desire takes up another cultural logic of the day—one that is specifically embedded in late nineteenth-century commodity culture's new economy of desire. Unlike the Baudelairean "flower of evil," lesbian eroticism is not, essentially speaking, an impossible demand for Vivien; rather, she seeks to emphasize the paradoxical predicament of the modern Sapphist, who must inhabit a world in which desire is both multiplied and unsatisfied. In this way, Vivien makes the decadent or perverse Sapphist a privileged emblem for the melding of commodification, seduction and aesthetics in fin-de-siècle society. Baudelaire captures this convergence of economics and aesthetics in his journals when he wistfully asserts that modern beauty "conveys an idea of melancholy, of weariness, even of satiety—and at the same time a contrary idea: an ardor, a desire to live, coupled with a recurrent bitterness, such as might come of privation or despair" (*My Heart Laid Bare* 163). The yoking of pleasure and sorrow—satiety and longing—is an enduring feature of the experience of capitalist modernity. In his essay, "Desire in Exchange Value," Baudrillard argues that the sphere of value is haunted by a fundamental "ambivalence" that takes the form of lack or "deficit":

> The commodity is the incarnation of the sublime in the economic order. The radical demand of the subject is sublimated there in the ever renewed positivity of his demand for objects. But behind this sublime realization of value, there lies something else. Something other speaks, something irreducible that can take the form of violent destruction, but most frequently assumes the cloaked form of deficit, of the exhaustion and refusal of cathexis, of resistance to satisfaction and refusal of fulfillment. (207)

Here, Baudrillard describes the contrary demands produced by capitalist social relations—the demand for a full, positive world and the necessity of lack and negation; as he suggests, the latter is necessary because it ensures that the former demand is "ever renewed." Baudrillard frames these opposing demands in terms of ambivalence, not contradiction, a term that shares with contradiction the dialectic in which gain and loss occur simultaneously (Lefebvre 233). As I have been arguing, Vivien formulates lesbian identity not only as an immeasurable and insatiable demand, but also as a sublime guarantor of fulfillment. For her, lesbian identity is a contradiction; it is both a form of radical lack (the refusal of fulfillment) and a fetishistic fascination with the realization of desire (the desire to make whole what is lacking). If for so many cultural commentators, the lesbian has been seen as an icon of modernism, this is because the model of lesbian identity I have just described is the incarnation of the contradictions inherent in the social experience of modernity.

In her poems that invoke Mytilène and Lesbos, Vivien imagines a world that is structured according to what Baudrillard calls the "phantasmic organization" of the exchange system—a world where "desire is fulfilled and lack resolved" (206). It is no wonder that she declares, "Happiness awaits us on this fragrant isle"—"Le bonheur nous attend dans cette île odorante" ("Vers Lesbos" ["Toward Lesbos"], *Poèmes de Renée Vivien* 20). In her vision of Lesbos, graceful and lovely women experience infinite pleasures while they recline on soft cushions, exchanging "lunar kisses"—"nos lunaires baisers"—and melodious caresses while sipping "nectar full of joy"—"le nektar rèmpli de joies"—served by Sappho herself ("Psappha revit" 33; "Ainsi je parlerai . . ." 52). In this Sapphic paradise, lesbian subjectivity is emblematic of wholeness and desire's satisfaction; it is, as Vivien puts it, the "passionate quest/Toward happy dreams"[32] that, paradoxically enough, ultimately allows the lesbian subject to "melt away and dissolve" ("je me fonds et me dissous") in an ecstatic communion with the "ancient soul"—"âme antique"—she sets out to recover ("En débarquant à Mytilène" ["Landing at Mytilène"], *Poèmes de Renée Vivien* 11, 19). Of course, this premodern, organic community is far removed from commodity culture's artificial paradise where the phantasmatic promise of satisfaction achieves its quintessential form. Indeed, in her Sapphic poems, Vivien inverts the dandy's desire to complete oneself in and through objects—through value—as a means of transcending nature. In Vivien's reworked model of queer identity, it would seem that nature trumps value as the naturalized world of Sapphic pleasures becomes a means of transcending commodification by banishing ambivalence, negativity, and lack.

Vivien juxtaposes this Sapphic and decidedly utopian vision of lesbianism with her decadent conception of lesbian desire as a torturous form of ecstasy: "the cruel pleasure that persists and torments" (*Sweet Hour* 20)—"le cruel plaisir qui s'acharne et tourmente" ("Je t'aime d'être faible . . ." ["I Love You for Being Weak"], *Poèmes de Renée Vivien* 12). As I have already indicated, this decadent vision of shared female eroticism both follows and departs from Baudelaire's influential depiction of lesbians as *femmes damnées* in *Les Fleurs du mal.* Because Baudelaire sees the lesbian as fundamentally sterile, he believes lesbian eroticism to be a desire never capable of achieving fulfillment. Addressing his fiery "flowers of evil," he declares, "never will you find your passion satisfied,/And your torment will be your pleasure's awful child."[33] Although she shares with Baudelaire this sense of lesbian love as an unquenchable thirst, Vivien revalues satisfaction itself, ultimately offering a radically different vision: "Toward you rises the pure aspiration of my soul./My anguish does not seek to quench itself at all" (*Muse* 13–14)—"Vers toi le songe pur de mon âme s'élève,/Mon angoisse ne cherche point à s'apaiser" ("A la Divinité inconnue" ["To the Unknown Divinity"], *Poèmes de Renée Vivien* 13–14). For Vivien, lesbian eroticism is a form of fierce love that *refuses* to fulfill desire, privileging the trembling caresses and ardent sufferings of a love with no beginning and no end. In the poem "Le Toucher" ("The Touch"), for instance, the speaker's trembling fingers worshipfully climb the contours of her lover's body and become an emblem for a love that does not demand or impose satisfaction. Vivien declares, "In your white voluptuousness my desire rests,/Swooning, refusing itself the kisses of your lips" (*Muse* 11–12)—"Mon désir délicat se refuse aux baisers:/ Il effleure et se pâme en des voluptés blanches" ("Le Toucher," *Poèmes de Renée Vivien* 11–12).

It is tempting to romanticize this refusal to fulfill desire, since in Vivien's model the resistance to satisfaction is a form of self-dispossession, making surrender a precondition for pleasure. But the complex fascination with lack, negativity, and dispossession that drives her definition of lesbian passion as "bitter ecstasy" locates Vivien squarely in a decadent tradition that empties the ideal of love by exposing its hollowing out and disfigurement by capitalist relations. In this respect, her Sapphic decadence has much in common with the decadent aestheticism and dandyism of Baudelaire, Wilde, or Huysmans. Of course, we cannot forget that Vivien's representation of lesbianism as a slakeless hunger makes the lesbian the very emblem of desire and corporeality, which the dandy's asceticism always aims to rise above. As a result, Vivien's perverse lesbian is chained to the body and its desires despite her own ascetic tendencies toward self-dispossession. At the same time, the decadent lesbian subject who refuses satisfaction critiques the concept of need itself, very much like the dandy who strives to transcend commodification by liberating desire from the tyranny of instrumental need. However, as I have demonstrated, in her poems that invoke Sappho and Lesbos, Vivien presents a naturalized and utopian vision of lesbian desire that promises wholeness and fulfillment. Caught between the contradictory imperatives of capitalism, Vivien's image of the decadent Sapphist is a privileged emblem for the modern, desiring subject who seeks both to realize and resist the economy of value. To be sure, this form of split subjectivity is the hallmark of a modern culture that turns us all into feminized—that is, insatiably desiring—subjects.

FUGITIVE FORMS AND OTHER SHADOWS OF INFINITY

If for Vivien Sapphic desire is an impossible demand, this is perhaps because she theorizes lesbian identity as an elusive and fleeting form, a "chimera one can see/That one strives for, reaches for and, over and over, forever misses" (*Muses* 9–10)—"ainsi que la Chimère/vers qui tendent toujours les vœux inapaisés . . ." ("Ta forme est un éclair . . ." ["Your Form Is a Gleam . . ."], *Poèmes de Renée Vivien* 9–10). This notion of the lesbian as a gleaming subject on the run—"a fluid parting" who always escapes containment ("Ta forme fuit, ta démarche est fluide")—is characteristic of Vivien's decadent poetry, which often invokes metaphors of velocity and instantaneousness to represent the lesbian subject ("Ondine" ["Undine"], *Poèmes de Renée Vivien* 5). Vivien invokes the temporal experience of modern city life as she depicts the decadent Sapphist as a subject in perpetual motion, in flight. In several poems, she uses the quintessentially urban image of the passer-by to describe the modern lesbian's restless motion. In this work, the object of the poet's desire is seductive and irresistible *because* she is just passing through. Consider the following verses: "When you pass, holding a subtle smile for me,/. . ./I dream of the splendor of your body naked and free" ("Sonnet" 12, 14); "And oh, Beloved, when you pass/What trembling of the air!" (*Muse* 3–4)—"Et tu passes, ô Bien-Aimée,/Dans le frémissement de l'air . . ." ("Chanson," *Poèmes de Renée Vivien* 5–6); and, finally, these lines from the opening of "Elle passe" ("She Passes")

> The sky frames her like a shrine,
> And I would live one hundred years without seeing her again,
> She is the sudden: she is the miracle of evening.
> The religious moment blazes and tolls . . . she passes . . .
> (*Sweet Hour* 1–4)[34]

Vivien is fascinated by the eroticism of fugitive forms—forms that provoke not love at first sight but "love at last sight" (Benjamin, *Charles Baudelaire* 45). In another "Sonnet," Vivien explores the ambiguity and anguish that constitute this longing for fleeting forms:

> Oh form that hands will never know how to retain!
> Elusive as a brief rainbow after rain,
> Your smile, disappearing, leaves more empty, more drear,
> The heart that mourns after a too-sweet souvenir.
> (*Muse* 1–4)[35]

The "disappearing" smile Vivien describes is a metonym for the seductive appeal of the elusive and disappearing lesbian. And yet this "Sonnet" pursues a twinned aesthetic that, as we have seen, characterizes Vivien's work as a whole. Longing for the "too-sweet" souvenir that represents an eternity of fulfillment, she nostalgically "mourns" the eclipse of the permanent by the transitory, while simultaneously fetishizing the elusive object of desire as a "souvenir" not of her presence but of her absence.

To put it another way, we might say that Vivien's longing for fleeting forms is matched by an equally powerful yearning for permanence. In the poem "Qu'une vague l'emporte . . ." ("May a Wave Carry It Away . . ."), Vivien uses the image of the "eternal ocean" as an emblem of the monumental and transhistorical into which the modern lesbian subject longs to merge. Vivien declares: "I am tired of loving fugitive forms./Standing tall, I take my heart where yesterday love was/So vibrant, and here: I throw it into the ocean"

(*Muse* 4–6)—"Je suis lasse d'aimer les formes fugitives./Debout, je prends mon cœur où l'amour fut hier/Si puissant, et voici: je le jette à la mer" (*Poèmes de Renée Vivien* 4–6). Vivien's desire to merge with the "deep work" ("profond travail")[36] of the eternal in the face of the flux and ephemerality of the present is most vividly expressed in her poetry about Lesbos, which the poet imagines as a magical place "where exalts a fragrance of eternal flowers"—"où s'exalte un parfum/De fleurs éternelles" ("Pour Androméda . . . ," *Poèmes de Renée Vivien* 7–8). In contrast with the Parisian world of 1900, where temporal processes are ceaselessly accelerated, Vivien's lesbian city of Mytilène possesses the stillness and silence of eternal forms, enfolding its inhabitants in an endless shower of golden dawns and silver evenings. In this way, Lesbos transcends temporality and so enables the Sapphic searcher to "aspire to the infinite that one no longer acquires"—"J'aspire aux infinis que l'on n'atteindra pas" ("Mon Ami le Vent . . ." ["My Friend the Wind . . ."], *Poèmes de Renée Vivien* 7). Accordingly, in the Mytilène poems, Vivien describes love between women as an eternal desire liberated of time and space. In the poem "Union," for example, Vivien celebrates an affinity between women so transcendent that it attains mythic dimensions:

> Our love is part of infinity,
> Absolute as death and beauty . . .
> See, our hearts are joined and our hands are united
> Firmly in space and in eternity.
> (*Muse* 17–20)[37]

Conceptualizing lesbianism as "an ecstatic timeless communion," Vivien offers a redemptive image of lesbian identity relieved of the tyranny of time (Blankley 54). Accordingly, the lesbian subject is simultaneously the quintessential fugitive form and the embodiment of all that is infinite and immutable; like Mytilène itself, "ornament and splendor of the sea," she remains both "versatile and eternal"—"Mytilène, parure et splendeur de la mer,/Comme elle versatile et comme elle éternelle" ("En débarquant à Mytilène" ["Landing at Mytilène"], *Poèmes de Renée Vivien* 37–38).

Approaching Vivien's poetry from this dual perspective, we can see that her decadent and Sapphic poetics are not separate and independent (as critics such as Benstock, Blankley, and Engelking have suggested) but, instead, mediate each other in complex ways. Vivien's insertion of the lesbian subject in the dialectic between the ephemeral and the eternal expresses not only the priviledged modernity of the decadent Sapphist, but also a particularly affirmative framing of this figure's utopian possibilities. It is worth noting that her double sense of the lesbian as both eternal and ephemeral recalls Baudelaire's famous definition of the modern artist as the one who undertakes "to extract from fashion whatever element it may contain of poetry within history, to distill the eternal from the transitory" (*Painter of Modern Life* 12).[38] For Baudelaire, what distinguishes modern artists is their attempt to locate the universal in the particular. By extracting the immutable and the monumental from the fleetingness of fashion and historical change, the modern artist lays bare the dialectical construction of modern life; like beauty itself, which fuses general and invariable elements with those that represent the relative and the particular, the culture of capitalist modernity ceaselessly mixes the eternal and ephemeral. Offering a dialectical image of the lesbian as a visionary seeker who immortalizes the moment, Vivien's work suggests that the decadent Sapphist is an artist of modernity who illuminates the threshold between the eternal and the ephemeral.

The lesbian subject of Vivien's decadent poetry inhabits a world of "everlasting uncertainty and agitation" in which "all fixed, fast-frozen relationships . . . are swept away (Marx and Engels 38). Embodying the temporality of a commodity society that is enraptured with ephemerality, the perverse lesbian is a mercurial creature, "changing as the sunsets of summer, changing as the motion/Of waves and flames" (*Muse* 7–8)—"Changeantes ainsi que les couchants d'été,/Les flots et les flammes" ("Le Dédain de Psappha" 7–8). In the poem "Ta forme est un éclair . . . ," Vivien's lesbian subject is the recognizable emblem for the fleetingness of modern social life:

> Your form is a gleam that leaves me clutching emptiness.
> Your smile is the moving instant that one can never clasp.
> You flee when my avid lips implore you, seek you, press
> Upon you, escaping my grasp.
> (*Muse* 1–4)[39]

The lesbian is the epitome of modernity's impatient rhythms precisely because she has incorporated the experience of modernity into her very being; a glittering symbol of the ceaselessly "moving instant," she has become the flux and ephemerality that surround her in the modern, capitalist world where, as Marx is famous for saying, "all that is solid melts into air" (Marx and Engels 38).

Unfolding the contradictions of Vivien's lesbian subject, we can trace an interpenetration of opposites in the poet's work. In "Ta forme est un éclair . . . ," she links the impermanence of the decadent lesbian to her coldness and inaccessibility: "More cold than visionary hope, your cruel caress/Dies like a pale reflection, passes like a faint perfume" (*Muse* 5–6)—"Plus froide que l'Espoir, ta caresse cruelle/Passe comme un parfum et meurt comme un reflet" (5–6). Although she is an emblem of the ephemeral—a "moving instant that one can never grasp"—the perverse lesbian of "Ta forme est un éclair . . ." is inaccessible and out of reach just like Vivien's eternal and virginal lesbian of Mytilène (see, for example, such poems as "Ainsi qu'une pomme . . ."). In a number of poems, the transhistorical Sapphist who remains "virgin as the serene snow"[40] possesses the same icy eyes—"Tes yeux sont des hivers pâlement étoilés" ("Lucidité" 9)—and "cold kisses"—"tes froids baisers" ("Ondine" 5)—as the transient, decadent lesbian. Furthermore, by portraying the lesbian as an icy and indifferent object of desire, Vivien imagines the lesbian in terms that suggest the dandy's famous detachment or "coldness" (Baudelaire, *Painter of Modern Life* 29). Vivien's decadent Sapphist is perpetually unappeased because, like the dandy, she is "exasperated of ecstasy"—"exaspéré d'extase" ("Sonnet," *Poèmes de Renée Vivien* 10); deflecting attachments, she veils her emotions in the graceful rhythms of her own weary desire, attaining a detachment so pure that, for Vivien, it borders on the divine. But the "coldness" of her lesbian subject does not simply mirror the dandy's "glacial indifference" (D'Aurevilly 54). As I have suggested, although she invokes the tropes of artificiality and inauthenticity to describe the lesbian's detachment, these qualities do not assume the centrality that they have in discourses about the dandy. Ultimately, I believe Vivien attributes the lesbian's inaccessibility to her fluidity, a trope that appropriates the mobility of the flâneur for the decadent Sapphist. As we have seen, she depicts the lesbian as an elusive and fugitive subject: "In your robe, fluid, imprecise as the waves of the sea,/You are like an algae" (*Muse* 5–6)—"Dans ta robe ondoyante, imprécise et fluide,/Tu me parais une algue" ("Ressouvenir" ["Remembrance"], *Poèmes de Renée Vivien* 5–6). Variable and capricious, Vivien's figure of the lesbian is perpetually unavailable because she is a protean form; in short, her elusiveness ensures that she will not stay the same long enough to be captured or conquered.[41]

As I have been arguing, Vivien presents the lesbian subject as a dialectical contradiction of ephemeral and eternal elements. In the hauntingly ambivalent poem "Naïade moderne" ("Modern Naiad"), both the speaker and the object of her desire are caught in the dialectic of attraction and repulsion that ensnares the lesbian subject "in tangled strands/Like seaweed" (*Muse* 5–6). Investigating the merging of opposites at the heart of lesbian identity, Vivien frames the classical figure of the water nymph in distinctly modern terms: "The pace of the times swirls in the cut of your dress./Your body seems a net of wires, twisted by stress" (*Muse* 1–2).[42] Here, she invokes images of a new industrialized, technological nature to theorize the lesbian subject as an incarnation of the fleeting beauty of fashion—a quintessential emblem of the modern because it is, in Baudelaire's formulation, "a sublime deformation of Nature, or rather a permanent and repeated attempt at her reformation" (*Painter of Modern Life* 33). But the lesbian subject is not just an emblem of modern restlessness and flux; when Vivien goes on to declare, "Your forehead recalls the surface glass of the sea" (9–10)—as we have already seen, the ocean is a symbol of the eternal for Vivien—she presents lesbian identity as both an emblem of modern restlessness and luminous, eternal beauty. Locating the eternal elements of classical antiquity in the transitoriness of the modern moment, Vivien's dialectical optic perceives the eternal as ephemeral, and the ephemeral as eternal.

This intersection of Vivien's decadent and Sapphic poetics is also visible in the poem "La Fusée" ("The Rocket"). In this poem, Vivien's lesbian subject is a dynamic symbol of speed and modernity who "dizzily" rockets through the night ("Vertigineusement, j'allais vers les Étoiles . . .") in a "wildly joyous ascending nuptial flight" (33)—"Et mon vol déchirait, nuptial et joyeux" (*Poèmes de Renée Vivien* 1, 3). And yet the restless pursuit of velocity ultimately leads to the realm of the eternal, since, after her ascent, the speaker declares that "I attained Eternal Silence"—"J'atteignais le Silence Éternel" ("La Fusée" 10). We should be reminded again of the dandy, whose vocation for elegance represents the "sunset" of heroism precisely because he is able to extract timeless beauty from the ceaseless flux of modern life (Baudelaire, *Painter of Modern Life* 26–29). A lesbian incarnation of the flâneur-dandy, Vivien's decadent Sapphist is a visionary traveler between times and places, who dazzles us with her ability to "immortalize/The kisses of an hour"—"Je suis l'immortel souvenir/Des baisers d'une heure" ("Inscription à la base d'une statue" ["Inscription at the Base of a Statue"], *Poèmes de Renée Vivien* 11–12). In the poem "Dans les lendemains . . . ," she uses Sappho's fragment "Someone, I believe, will remember us in the future" to conceptualize lesbianism not as a self-immolating desire of the moment but as a transcendent union in which eternity is present in the here and now (41). For Vivien, then, lesbian love becomes an emblem of "the passing moment and of all the suggestions of eternity that it contains" (Baudelaire, *Painter of Modern Life* 5):

> The fluctuating days, the perfumed nights to ensue
> Will come to make eternal across the abyss
> Of time the joy, the ardent suffering we knew,
> Our tremblings, our embrace, our kiss.
> ("On tomorrows . . . ," *Muse* 9–12)[43]

Struggling against the "shadow of oblivion" ("l'ombre du trépas"), Vivien's speaker is transfixed by the way the transitory moment—the trembling embrace, the fragile kiss—ultimately vanishes before her only to reveal the glimmer of infinity contained within it, "all of eternity in that one brief moment" ("Like This I Would Speak," *Sweet Hour* 20)—"Cherchant l'éternité dans la minute brève" ("Ainsi je parlerai . . . ," *Poèmes de Renée Vivien* 20). A brilliant fusion of the distinct and multidimensional moments embodied within decadence's utopian promise, Vivien's lesbian subject does not resolve the contradictions of modernity but inhabits them relentlessly.

3

Radclyffe Hall and the Lesbian Dandy

[The] lesbian's dandyism is her androgyny.
—Elizabeth Wilson

In her classic essay on Paris lesbianism, *The Pure and the Impure* (first published as *Ces plaisirs* in 1932), Colette constructs two overarching categories of lesbian subjectivity: the perverse lesbian and the mannish lesbian. The feminized, perverse lesbian is grounded in fin-de-siècle images of excess and exoticism, best represented by the Sapphic decadence of artists such as Renée Vivien. The mannish lesbian or female "invert" (to use the term popularized by turn-of-the-century sexology) remains our most enduring stereotype of lesbian identity, representing female inverts as men trapped in women's bodies—a so-called third sex. Although scholars such as Elaine Marks have pointed out the way in which Colette's lesbians fall into these two stereotypical categories, critics have tended to overlook the persistence of these categories as oppositions undergirding contemporary studies on Sapphic modernism. For example, in her anthology of lesbian literature, *Chloe Plus Olivia*, Lillian Faderman neatly separates "carnivorous flowers" from "men trapped in women's bodies," implying that modern lesbians were either beautiful and deadly *femmes damnées* or handsome and defiant androgynes. In a similar move, Shari Benstock's *Women of the Left Bank* describes the Paris lesbian scene as a "Lesbos divided," contrasting a sensual and feminized image of the lesbian—embodied in Natalie Barney and Renée Vivien—with the mannish image favored by a younger generation of lesbians, like Radclyffe Hall (Figure 3.1), Romaine Brooks, and Janet Flanner. In my view, such treatments present stylized and countervailing versions of Sapphic modernism that minimize the continuities *within* lesbian identities and *between* lesbian and gay male subjectivities. For this reason, it is my contention that "Paris-Lesbos" was not as divided—nor as separate—as we have been led to believe.

Disrupting established gender polarities with her cropped hair, smoking, and mannish dress, the monocled lesbian dandy is the newest face of homosexual aestheticism; exuding an "aura" of "highbrow modernism," she is both an extension and reinterpretation of nineteenth-century dandyism. Discussing the art of Romaine Brooks, Joe Lucchesi has persuasively argued that, in works such as *Self-Portrait* (1923) and *Una, Lady Troubridge* (1924: Figure 3.2), the dandy functioned as a "performative marker" of lesbian desire for Brooks:

> Through the visual rhetoric of the modern woman, Brooks transfigured the *male* cultural connotations of the dandy in early-twentieth-century Paris and London to suggest a potential *female* homoerotic sexuality as she explored the possibilities and limits of a visible lesbian identity within a culture based on normative heterosexuality. (155)

Despite dandyism's appeal and usefulness for modernist lesbians, its appropriation is complicated by the model of sexual inversion, which conceptualizes mannish lesbians as a deformed "third sex" tormented by the struggle between body and mind. In her recent work on female masculinity in the 1920s, Laura Doan has challenged the notion that the pervasive image of the short-haired, monocled, and tuxedoed female dandy is necessarily a lesbian at all. Doan argues that, given the fashionable "masculine mode" in women's attire of the period, masculinity in women such as Radclyffe Hall did not signify lesbianism per se, but rather affirmed the fashionable modernity of the boyish, "Modern Girl." Just as Alan Sinfield argues that, prior to Oscar Wilde's trial of 1895, effeminacy did not necessarily signal homosexuality (as it does for us now), Doan's work on the relation between mannishness and lesbian identity seeks to undo the equation of gender variance and same-sex desire. It was not until the obscenity trial of Radclyffe Hall's *The Well of Loneliness* in 1928, Doan argues, that the mannish look was fixed as a distinctly lesbian style in public culture. "What we have been accustomed to reading as distinctly lesbian represents something else, perhaps something Modern" (681). Approaching these issues from another angle, I propose that the flexibility and pervasiveness of the "Modern Girl" enabled lesbians such as Hall, Gluck, and Claude Cahun to appropriate this mannish style for their own purposes—and subtly rework it by combining it with the decadent aestheticism of Aubrey Beardsley and Oscar Wilde.

FIGURE 3.1. Radclyffe Hall (1928). Photo by Russell/Getty Images. Hulton Archive/Getty Images.

FIGURE 3.2. Romaine Brooks, *Una, Lady Troubridge* (1924). Oil on canvas. 50 1/8 x 30 1/8 in. (127.3 x 76.4 cm.). Smithsonian American Art Museum, gift of the artist.

Usually excluded from discussions of homosexual aestheticism and decadence, Radclyffe Hall's *The Well of Loneliness* is typically understood as an attempt to separate the long-standing cultural conjunction of queerness and artifice by using modern sexual science, along with other naturalizing tropes for lesbian identity, to challenge the terms in which homosexuality had previously been conceptualized. When Hall's "sexually inverted" protagonist, Stephen Gordon, declares her transgressive sexual and gendered identity to be inborn and therefore authentically realized, she signals a new prominence of the body and nature in queer subject formation. Nevertheless, like Oscar Wilde's dandy and Renée Vivien's decadent Sapphist, Hall's figure of the mannish lesbian theorizes queer—and specifically lesbian—subjectivity as fundamentally contradictory. Although Wilde and Hall are often offered up as examples of the fundamental differences between gay male and lesbian subject formation, it is worth noting one particularly important similarity between these authors. As we saw in chapter 1, Wilde's presentation of the mind-body split is grounded in what Lukács calls the bourgeois antinomy of thought and existence, which conceptualizes the mind-body split as a specifically middle-class experience of duality and division. If, as I have been arguing, gay identity is paradigmatic of this new, radically split form of consciousness that characterizes modern experience, then it is perhaps not a coincidence that Marx uses the concept of inversion to explain the opposition between exteriors and interiors engendered by capitalism. The hallmark of social conditions historically specific to capitalist modernity, inverted consciousness, according to Marx, is not an epistemological distortion of reality (Larrain, *Marxism and Ideology* 124–25); to the contrary, as we shall see, the sexual invert's contradictions correspond to a fundamental inversion "particular to and characteristic of capitalist production"—that of appearance and essence (Marx, *Capital* 425).

I want to emphasize that, because Hall grounds her work on new medical formulations of sexual inversion, she articulates a conception of queer identity that manifests its essential contradictions in a new way. Building on my earlier arguments for the importance of dandyism and decadence in lesbian subject construction, this chapter demonstrates the continuities between the modernist, lesbian dandy and other queer heroes of modern life. At the same time, I am particularly interested in the differences Hall seeks to establish between the mannish lesbian and the dandified aesthete, thereby presenting lesbian dandyism as a mode of queer identification that paradoxically repudiates decadence, artifice, and femininity. Unlike the Baudelairean or Wildean dandy who seeks to dispense with the body and nature, Hall's figuration of the lesbian articulates a seemingly paradoxical form of dandyism that is defined through an incorporation of nature. For precisely this reason, many literary and cultural critics have argued that Hall's novel seeks to naturalize same-sex love in order to gain social acceptance for homosexuals and lesbians. Although it pertains specifically to gender-variant or cross-gendered homosexuals, the trope of sexual inversion embodies in a new form the oppositions I have been defining as constitutive of modern gay and lesbian identities: appearance/essence, production/consumption, and work/play. My project is to show that Hall's theory of the mannish lesbian as "a fact in nature" actually produces this new subject as the very embodiment of modernity's contradictions.[1] Or, to put it another way, it repeats in another register what the latter mystifies.

INVERSION, CONTRADICTION, AND THE MANNISH LESBIAN

In *The Well*, the now familiar image of the mannish lesbian coheres for the first time in English literature: she shares the nineteenth-century dandy's aristocratic nostalgia for a bygone age, but, unlike the figure of the gay male dandy, she is in "physical bondage"—her inherent masculinity makes her at once handsome and freakish, dapper and doomed (218). Banned after it was declared "an obscene libel" and "an offence to public decency" in the trial of 1928, Hall's groundbreaking novel is best known today as a polemic that aims to render both cross-gender identification and same-sex desire "natural" by inscribing them on the body as "inversion."[2] As the queer theorist and cultural critic Mandy Merck has asserted, Hall's novel "can be seen as the textual culmination of an entire sociomedical tradition which sought to 'embody' sexual deviance" (87). Like the English sexologist Havelock Ellis, whose study *Sexual Inversion* is typically seen as the theoretical armature of *The Well*, Hall seeks to free "contrary sexual feeling" from the moral taint of perversity by reconceptualizing it as "a fact in nature—a simple, though at present tragic, fact" (Dickson 140). This shift from perversion to inversion, and from sin to sickness, requires Hall to locate the "essence" of lesbian sexuality in a body that is deviant and abnormal, despite also being natural.

This shift to the discourse of sexual inversion privileges gender over sexuality—a fact that far too many literary and cultural critics have overlooked. In his important critique of lesbian and lesbian-feminist readings of *The Well* since the 1970s, Jay Prosser asserts that critics have "made a categorical slide from invert to lesbian" and thus "wrongly reduced sexual inversion to homosexuality" (*Second Skins* 137).[3] Prosser argues, persuasively I think, that when critics read inversion as a metaphor for homosexuality, they fail to recognize that both Hall's work and sexological texts insist on a literal definition of sexual inversion as gender inversion, or transgendered identification. Similarly, Judith Halberstam sees Stephen Gordon's female masculinity as a form of cross-gendered aspiration, arguing that Stephen "embodies a sexual and gender identity that is not fully contained by the term 'lesbian'" (*Female Masculinity* 97). Interestingly enough, such transsexual or transgendered readings of *The Well* shed light on the problems that lesbian-feminist critics have long had with the character of Mary Llewellyn, Gordon's feminine lover, and Hall's aporia regarding femme lesbian identity more generally.[4] As Esther Newton points out, the notion of a feminine lesbian contradicts the theory of inversion, so sexologists therefore did not consider such women to be "true inverts." (293). Building on Newton's work, Leslie J. Henson's reading of *The Well* argues: "the dominant claim of the text is that the upper-class masculine invert alone represents the entire class of suffering inverts" (62). Critics such as Henson and Newton have failed to notice that, although Mary certainly demonstrates lesbian desires, she is not, in fact, an invert.[5] By rendering inversion and homosexuality synonymous, lesbian feminists perpetuated a different but equally troubling erasure, often rendering the long history of female masculinity as little more than a fictional construct.[6]

Although I do not want to collapse the category of inversion into same-sex desire, I think it would be a mistake to downplay its origins in the emergence of gay and lesbian identities. As Havelock Ellis states at the very outset of his landmark study, "sexual inversion, as here understood, means sexual instinct turned by inborn constitutional abnormality toward persons of the same sex. It is thus a narrower term than homosexuality" (1). Although this statement theoretically separates these two terms, Ellis nonetheless conflates them throughout his work, as even Prosser himself admits ("Transexuals and Transsexologists" 120). This conflation of sexual inversion and gender inversion, I want to assert, is part and parcel of the history of homosexuality.[7] Furthermore, as the historian George Chauncey has demonstrated, this association has been especially significant in the construction of lesbian identity, since medical and scientific paradigms of female inversion were slow to differentiate the gender of a subject's sexual object choice from that subject's conformity to her conventional gender role. Although medical writings about female sexual deviance increasingly participated in the cultural turn away from gender and toward sexuality, thus privileging object choice over gender role in the construction of lesbian identity, doctors and sexologists nonetheless insisted upon the intersection of sexual and gendered forms of inversion for women.

In *Three Essays on the Theory of Sexuality*, for example, Freud links cross-gendered identity or "character-inversion" to same-sex desire but notes that "it is only in women that character-inversion of this kind can be looked for with any regularity. In men the most complete mental masculinity can be combined with inversion" (8). Like Ellis and other turn-of-the-century sexologists, Freud claimed that such "character inversion" was a hallmark of inversion in women *only* (Chauncey, "From Sexual Inversion to Homosexuality" 125). If, unlike their male counterparts, female inverts found that their sexual desires and relations were ceaselessly yoked to gender deviance, then this testifies not only to the profound challenges presented by the developing feminist movement but also to the wide-ranging backlash such challenges produced (Chauncey, "From Sexual Inversion to Homosexuality" 140). Therefore, it is my contention that we cannot understand modern lesbian history or the figure of the mannish, lesbian dandy without paying attention to the complex and often contradictory union of sexuality and gender that characterizes her inversion. Furthermore, the cultural entanglement of lesbian eroticism and gender variance must be understood as one aspect of the oppressive regime of gender that the figure of the invert so forcefully subverts. Unfortunately, critics have paid little attention to the novel's radical critique of those ideological and social systems that are "insistent upon sex distinction" (Hall 77).[8] It is my contention that this is, in part, because such readers have not fully contextualized Hall's theory of inverted lesbian identity, and so have not theorized the relationship between this form of subjectivity and the social structures unpinning its construction.

Although she rails against the injustices of contemporary sexual and gender arrangements, the mannish lesbian never ultimately contests the inequalities and hierarchies of bourgeois society. This should alert us to a highly significant displacement. Hall uses economic power to compensate for the gender privilege Stephen Gordon lacks. In so doing, Hall naturalizes the dynastic control of private property in land and self-sustaining economic growth that was uniquely characteristic of English property relations (Wood 58; 173–74). With all traces of political and economic domination erased, Hall may affiliate the lesbian dandy with an idealized landed gentry through the nostalgic rendering of Stephen's tie to her ancestral home, Morton. Saturated in a sense of the past and memory, Morton is "a place of remembering" that holds Stephen in its grip throughout her life (122):

> [Stephen] belonged to the soil and the fruitfulness of Morton, to its pastures and paddocks, to its farms and its cattle, to its quiet and gentlemanly ordered traditions, to the dignity and pride of its old red brick house, that was yet without ostentation. To these things she belonged and would always belong by right of those past generations of Gordons. (108)

The notion of Stephen as a "law-abiding outlaw [with an] inherent respect for the normal" (394, 430) finds its genesis in passages such as this one, in which Stephen's love for the countryside and its "gentlemanly" traditions is captured in a decidedly romantic image of England's preindustrial and precapitalist past. Like the Baudelairean dandy who resists an increasingly intrusive urban and industrial society, and like the perverse lesbian or decadent Sapphist who seeks to revive Sappho's island utopia in Paris, Hall's figure of the lesbian dandy is conceptualized as a quintessentially modern gender outlaw who nevertheless harbors a sentimental desire to escape modern mass culture and retreat into a more authentic past. Finally, *The Well*'s nostalgic presentation of Morton mystifies Stephen's investment in maintaining and reinforcing her own class privilege and personal property, thus veiling the capitalist logics that structure her relationship to modernization.

Hall was not unique in presenting the female invert as a paradoxical union of past and present. Colette, for example, depicts the mannish lesbian as a figure in, but not of, the modern world in a famous passage from *The Pure and the Impure*:

> some of them wore a monocle, a white carnation in the buttonhole, took the name of God in vain, and discussed horses competently. These mannish women I am calling to mind were, indeed, almost as fond of the horse, that warm, enigmatic, stubborn, and sensitive creature, as they were of their young protégées. With their strong slender hands they were able to break in and subjugate a horse, and when age and hard times deprived them of the whip and the hunting crop, they lost their final scepter. A garage, no matter how elegant, can never equal the smartness of a stable. . . . The exciting scent of horses, that so masculine odor, never quite left these women, but lingered on after the ride. I saw and hailed the decline of these women. They tried to describe and explain their vanished charm. They tried to render intelligible for us their success with women and their defiant taste for women. The astonishing thing is that they managed to do so. (65–66)

Like her nineteenth-century predecessors, the lesbian dandy is here linked to the "vanished charm" and elegance of a preindustrial past. She may wear a monocle and crop her hair, but this outward appearance of modernity should not prevent us from recognizing that, for Colette, these masculine women fascinate because they transcend the ugliness and vulgarity of modern metropolitan life. "The exciting scent of horses" and "dust of the bridle paths" suffuses these daring, bachelor ladies with the lingering aroma of a glamorous, bygone era—an era of style and leisure that predates the motorcar, here depicted as the emblem of modernity's drive toward rationalization and commodification. In short, Colette's mannish, lesbian dandy is conceptualized in opposition to the sterility and uniformity of mass culture, even as she is portrayed as the quintessentially modern, new woman. Boldy defying bourgeois conventions, she carries on the nineteenth-century dandy's contradictory relationship to modern industrial capitalism, making a paradoxical combination of seductive modernism and protest against modernity the key to her considerable sex appeal.

Despite the entrenched associations of Hall's work with immutable and eternal conceptions of gay and lesbian identity, *The Well* actually reveals that the inverted subject must also be understood in social and historical terms. It does this despite the fact that Hall's naturalizing representation of the mannish lesbian seeks to mystify those historical and material conditions that give rise to inverted subjectivity in the first place. In a frequently cited description of Gordon, Hall proclaims: "And yet there was a kind of large splendour about her—absurd though she was, she was splendid at that moment—grotesque and splendid, like some primitive thing conceived in a turbulent age of transition" (52). Most critics discuss this passage as an example of the novel's tormented rendering of the queer subject, and I certainly would agree with this reading. But Hall also forcefully suggests that the flux and ferment of modern life shape the forms that queer identity take. Magnificent and freakish, primitive and modern, the mannish lesbian's contradictions are emblematic of the profound antagonisms that define her world. But it should be stressed that, although the logic of *The Well* displaces the contradictions of modernity onto the figure of the invert, Hall simultaneously disavows this move by positioning the masculine lesbian outside the horizon of sociohistorical development. This results in *The Well*'s relentless return to the body as the site of inversion's authentic (albeit overdetermined) meaning. According to Hall, inversion embodies the mannish lesbian but simultaneously causes her to "live in great isolation of spirit and body" (217). I will explore this topic in more detail later. For now, I want to emphasize that the vocabulary of the mind-body split frames the invert in relation to the bourgeois antithesis of thought and existence, thus making Hall's model of lesbian dandyism a privileged emblem of capitalism's contradictions.

At the end of *The Well*, Valérie Seymour (a character widely known as Hall's homage to Natalie Barney) seems to sum up Stephen's predicament when she declares to her friend, "You're rather a terrible combination. . . . But supposing you could bring the two sides of your nature into some sort of friendly amalgamation and compel them to serve you and through you your work—well, then I really don't see what's to stop you. The question is, can you ever bring them together?" (407–8).[9] Of course, the answer to Valérie's question is no. Interestingly enough, Hall unwittingly creates a parallelism between the sympathetic and enlightened Valérie (whose lesbianism seems to transcend the repression and opprobrium of her time and place) and Stephen's brutal mother, Anna Gordon, who is the novel's most vivid emblem of society's cruelty toward the inverted. Although she is not "puzzled" by Stephen—"this creature who seemed all contradictions"—in the way that Stephen's mother is, Valérie, like Anna, refuses to allow Stephen's fractured self to realize its fundamental duality (32).

This fundamental duality points us toward one of my key arguments: Hall's medicalized definition of lesbian identity is founded on the appearance/essence split that it would seem to refute. At first glance, it may seem that Hall's concept of the invert does away with any disjunction between appearance and essence because it seeks to make lesbianism visible by picturing it as "written on the body." Indeed, Hall's embodiment of the invert is part of a larger cultural shift to a new, specifically modern subjectivity that is predicated on the "implantation" of sex in the body.[10] For queer subjects, this shift meant that homosexuality ceased to be contiguous with the practices of sodomy and was instead embedded as an identity formation in the body's anatomical details. As such, sexual inversion and other perversions are conceptualized by modern sexual science as "visible differences," subject to medical scrutiny and detection. In her contribution to *Sexology in Culture* (1998), Siobhan B. Somerville asserts that Havelock Ellis, "Like other sexologists . . . assumed that the 'invert' might be visually distinguishable from the 'normal' body through anatomical markers, just as the differences between the sexes had traditionally been mapped upon the body" (63). From this perspective, the mannish lesbian's "essence" is not buried or concealed—as it seems to be for Wilde's Dorian Gray, for example—but instead inhabits the surfaces of outward appearances. To put it another way, Hall's lesbian dandy *is*, immediately, what she appears to be. Her appearance is her essence. But to theorize the lesbian or sexually inverted subject in this way is both to fetishize phenomenal forms and divorce them from their inner connections. Theorized in relation to its own history as a modern ontological category, the trope of sexual inversion does not erase or ideologically reify the appearance/essence contradiction but rather inhabits it immanently.

Stephen's experience of self-alienation simultaneously reproduces and yet refunctions the classically bourgeois struggle between thought and being, which materializes capitalism's contradiction between appearance and essence through the body. With this in mind, it is worth noting that Hall portrays Stephen Gordon's relationship to her body in fundamentally contradictory terms. With her father's striking facial features, Stephen is dashing and majestic, possessing an elegant athleticism and graceful refinement. As Hall writes, "Stephen's figure was handsome in a flat, broad-shouldered and slim flanked fashion; and her movements were purposeful, having fine poise, she moved with the easy assurance of the athlete" (72). At the same time, Hall indicates that these very same qualities also make Gordon awkward and freakish, a "ridiculous figure" who is haunted by her abnormality (52). In this way, Hall introduces the notion that inversion instantiates a splitting or division of identity, a doubleness that challenges conceptual paradigms for categorizing bodies. But this doubleness is a source of tremendous anguish for the invert, who is enslaved to the body and its desires. Imprisoned by the "constant and ruthless torment" that plagues her (184), Stephen discovers that her spirit is perpetually in the grip of the "chains of the flesh" (218). Although she defines the invert's body as "sterile," "maimed," and "flawed" (187, 204), Hall also emphasizes the strength and power of the invert's body. This is apparent in novel's infamous mirror scene, in which she portrays Stephen as simultaneously defrauded and governed by the body:

> That night she stared at herself in the glass; and even as she did so she hated her body with its muscular shoulders, its small compact breasts, and its slender flanks of an athlete. All her life she must drag this body of hers like a monstrous fetter imposed on her spirit. This strangely ardent yet sterile body that must worship yet never be worshipped in return by the creature of its adoration. She longed to maim it, for it made her feel cruel; it was so white, so strong and so self-sufficient; yet withal so poor and unhappy a thing that her eyes filled with tears and her hate turned to pity. She began to grieve over it, touching her breasts with pitiful fingers, stroking her shoulders, letting her hands slip along her straight thighs—Oh, poor and most desolate body!
>
> Then, she for whom Puddle was actually praying at that moment, must now pray also, but blindly; finding few words that seemed worthy of prayer, few words that seemed to encompass her meaning—for she did not know the meaning of herself. But she loved, and loving groped for the God who had fashioned her, even unto this bitter loving. (186–87)

In an inversion of the Hegelian master-slave relation, the invert's body usurps the mind precisely at the moment when Stephen most seeks to repudiate her corporeal self. Furthermore, the violence and darkness of this passage are suggestive of the decadent sensibility that invades Hall's descriptions of the invert, who is both a morbid emblem of degeneration and an object of fascinated longing. Although it is seldom linked to Sapphic decadence, Hall's construction of inversion as a form of "bitter loving" has a great deal in common with nineteenth-century decadent conceptions of lesbian love as a form of bitter ecstasy, sterile and doomed—a state of relentless longing that defers satisfaction.[11] In the mirror scene, Hall's text eerily repeats the dialectic of desire that Renée Vivien captures in her decadent poems. As biographer Sally Cline has documented, Hall was fascinated by Vivien and her tragic rendering of lesbian identity. Visiting Vivien's grave several times in October 1926 when she began writing *The Well*, Hall found that Vivien's vision "powerfully permeated her own novel" (Cline 230–31). As the reader may recall, in Vivien's poems such as "Je pleure sur Toi . . ." ("I Cry Over You . . .") and "Sommeil" ("Sleep"), Sapphic love is represented as a form of mourning, and the lesbian subject whom the speaker adores most often remains serenely out of reach, ghostly pale, and reified. Hall uses the paradigm of the mind-body split to insert this very same dialectic of lesbian passion into her novel. Now, however, the fraught lesbian relationship between ardent lover and inaccessible beloved is reworked as the contradictory and mutually exclusive aspects of inversion, and thus inscribed within the being of the mannish lesbian herself.

My goal here is to complicate our understanding of *The Well* by offering new ways to understand an all-too-familiar passage. To say, as many lesbian and feminist critics have, that the mirror scene exemplifies Hall's insurmountable limitations and lesbian self-hatred is to fail to recognize the potentially disruptive cultural work that this text performs. Theorizing the contradiction between appearance and essence as the driving force of inverted identity, Hall reinterprets the nineteenth-century representation of lesbian passion as fundamentally narcissistic. Although the depiction of Stephen standing before her own taunting mirror image, reflected in the coldness of the glass, is a commonplace emblem of lesbian narcissism, this untouchable and petrified body—which is represented in the vocabulary of negation (she longs to maim it, deny it, repudiate it)—is dialectically linked to a fragility that is irresistible *because* it cannot be assimilated to cultural norms. The logic of desire Hall theorizes is therefore not fetishistic—as Teresa de Lauretis has argued—nor is it simply a narcissistic eroticizing of the wounded self. Transfixed by her own duality and contradictions, alienated and dispossessed, Gordon loses herself in a reverie that seeks—blindly, gropingly—to transcend the limitations of her inverted consciousness. For Gordon as for Hall, this language of longing performs a double function: it is a mournful yearning that, embracing its inability to be satiated, intertwines rapture and loss. Hollow, exhausted, and condemned, the invert nevertheless partakes of the sacred. Indeed, Gordon's plea to "the God who had fashioned her" underlines a reversal of internal relations at another level as well; clearly, the masculine lesbian is subject to a second inversion, which presents the process of objectification and alienation previously discussed as natural.

THE TRAGIC DECADENCE OF THE LESBIAN DANDY

In contrast with the fin-de-siècle figure of the perverse, Sapphic temptress, whom Vivien imagines as the apotheosis of the aesthetic, Hall's characterization of the mannish lesbian seeks to remove the lesbian body from the shadow of Baudelairean decadence once and for all. Although *The Well* is saturated with such motifs, in Hall's work artifice, decadence, and aestheticism persist primarily as outdated models of homosexuality, a nineteenth-century legacy that is superseded by the scientific discourse of sexology. Of course, sexology's definitions are themselves embedded in these literary and aesthetic motifs, as my previous discussion has demonstrated. Nevertheless, since Hall is not sympathetic to those queers who succumb to the "terrible nerves of the invert" (184) and fall into decadence and morbidity (decadent aestheticism, idleness, drug addiction), it would at first seem to make sense to read *The Well* as a revision of nineteenth-century notions of same-sex desire and identity—an effort to challenge the oppressive reign of "the love that dare not speak its name" by utilizing the legitimating vocabulary of modern sexual science. However, despite this shift from a decadent literary-aesthetic model to a modern medical model, Hall's revision of queer identity remains caught within the terms of the model it seeks to supplant. This is not simply because decadent themes persist in *The Well*, but—more important—because Hall's portrayal of the lesbian dandy seeks to "invert" the decadent aesthetic itself.

The Well both participates in the decadent impulse to depict the queer (both male and female) as a spectacle of artifice and perversion *and* aims to refashion masculine lesbian identity as the very apotheosis of bourgeois ideology—as, in other words, antidecadence. We can see this double move at work in Hall's rendering of the figure of the mannish lesbian as a rewriting of the leisured, dandified aesthete. As I will demonstrate, *The Well* highlights a transitional moment in the history of the queer image when the very same expressions of dandyism that had once signified the gay male aesthete's effeminacy also came to be emblematic of the lesbian's masculinity and, by extension, her queerness. Hall writes that on one shopping trip to London, Stephen

> bought twelve pairs of gloves, some heavy silk stockings, a square sapphire scarf pin and a new umbrella. Nor could she resist the lure of pyjamas made of white crêpe de Chine which she spotted in Bond Street. The pyjamas led to a man's dressing-gown of brocade—an amazingly ornate garment. Then she had her nails manicured but not polished, and from that shop she carried away toilet water and a box of soap that smelt of carnations and some cuticle cream for the care of her nails. (186)

Like the dandies whose style she emulates, Gordon pays attention to the details of dress and appearance because she views clothes as "a form of self-expression" (Hall 73). Indeed, with her interest in style and fashion, her class privilege, and her notion of art as protest, Stephen bears more than a passing resemblance to the nineteenth-century dandy. Hall herself cultivated an image that suggested a similar kinship with dandyism and decadent aestheticism. Sally Cline, for example, notes a "startling" photograph, which appeared in 1928 after *The Well*'s publication, of Hall in her gentleman's silk smoking jacket: "She looked languid, elegant—with a hint of the haughty, the decadence of the dandy, a lingering memory of Beardsley and Wilde" (Cline 243). This deliberate effort to adopt the iconography of decadence is apparent in a striking photographic portrait of Hall and Troubridge, whose partnership lasted almost thirty years (Figure 3.3). The portrait does not suggest cozy or

FIGURE 3.3. Radclyffe Hall and Una Troubridge (1927). Photo by Fox Photos/ Stringer. Hulton Archive/Getty Images.

tame domesticity but rather a willingness to play with stereotypes of exotic lesbian passion (note the leopard rug) in order to create a fusion of Sapphic decadence and dandyist refinement and luxury. Despite such affiliations, I am not arguing that Hall's model of inverted subjectivity turns the mannish lesbian into a dandified aesthete; on the contrary, because it is a revision of that earlier male model of the dandy, Hall's portrayal of the female invert ultimately hinges on the distinctions she introduces between the lesbian dandy and the decadent, gay aesthete.

In order to trace these distinctions, we need look no further than the character of Jonathan Brockett, the dandified playwright who makes up his mind to befriend the utterly ambivalent (and overwhelmed) Gordon. Although he, like Stephen, is also described as being an opposition of outward appearance and inner essence, this dialectic plays out differently for Brockett. With his irrepressible enthusiasm for living and his beautiful reindeer gloves, Brockett swoops in and out of Stephen's life bearing gifts, valuable advice, and lobster salad. "Dropping in on [Stephen] whenever the spirit moved him," the carefree Brockett seems neither to worry nor to work. He is such a remarkable figure in the world of the novel that Terry Castle has wittily remarked: "he belongs in some other work—*The Well of Sociability*, perhaps, or *The Well of Feeling Better*, or *The Well of Having a Good Time*" (55). Unlike the more restrained Stephen, Brockett is not afraid to attract attention. Sporting flashy platinum and emerald cuff links and wearing clothes that are "just a trifle too careful," Brockett is a Wildean figure who worships luxury, style, and—of course—himself (Hall 226). Indeed, like Ireland's most famous dandy-dramatist, Brockett combines the pursuit of elegance—the dress and manners of fashionable society—with a dedication to the project of aesthetic and literary distinction. And like Wilde's hero Dorian Gray, Brockett seems perpetually in "search of sensations," combating boredom in a ceaseless quest for stimulation, pleasure, and the revitalization provided by the fresh shapes and colors of new surroundings (Wilde 115). However, Hall makes it clear that this search for sensations is fundamental to Brockett's art and so it must be understood not simply as an emphasis on the positive value of pleasure but, more precisely, as an effort to aestheticize experience itself.

Despite providing a liberated and cosmopolitan sensibility to the novel, Brockett's dandyism is rendered in satirical and comic terms. Stephen is both attracted to and repelled by this queer man—whose soft, white hands make "odd little gestures"—a recurring image that signifies an authorial attitude that is, at best, ambivalent about Brockett's effeminacy: "Stephen was never able to decide whether Jonathan Brockett attracted or repelled her. Brilliant he could be at certain times, yet curiously foolish and puerile at others; and his hands were as white and soft as a woman's—she would feel a queer little sense of outrage creeping over her when she looked at his hands" (Hall 226).

Although Stephen's aversion is presented as a "natural" reaction to Brockett's transgressive gender variance, Brockett refuses to be ashamed of his effeminacy and, unlike Stephen, he chooses to celebrate his "inversion." On one occasion, he arrives at Stephen's home, jubilant and festive, his arms full of overstuffed packages of food, and heads straight for the kitchen. He was, according to Hall, "in his most foolish and tiresome mood—the mood when his white hands made odd little gestures, when his laugh was too high and his movements too small for the size of his broad-shouldered, rather gaunt body" (229). As Stephen and her "parlourmaid" watch, Brockett proceeds to put on the maid's "ornate frilled cap" and small apron and declares, "'How do I look? What a perfect duck of an apron!'" (229). The maid giggles and, despite her disapproval, even Stephen laughs. Moments such as this demonstrate that although there is a considerable stigma attached to his divergence from normative manly behavior—not just his behavior but his very being is depicted as pathological, perverted—the womanly behavior of the effeminate invert ultimately makes him little more than a campy joke. Hall's novel recodes gay and lesbian identities, setting up a dialectic in which the gay male aesthete becomes the comic inversion of the tragic but noble lesbian dandy. This aspect of *The Well* is typically modernist in that the dandy is no longer depicted as a dangerous monster; now he is harmless and even endearing—a witty and urbane jester.

Although disparaged for his effeminacy and narcissism, Brockett the artist is nevertheless taken quite seriously by Hall. Like the Wildean dandy, he "belonged to his art—the one thing in life he respected" (231). Nevertheless, Brockett is simultaneously demeaned by Hall for this very aestheticism, since he not only writes plays but also takes up the dandy's project of creating for himself a personal originality. By turning himself into an aesthetic object, Brockett resists the bourgeois work ethic that Gordon embraces. It is worth remembering that Radclyffe Hall herself worked obsessively, following a brutal and rigid schedule that, over the years, seriously impaired her health and eyesight. Once Hall became a novelist, she—like her creation Stephen Gordon—did not "compose or write for pleasure as she had as a poet and songwriter. The enjoyment of her spontaneity was now seen as immature. Certain stringent forms must be adhered to if impulse and sensation were to be made to serve the ends of the imagination" (Cline 155). Given such beliefs, it is not at all surprising that *The Well* condemns Brockett for insisting on the freedom to be spontaneous, the privilege to pursue inspiration in all its various forms, and the right to be lazy. The following quotation demonstrates this authorial rebuke: "Stephen often wondered when his fine plays got written, for Brockett very seldom if ever discussed them and apparently very seldom wrote them; yet they always appeared at the critical moment when their author had run short of money" (226). Occupying a double bind produced by capitalist imperatives, the playwright is demeaned both for resisting and performing the imperative to work—that is, to produce value. This representation of Brockett's art contrasts with Hall's depiction of Gordon as the "true" writer—obsessive and selfless, more ascetic than aesthetic.

Valorizing the masochistic professionalism of Stephen over the antibourgeois aestheticism of Brockett, Hall downplays Gordon's considerable fortune, which, of course, is what enables Stephen to "transcend" market imperatives and write not for money but for high-minded artistic, moral, and political purposes. Indeed, Hall seeks to present Stephen's art not as excess or self-gratification but as a form of ennobling work, thereby reconfiguring the mannish lesbian as a productive member of society. In fact, the novel suggests that great art is proof of the lesbian's worth to society (Cline 190). In her only written account of *The Well*'s publication, Hall emphasizes that one of the main purposes of the book, in her mind, was to fortify "the inverted" by encouraging them to adopt a code of bourgeois earnestness and productivity: "I hoped that it would give even greater strength than they already possess to the strong and courageous, and strength and hope to the weak and the hopeless among my own kind . . . to make good through hard work, faithful and loyal attachments . . . this against truly formidable odds" (Cline 264). Seen in this light, Hall's representation of gay male dandyism as the epitome of superficiality serves as a reminder that, within this cultural logic, Brockett's refusal to conform to bourgeois values and conventions is a considerable failure indeed. Fittingly, Hall returns to nineteenth-century motifs of the decadent aesthete in order to distinguish the female invert from her male counterpart. Beneath the shimmering spectacle of his dandified indolence, Brockett is the "carnivorous genius" who feeds his art on "live flesh and blood" (234). This vampiric image of the dandy is symptomatic of Hall's desire to define Brockett's aestheticism in the vocabulary of decadence, presenting his art as a diabolical and degenerate form of consumption. Stephen's art, on the other hand, is framed as productive and honorable because it aims to educate, and therefore perfect, the world.

As I have been arguing, Hall seeks to contrast and privilege the mannish lesbian dandy over and against the effeminized gay male dandy. In one of *The Well*'s most overlooked strategies, Hall ultimately reduces the dandy-aesthete to an inglorious cliché while embodying the lesbian dandy with the athletic masculinity and loyalty to empire that is itself the modern, nationalistic definition of virile, British manhood. Brockett is an abject figure because his is the image of a defeated version of manhood (defeated since Wilde, of course)—the effeminate dandy whose preference for aesthetics over athletics was exposed, after Wilde's trial, as evidence of his degenerate and inverted desires.[12] Weak and passive, Brockett is the homosexual as agent of imperial decline—a soldier who lacks patriotism, grows faint at the sight of blood, and indulges in caramel creams while in the trenches. In contrast, Stephen Gordon is celebrated for her superior valor and gentlemanly heroism, finally wearing a prominent scar and military medal that prove her allegiance to country and empire.

In *The Well*, the figure of the gay male dandy comes to represent a retreat from politics and history into art, style, and pleasure. The lesbian dandy emerges as the defender of bourgeois society, fighting against the feminization of modern culture as she upholds the value of industry, repression, rationality, and nationalism. However, Hall demonstrates that both Stephen and Brockett are split subjects caught within the countervailing forces that produce queer identity—the oppositions between appearance and essence, production and consumption, work and play—oppositions that are characteristic of capitalism's historical contradictions. But by dividing these dualisms between the effeminate dandy and his masculine lesbian counterpart, Hall ultimately seeks to attribute the aesthetic, feminized, and perverse aspects of queer identity to the gay male dandy alone. It is because this act of projection and disavowal will not stick that Stephen Gordon is finally inscribed in a narrative of loss—a loss that is orchestrated by Gordon herself, who pushes her lover into the arms of a man. This sets in motion a tragic unraveling that reinforces received ideas about the fate of the androgynous figure "never to be happy" but, instead, to bestow her "seraphic suffering" upon the world through a trail of "glimmering tears" (Colette 68). In this way, *The Well*'s notoriously pessimistic conclusion intersects with the nineteenth-century decadent definition of lesbian love as sterile and doomed, a desire that is never capable of achieving fulfillment. Whereas Vivien's vision of the decadent Sapphist embraces the split self and its contradictions, Hall yearns to banish ambiguity and contradiction, even as she theorizes lesbian eroticism as a form of radical lack and the mannish lesbian herself as a fundamentally divided subject: decadent and bourgeois, deviant and natural, feminized consumer and manly producer. If Stephen Gordon seems to write herself out of her own story at the end of the novel, it is because she fails to recognize that the reversal of inner relations that she experiences as a process of dispossession and alienation is, in fact, the palpable reality of a modern world turned upside down.

4

Harlem's Queer Dandy and the Artifice of Blackness

There is perhaps no greater refutation to the bifurcating logic that opposes racial and queer identification than Harlem's modern black dandy. A figure of urbanity, decadence, and polished elegance, the black aesthete makes dandyism a badge of openly queer desire and antibourgeois politics during the Harlem Renaissance—the African American cultural, intellectual, and political movement that flourished in Harlem in the 1920s. When acknowledged in cultural criticism, however, the figure of the black dandy is often deracialized, following the masculinist logic that sees the bisexual or gay African American as a threat to racial unity and the notion of "authentic"—that is, masculine—blackness it is implicitly founded on. Even when such ideologies are critiqued, as in Michael L. Cobb's essay "Insolent Racing, Rough Narrative," there seems to be no way to get around the reading of queer identity as a "racial death-sentence" (332). Nevertheless, it should be noted that (as the work of Cobb and others indicate) the ambivalent and/or hostile reaction to the black dandy has its roots in the contradictions of the Harlem Renaissance itself, as well as in the increasing association of dandyism with homosexual "vice" in the early part of the twentieth century.[1] As a wide range of critics and historians have demonstrated, the established black bourgeoisie and representatives of the Talented Tenth such as Du Bois came to see the dandy—and his queerness in particular—as the embodiment of a form of decadence that they believed threatened to overtake the Renaissance and tarnish the "New Negro," thus making the dandified aesthete a widely recognized symbol of the social disintegration and corruption associated with modernization and urban life.[2]

Investigating the complexities and contradictions of dandyism as symbol and oppositional act, this chapter seeks not only to make legible the epistemic relation between racial and sexual categories in modern American society, but also to demonstrate how this relation emerges out of the dialectic between primitivism and decadence that defines the construction of African American cultural modernity. When contemporary literary and cultural critics represent the black dandy only or primarily as the condensation of African American anxieties about racial uplift (anxieties that equate racial and sexual respectability), they actually reinforce an ideological fiction about the "threat" of queerness to black identity and leave unaddressed the important critical task of theorizing race and sexuality together. By examining Wallace Thurman's novel *Infants of the Spring* (1932), Richard Bruce Nugent's notoriously decadent contribution to *Fire!!*—the modernist stream-of-consciousness story "Smoke, Lilies and Jade" (1926)—and his striking illustrations entitled "Drawings for Mulattoes" (1927), I will demonstrate that the bohemian aesthete was not only central to the battle over the black image that characterized African American modernism but also was the privileged emblem of the political challenge posed by the second generation of the Harlem Renaissance. If the dandy was and still often is seen as a threat to the integrity of black selfhood, I would argue that this is because he subverts the cult of authenticity that not only surrounded the construction of African American identity during the Renaissance, but also persists today as a central motif for black identity and culture. For Thurman and Nugent, the African American dandy's revision of nineteenth-century European models of dandyism and decadence serves a strategic purpose; his transformative appropriation of decadence enables him to offer a critique of authenticity and primitivism, while simultaneously mobilizing a radical recombination of primitivist and decadent aesthetics that disrupts the commodity relation to African American culture.

It is not a coincidence that the black dandy comes to prominence during the Harlem Renaissance's inauguration of the so-called New Negro. As an emblem of the new forms of identity and agency emerging in the modern cities of the North, the figure of the black dandy queers the notion that even urban black cultural identity is primarily rooted in rural, southern folk traditions. The Great Migration of over one million blacks from the South to the urban North during the 1917–1930 period had enormous social and political consequences since this movement northward fundamentally restructured the forms and meanings of African American identity and its cultural expressions (Maxwell 37).[3] As Alain Locke succinctly puts it in the introduction to his classic contribution to the Renaissance, *The New Negro* (1925): "In the very process of being transplanted, the Negro is becoming transformed" (6). For Locke, the New Negro becomes a kind of superman, "shifting from countryside to city," able to "hurdle several generations of experience at a leap" (4). Still, a question lingers: the African American is becoming transformed, but transformed into what? I would argue that the tide of black migration reconceptualized African American identity in relation to the central contradictions of modernity. The opposition of a newly industrialized and rationalized urbanity with the vital, organic community of traditional, rural life was literally mapped out on the black body, as the Old Negro increasingly became associated with the rural South and the New Negro was depicted as the emblem of the urban, industrial North. But it is important to note that the renewal and dynamism that is found in the new life of black community transforms for Locke not only the African American but also the nation as a whole. "With each successive wave of it, the movement of the Negro becomes more and more a mass movement toward the larger and the more democratic chance—in the Negro's case a deliberate flight not only from countryside to city, but from medieval America to modern" (6).

The opposition of northern and southern, rural and urban, is obviously nothing new in terms of the cultural representation of blackness. As Eric Lott has demonstrated in his important study of blackface minstrelsy and American working-class culture, this opposition dates back to antebellum minstrelsy and the juxtaposition of the plantation rustic or southern slave (Jim Crow) and the urban dandy (Zip Coon) (22). From this sectional break, the black dandy emerges in American popular culture as an emblem of the fascination and dread white Americans felt for a specific construction of racialized gentility, embodied in minstrel songs such as "Long Tail Blue" (1827), "Old Zip Coon" (1834), and "De Blue Tail Fly" (1844). Despite such stereotypical conventions, we must be careful to recognize the complexity, variability, and improvisation inherent in the performance of minstrel stage types. As Barbara L. Webb has demonstrated in her work on the black dandyism of George Walker, the minstrel dandy "was not a coherent stage type, but a spectrum of performance options" (8). As a displacement and projection of race and class struggles, the Zip Coon character was a racist rendering of dandified, urban blacks with enormous influence in white working-class culture; as such, it reveals a racist and "class animus" toward the black dandy and the threats of miscegenation and amalgamation he was thought to embody (Lott 134). The fantasy that propelled the fascination with the black dandy was also fundamentally a sexual one, which, according to Lott, reveals the homoerotic desire that was a central part of the minstrel tradition. In songs such as "Jumbo Jim" (1840), the dandy type is a covert object of sexual interest for the white male audiences who admire his sexual virility. Because "white men's investment in the black penis" defined the minstrel show, Lott suggests that jealous white male fears of miscegenation are embedded in "homosexual fantasies, or at the very least envy, of black men" (121). As I will demonstrate, the dandies of the Harlem Renaissance appropriate the queer subtext of the American minstrel show and its working-class, white representation of the black dandy and combine this figure with the European, decadent tradition of dandyism as a form of intellectual and artistic rebellion.

Despite the status of homosexuality as an "open secret" in Harlem during the 1920s and 1930s, queer identity and identification have long been seen as a problem for the political project of the Renaissance. For example, in the introduction to his recent edition of Alain Locke's *The New Negro*, Arnold Rampersad describes writer and artist Richard Bruce Nugent as "far more concerned with his gay identity than with this sense of race or ethnicity" (xxi). A bohemian and decadent aesthete in the tradition of Wilde, Nugent was "the perfumed orchid of the New Negro movement" and the Renaissance's most famous incarnation of the black dandy (Watson, *Harlem Renaissance* 90). Nugent was a part of the "decadent" colony of artists and writers of the Renaissance's second generation—a self-consciously unconventional circle whose "central and dominant character" was the writer Wallace Thurman (Wintz 88). The magazine *Fire!!* (1926), which Thurman organized and edited and to which both he and Nugent contributed fiction, is commonly read as a defining moment in which the younger generation of artists separated from the bourgeois, race-building politics of Harlem's old guard. Writing about controversial topics such as prostitution, drug use, homosexuality, and bisexuality, Thurman and Nugent departed from the code of what had previously been considered appropriate representations of African American identity and culture. As Steven Watson asserts, one critic called *Fire!!* "effeminate tommyrot"—thus decrying what was seen as the movement's fall into decadence and excess (*Harlem Renaissance* 92).

It is well known that, during the Renaissance, black identity was encoded in a cultural logic that depicted it as a supposed counterforce to the rationality and sterility of capitalist modernity. By the mid- and late twenties, "Harlemania" had taken hold of New York, propelled in large measure by the enormous influence of Carl Van Vechten's *Nigger Heaven* (1926). Writer, photographer, Wildean aesthete, and gay dandy, Van Vechten almost single-handedly popularized the white trend of "going uptown," and his novel's success established his status as Harlem's most famous tour guide.[4] The publication of Van Vechten's controversial bestseller was, according to literary historian and critic Cary Wintz, "the most important single event in creating the Negro craze and sending thousands of whites into Harlem's speakeasies and clubs" (94). In addition to the influence of *Nigger Heaven*, the vogue for black culture was fostered by white-produced musicals of African American experience that were featured on Broadway, which sometimes combined whites in blackface along with African Americans. Black musical reviews such as *Shuffle Along* (1921), *Runnin' Wild* (1923), *Chocolate Dandies* (1925), and *Porgy* (1926) marketed whites' fascination with a primitivist vision of the intensity, warmth, and rhythm of black life.[5] Whites responded to these productions by flocking to the "World's Greatest Negro Metropolis" in record numbers, setting up a division between the Harlem residents (whose everyday lives and labor were rendered invisible) and the white thrill-seekers who visited speakeasies or cabarets such as the Cotton Club where "the only Harlemites seen by seven hundred white revelers each night were high-stepping, high-yellow chorines ('Tall, Tan and Terrific') and tuxedoed musicians belonging to Andy Preer's or Duke Ellington's orchestra" (Lewis 209).

In short, Harlem had become a commodity—primitivism for export. Unlike in Paris, for example, where the fascination with the apparent elementality of blackness took a different form, white American primitivism was distinguished by its single-minded fetishizing of race as sex.[6] Despite the intellectual and artistic efflorescence of the Renaissance, white American primitivists only saw African Americans as a form of sexualized exoticism packaged and sold as blackness. The black dandy deploys a decadent aesthetic in order to disrupt the fetishizing of the primitive that drove both the so-called Negro craze and (in a different but no less significant manner) the nostalgia for an African heritage that infused the New Negro movement. Renouncing the toil and industry of capitalist production, Thurman's and Nugent's dandies rebel, like other leftists and bohemians, not only against wage slavery, but also against the imperative to perform a racialized construction of Otherness in the cultural marketplace. It is my contention that dandyism enables the artists of the Renaissance's second generation to contest the commodification and fetishizing of blackness that has characterized the experience of modernity for African Americans. In doing so, the black dandy gives birth to a new aesthetic that combines the naturalized simplicity and vigor of primitivism with the artifice of decadence—making legible a distinctly African American incarnation of the queer forms of desire, identity, and community emerging in modern, urban culture.

THE BLACK DANDY AND THE CULTURE OF CAPITAL

The single most influential characterization of the black dandy to emerge from the Harlem Renaissance, Paul Arabian of *Infants of the Spring* is positioned by Thurman as a privileged emblem of the avant-garde project of Niggeratti [*sic*] Manor, and his dandyism is pictured as a form of individual rebellion against capitalist modernity and its various hierarchies of power. A Wildean aesthete and self-proclaimed genius, Paul subverts conventional moral sensibilities and earns a reputation as self-consciously outrageous, controversial, and decadent. Wearing neither tie, socks, nor underwear, he affects a "musty and disheveled" appearance that is the polar opposite of the polished respectability of the New Negro (21). Simultaneously "delightful" and "obscene," Paul is a spectacle of contradiction who defies categorization—"a person" who, according to Raymond, "you've got to see to appreciate" (18). Thurman captures the contradictions of the black dandy in the following passage, which presents Paul as a fascinating combination of intellectual refinement and lowdown scruffiness, classic elegance and cultural dissidence:

> He observed him now, sitting tailor fashion on the floor, his dirty yellow face aglow with some inner incandescence, his short stubborn hair defiantly disarrayed, his open shirt collar forming a dirty and inadequate frame for his classically curved neck. He was telling about his latest vagabond adventure. His voice was soft toned and melodious. His slender hands and long fingers described graceful curves in the air. As usual when he spoke, everyone remained silent and listened intently as if hypnotized. (44)

A merging of decadence and bohemianism, Paul represents an African American incarnation of the Baudelairean tradition that joins the dandy and the *bohème*, thus transforming the black dandy into a cultural bohemian whose "defiant" appearance and "vagabond adventures" signal his rebellion against middle-class values—a bohemianism that makes him, in other words, our stereotype of the modern artist.[7]

For the black aesthetes of Thurman's novel, as well as the decadent protagonist of Richard Bruce Nugent's "Smoke, Lilies and Jade," to be an artist is to be in opposition to the work ethic of capitalism. Nugent's Alex turns "idleness" into a verifiable art form, lying on his bed surrounded by a cloud of blue smoke, "smoking a cigarette thru an ivory holder . . . inlaid with red jade and green" (34). My point here is not to position the black dandy as in some way outside of capitalist modernity, but rather to theorize the political critique implicit in his decadent aesthetic—itself a campy comment on racist ideologies that define African Americans as "naturally" lazy. Thurman's Paul and Nugent's Alex exemplify the black dandy's refusal to be a commodity to be bought and sold in the form of a fetishized black body or in the form of wage labor. Of course, the decadent, bohemian aesthete is hardly the only figure who finds work to be an anathema during the Renaissance. In Thurman's novel, the distinguishing feature of Niggeratti Manor is that nobody wants to work, and rarely does; transforming every day into a holiday, these artists subvert the modern industrial code that inflicts ceaseless compulsory labor on the worker, cultivating an individual expressivity grounded in what Paul Lafargue calls "the right to be lazy." This aestheticization of laziness results in the landlady Euphoria ultimately closing down the house, so it is no exaggeration to say that the fall of Niggeratti Manor is attributable to a collective refusal on the part of its inhabitants to devote their energies to "useful" production. Instead of working, this young assortment of writers and artists throw interracial parties where Harlem jazz musicians mix with Greenwich Village "uranians" (homosexuals), and pimps mingle with college boys. Although the revelry and social equality of their parties embody the spirit of the second generation of the Renaissance, a newspaper editorial (presumably representing the established black middle class) criticizes the residents of Niggeratti Manor for neglecting their work and indulging in decadent pleasures: "They were satisfied to woo decadence, satisfied to dedicate their life to a routine of drunkenness and degeneracy with cheap white people, rather than mingle with the respectable members of their own race" (197). Although decadence comes to stand in for a whole range of deviant behaviors, including interracial relationships and homosexuality, I would argue that the black dandy is the most visible symbol of the Renaissance's alleged slide into "degeneracy" and so is the privileged emblem of the second generation's refusal to be "respectable"—or, as Raymond puts it, "to beg and do tricks" (200).

Unlike those African Americans who seek to exploit "Harlemania" for their own advancement, the figure of the bohemian aesthete will not perform blackness for white audiences. To make this point, Thurman contrasts the characters of Raymond and Paul with effervescent and ribald Sweetie May Carr, who is widely known as Thurman's fictional representation of the writer Zora Neale Hurston. Posing as a promising young writer in order to get "kind hearted o'fays" to pay her tuition at Columbia, Sweetie May declares that "being a Negro writer these days is a racket and I'm going to make the most of it while it lasts. Sure I cut the fool. But I enjoy it, too" (230). Actually, she has a lot in common with writers like Paul and his friend Raymond, who also produce very little actual literary work and share her cynicism about the so-called Negro literary renaissance. However, Thurman makes it clear that Carr's success must be attributed to the fact that she lives up (or down) to her white patrons' conception of what a typical "Negro writer" should be: "Given a pale-face audience, Sweetie May would launch forth into a saga of the little all-colored Mississippi town where she claimed to have been born. Her repertoire of tales was earthy, vulgar and funny. Her darkies always smiled through their tears, sang spirituals on the slightest provocation, and performed buck dances when they should have been working" (229). Recognizing that blackness is a valuable form of cultural capital, Sweetie May offers an ironic critique of racist ideologies while selling the stereotype of African American identity white people want to buy. Although Carr's performance of blackness satirizes racist stereotypes as much as it reiterates them, Thurman ultimately depicts her as an opportunistic storyteller who conspires with racist myths by willingly becoming a blackface caricature for whites. However, Sweetie May's function as a *debased* form of comic relief points to an elitist and masculinist disavowal of the feminine by gay male artists of the Renaissance such as Thurman—what James Kelley persuasively calls an "unexamined reinscription of patriarchal authority" (513). If Thurman portrays Carr in the style of the minstrel, I would argue that he does so at least partly to delegitimate her feminized "low" art and thus distinguish it from the homosocial avant-gardism of Raymond and Paul, who, garnering neither public recognition nor financial rewards for their writing, perpetuate another stereotype—the notion of the masculine bohemian as "the creator of transcendental art" (Gluck 352).[8]

Since the black dandy defines himself in opposition to bourgeois modernity, it should not be surprising that he seeks to escape from the nightmare of capitalist domination. In both Thurman and Nugent's work, the figure of the bohemian aesthete tries to transcend market imperatives. In Richard Bruce Nugent's "Smoke, Lilies and Jade," for example, the main character Alex imagines his mother asking him, "how do you feel Alex with nothing in your pockets . . . I don't see how you can be satisfied. . . . Really you're a mystery to me . . . you won't do anything to make money . . . wake up Alex" (34). In refusing to uphold "the dogma of work" (Lafargue 10), Alex conceptualizes wage labor as a form of slavery. Paul Gilroy argues that such an opposition to alienated labor has a specificity for African Americans and other members of the African diaspora: "for the descendants of slaves, work signifies only servitude, misery, and subordination"; furthermore, it is because of the brutalizing legacy of slavery that, according to Gilroy, artistic expression "becomes the means of individual self-fashioning and communal liberation" (40). Thurman makes the association of labor and slavery explicit in the character of Pelham (George Jones). Raised by his "Grandma Mack" to believe that "niggers were made to be servants" (120) (Grandma Mack was herself born into slavery), Pelham acts as a servant in the house, performing the domestic labor that allows the other residents of Niggeratti Manor to devote themselves to their art. While Pelham is depicted as a "natural born menial" who would be "perfectly miserable" if the others were to treat him as an equal, the bohemian aesthete makes his inner intellectual and artistic superiority known by putting others to work for him (49).

It should be clear by now that the black dandy is as much a product of capitalist modernity as he is a rebel against it. This is aptly illustrated by Nugent's languid and dreamy story, in which Alex rebels against capitalist imperatives: "why wasn't he worried that he had no money . . . he *had* had five cents . . . but he had been hungry . . . he *was* hungry and still . . . all he wanted to do was . . . lay there comfortably smoking" (33). Even hunger does not drive the true dandy to wage labor, since his aestheticization of reality allows him seemingly to transcend such mundane concerns. But Alex's appetite should alert us to the fact that, even as he resists the tyranny of work and celebrates the right to be lazy, his rebellion epitomizes the logic of consumption and its endlessly deferred satisfaction. On this point, Alex muses, "was it Wilde who had said . . . a cigarette is the most perfect pleasure because it leaves one unsatisfied" (35). To excite the appetite—that is the fundamental goal of both the cigarette and the commodity. And who better than Wilde to remind us that the culture of commodity production depends on mobilizing the promise of a satisfaction that it will never, can never, deliver? I want to emphasize that the cigarette and wandering blue smoke around which Nugent's story is constructed are at once emblems of the contradictions of consumer society—in which the sphere of value is haunted by lack and negativity—and emblems of a new form of desire (queer, urban, mobile) that the black dandy embodies.[9]

THE DIALECTIC OF PRIMITIVISM AND DECADENCE

I have been arguing that the strategic use of the tropes of dandyism and decadence by certain of the Harlem literati has not been recognized by most literary and cultural critics because of the tendency to view the dandy as a race traitor. Thurman's presentation of Paul Arabian sets up dandyism simultaneously as an attempt to fulfill the wish of racial transcendence and as a mode of white aspiration/identification:

> Paul has never recovered from the shock of realizing that no matter how bizarre a personality he may develop, he will still be a Negro, subject to snubs from certain ignorant people. The fact distresses him, although he should ignore both it and the people who might be guilty of such snubs. He sits around helpless, possessed of great talent, doing nothing, wishing he were white, courting the bizarre, anxious to be exploited in the public prints as a notorious character. Being a Negro, he feels that his chances for excessive notoriety à la Wilde are slim. Thus the exaggerated poses and extreme mannerisms. Since he can't be white, he will be a most unusual Negro. (59)

In its explicit association of dandyism with class and race longing, this is Thurman's most damning assessment of the decadent bohemian. Nevertheless, his representation of queerness as a pose that masks a fundamental desire for whiteness is hardly the last word on the black dandy. In fact, what is fascinating about the representation of Paul is that his voluptuously phallic "spirit portraits"[10] synthesize black spirituality with an openly queer aesthetic. Paul's bold homoerotic drawings and designs of "highly colored phalli," which are featured prominently in Niggeratti Manor, conjure up suggestions of fin-de-siècle decadence, especially the unabashed phallicism of Aubrey Beardsley's late work.[11] Like Alex of Richard Bruce Nugent's "Smoke, Lilies and Jade," who celebrates the "symmetry and music" of the beautiful, male body, Paul insists upon the positive value of pleasures both erotic and aesthetic. This should not be taken to mean that Thurman's depiction of the black aesthete merely mimics the stylistic project of the nineteenth-century dandy, offering a blackfaced portrayal of what is commonly believed to be a white, European tradition. For Thurman and Nugent, the figure of the African American dandy employs decadence to contest modern culture's fetishizing of the primitive as a site of authenticity. In other words, decadence and artifice are the means through which the black dandy queers the New Negro's quest for origins.

In *Infants of the Spring*, Thurman distinguishes between the romantic primitivism celebrated by the established leaders of the "Negro" Renaissance and the African American dandy's refusal to legitimate any particular construction of racial identity as authentic. In the salon scene that features Dr. Parkes (widely recognized as Thurman's representation of Alain Locke), Parkes aims to convince these young artists of the value of "going back to your racial roots, and cultivating a healthy paganism based on African traditions" (235). This call for a return to African traditions is explicitly rejected by Paul, who causes the assembled crowd to gasp at his blasphemous declaration: "How can I go back to African ancestors when their blood is so diluted and their country and times so far away? I have no conscious affinity for them at all" (237). The African American dandy's critique of nostalgia for a "black pagan heritage" is a highly significant political move in the ongoing battle for the image of the race. By refusing to define blackness in the New Negro's terms—as, in other words, a nostalgic appeal to African origins—the black dandy challenges the primitivist aesthetic of the Renaissance.

During the salon scene, Thurman depicts the bohemian aesthete as having the courage to challenge a conservative construction of racial consciousness, which in his view is constraining the movement as a whole. For example, Raymond declares that Paul has "hit the nail right on the head," asking, "Is there really any reason why *all* Negro artists should consciously and deliberately dig into African soil for inspiration and material unless they actually wish to do so?" (237). Both Raymond and Paul critique the notion that Negroes are "all like" the subject of Countee Cullen's poem "Heritage," who, despite being "One three centuries removed/From the scenes his fathers loved" (7–8), still hears the "unremittant beat" (66) of Africa in "Great drums throbbing through the air" (22). Disrupting the group's collective dream of a return to Africa, Paul exclaims that he is "not an African" but rather "an American and a perfect product of the melting pot" (238). In this respect, Paul not only insists upon a diasporic identity that recognizes his ethnic complexity, which includes German, English, and Indian, as well as African ancestors, but also locates his own cultural production in the broader context of American cultural nationalism.[12] It is precisely this loss of specificity that is, I would argue, troubling to Dr. Parkes, and so it should not be surprising that the black dandy is ultimately scapegoated for challenging and disrupting the categories on which the project of pan-Africanism depends.[13] For the Lockean figure of Dr. Parkes, African revival is a necessary step to stem the tide of decadence—symbolized by the bohemian aesthete—that is overtaking the Renaissance. As we shall see, in the eyes of Parkes, the black dandy's rejection of an authentic African heritage puts the very future of the race in jeopardy.

As the fictional incarnation of the brilliant and impeccably tailored Locke—who was himself, ironically enough, a homosexual and a dandy—Parkes represents the Talented Tenth's criticism of Thurman's circle for precipitating "the New Negro movement's slide from uplifting propaganda to suspect beauty to unalloyed decadence" (Watson, *Harlem Renaissance* 92). Fearful of "the decadent strain" that seems to have infected the work of Niggeratti Manor's inhabitants, Parkes declares that the New Negro must not, "like your paleface contemporaries, wallow in the mire of post-Victorian license" (234). Thurman is here referring to the widespread belief that white artists and literati of the 1920s—the so-called lost generation (to use the phrase Gertrude Stein made famous)—rejected public duties and middle-class norms in order to escape into the bohemian world of aesthetics, excess, and sexual freedom. The affiliations and connections between the cultural rebellions of white writers of the twenties and the second generation of the Harlem Renaissance have not been explored nearly enough.[14] Although the relationship between white American and African American modernisms falls outside the scope of my present project, it is worth noting that the gin, jazz, and sex ethos of the twenties took similar forms in Harlem and Greenwich Village, as did the commentaries of those who attacked such libertine philosophies and practices. For instance, Du Bois's repeated claims in his magazine *The Crisis* that the Renaissance was succumbing to decadence echoed in important ways the objections made by a curious assortment of cultural critics from both the right and the left about the individualism and excess that characterized the bohemian subculture of the jazz age.[15]

However, despite such affinities and intersections between white American and African American traditions, what was distinctive about the nationalist enterprise taking shape under the sign of the "New Negro" (in contrast with white American modernism) was the widespread belief that both the problem and the solution—decadence and its antidote—could be found within the forms of community and consciousness emerging in modern culture. As a result, the Harlem Renaissance begins to take on a circular explanatory logic that locates the so-called New Negro in an internal contradiction.

According to this racial logic, blacks are, in the words of one of Dr. Parkes's protégés, "the only people in America not standardized. The feel of the African jungle is in their blood. Its rhythms surge through their bodies. Look how Negroes laugh and dance and sing, all spontaneous and individual" (241). As this quotation demonstrates, black identity is conceptualized as premodern (closer to nature, spontaneous, emotional, and sexual) and therefore as a much-needed counterforce to the rationality and sterility of urban capitalism. However, if black passion and vigor are the means to restore vitality to Euro-American modernity, this same supposed lack of civilization and self-control makes African Americans prone to the modern excesses of bohemian pleasure-seeking and other forms of urban decadence (sexual excesses that include, but are not limited to, homosexuality). This ultimately associates blackness as much with modernity as with premodernity. Despite, or perhaps because of, the danger presented by the slippage between primitive origins and decadent artifice, proponents of the New Negro such as Locke argued that the phenomenon of decadence could only be defeated by restoring African America to its "essential" blackness.

Subverting this cult of authenticity, the black dandy offers himself as a way out of the double bind of modern African American identity as I have been describing it. He embraces the contradictions of modernity and develops what I believe to be a characteristically African American idiom that combines the elemental energy of primitivism and the stylized modernity and artificiality of decadence. Richard Bruce Nugent's four "Drawings for Mulattoes," published in Charles S. Johnson's collection *Ebony and Topaz* (1927), represent African American identity as a dialectic between the tribal and the artificial (Figures 4.1–4.4). Nugent's queer aesthetic uses the image of the sexually ambiguous mulatto (Am I black or white? Woman or man?) to examine the divisions faced by black people and question the strictness of the oppositions that supposedly constitute them. For example, in drawing number 3 (Figure 4.3), the artist merges the image of a nude, African tribal dancer with the cosmopolitan and decadent image of the flapper. A testament to the aesthetic and political importance of the African American dandy's contribution to the Renaissance, Nugent's drawings bring together the decadent, formal preoccupations of art nouveau with African art's caricaturizing of the human body—reveling in the joined contradictions of naturalism and abstraction.[16]

At first glance, Nugent's debt to Aubrey Beardsley is apparent in his striking composition and mannered formalism.[17] Following the tradition of Beardsleyan ambivalence and contradiction, Nugent uses stylization and linear abstraction in all of his drawings to complicate the oppositions of black/white and male/female, creating androgynous figures who often seem to blur gender and racial polarities. In her study *Racechanges*, Susan Gubar argues that "Nugent's prints can be read as a series about ethnogenesis that moves

FIGURE 4.1. Richard Bruce Nugent, *Drawings for Mulattoes—Number 1* (1927). Courtesy of Rare Book Collection in the Inman E. Page Library, Lincoln University, Jefferson City, Missouri. Reprinted by permission of the National Urban League.

FIGURE 4.2. Richard Bruce Nugent, *Drawings for Mulattoes—Number 2* (1927). Courtesy of Rare Book Collection in the Inman E. Page Library, Lincoln University, Jefferson City, Missouri. Reprinted by permission of the National Urban League.

FIGURE 4.3. Richard Bruce Nugent, *Drawings for Mulattoes—Number 3* (1927). Courtesy of Rare Book Collection in the Inman E. Page Library, Lincoln University, Jefferson City, Missouri. Reprinted by permission of the National Urban League.

FIGURE 4.4. Richard Bruce Nugent, *Drawings for Mulattoes—Number 4* (1927). Courtesy of Rare Book Collection in the Inman E. Page Library, Lincoln University, Jefferson City, Missouri. Reprinted by permission of the National Urban League.

from depictions of the primitive to images of civilization, all of which emphasize the primacy of blackness as well as the aesthetic centrality of Africa in the evolution of twentieth-century Western culture" (107). Gubar is right that the four drawings move from the "primitive" jungles of Africa to the "civilized" urbanity of Harlem's speakeasies and cabarets, but not in the progressivist model she puts forth. In my view, Nugent's decadent aesthetic theorizes the primitive and the civilized as an ongoing dialectical relation, thereby disrupting the ideology of "progress" that undergirds Western racism. This is made clear in Nugent's rendering of the queer, biracial subject in drawing numbers 2 and 3 (Figures 4.2 and 4.3). Both images simultaneously suggest contradiction as well as unity in opposition. In drawing number 2, Nugent depicts a world both divided and united by racial thematics, using basic geometric forms to convey the monumentality of both premodern and modern cultures, and repeating and mixing those forms in order to question the very notions of "whiteness" and "blackness." Note that the facial forms of the black silhouette (to the left) are portrayed in the classical style of European art, while the facial structure of the white profile (to the right) conveys the aesthetic iconography and architectural composition of African sculpture. Nugent seeks to depict the puzzling ideological landscape of modernity, in which, for example, metropolitan skyscrapers seem to loom just beyond the native jungles of Africa (and vice versa). Such contradictions shape Nugent's dialectical image of the "mixed" subject, always in motion, whose rebellion against categorization and commodification demonstrates the complexities of racial and sexual becoming.

The relevance of this dialectic between primitivism and decadence for the black aesthete or dandy is evident in Thurman's portrayal of Paul as both male and female, innocent and corrupt, natural and artificial—a figure who delimits the horizon of both beginnings and endings because he embraces both, and neither. In a scene that is highly reminiscent of Nugent's story, "Smoke, Lilies and Jade," Thurman depicts Paul recounting a highly sensual and sensuous dream to the rapt audience at Niggeratti Manor:

> I was dreaming . . . a poignant, excruciatingly beautiful dream. I was in a flower garden, canopied by spreading oaks, and perfumed by fresh magnolia blossoms. The soil was pungent and formed a many colored blanket. White lilies, red lilies, pale narcissi, slender orchids, polychromatic pansies, jaundiced daffodils, soporific lotus blossoms. I was in Eden. The trees were thickly foliaged and only an occasional sunbeam filtered through. Above my head a bevy of full throated thrush caroled sweetly, insinuatingly. I lay down. Then I became aware of a presence. An ivory body exuding some exotic perfume. Beauty dimmed my eyes. The physical nearness of that invisible presence called to me, lured me closer. And as I crept nearer, the perfume pervaded my

> nostrils, inflamed my senses, anesthetized my brain. My hand reached out and clutched a silken forelock. Involuntarily my eyes closed and I was conscious of being sucked into it until there was a complete merging. For one brief moment I experienced supreme ecstasy. (45)

Like Nugent's Alex, Paul is depicted as an aspiring artist who yearns to escape from the workaday reality into a dreamworld of sensory experience, pleasure, and aesthetics. Thurman's representation emphasizes that the black dandy seeks to transcend sexual and gender categories: "Was the presence male or female?" (46), Samuel asks. Paul replies, "I really don't know. After all, there are no sexes, only sex majorities" (47). What I find interesting about this passage is the tension between everything that is characteristically decadent about it—the impulse to transform naturalistic detail into ornamental decoration, superabundance that slides into artifice, and the aura of enticing perversity—and a kind of primitivist pastoralism (lush foliage, sexual fertility, etc.) that nostalgically mourns the loss of organic sexual and spiritual communion. In this respect, the queer, African American form of dandyism we have been examining parts company with the nineteenth-century European dandy's effort to transcend nature and the body. The black dandy wishes to transcend the limitations of particular forms of embodiment—the biological essentialism that undergirds racial and sexual polarities—but he does not seek to dispense with the body altogether, nor does he entirely empty out the category of nature, as did his white male predecessor. Like Renée Vivien's decadent Sapphist or "perverse" lesbian, Thurman's interpretation of the dandyist tradition offers a seemingly improbable synthesis of artifice and nature, but one that specifically emerges from the black dandy's rearticulation of decadent and primitivist aesthetics.

DECADENT DISAVOWALS

I have asserted that Thurman does not present the black dandy (simply) as a representation of class and race longing that takes the form of a revival of the aesthetic project of the Wildean dandy. Nevertheless, it should be noted that Thurman does show us what happens when the black dandy disavows his racial identity and uses dandyism only as a form of racial passing. In order to explore these issues, we need to examine the character of Eustace Savoy and the novel's juxtaposition of Eustace and Paul. Actor, singer, and effeminate dandy, Eustace runs "a den of iniquity" in the basement of Niggeratti Manor (20), where he hosts nightly gin parties in his "ubiquitous green dressing gown" (42). Determined to divorce himself from the black aesthetic traditions of which he is ashamed, Eustace wants to be an opera singer—a "carbon copy of Caruso"—a desire that Thurman depicts as antithetical to the success of the Renaissance (112). I will return to this issue shortly, but for now I want to focus on how Eustace's dandyism is depicted as a preoccupation with dress and exterior elegance stripped of the social rebellion that is the badge of the bohemian dandy:

> Eustace was a tenor. He was also a gentleman. The word elegant described him perfectly. His every movement was ornate and graceful. He had acquired his physical bearing and mannerism from mid-Victorian matinee idols. No one knew his correct age. His face was lined and drawn. An unidentified scalp disease had rendered him bald on the right side of his head. To cover this mistake of nature, he let his hair on the left side grow long, and combed it side-wise over the top of his head. The effect was both useful and bizarre. Eustace also had a passion for cloisonné bric-a-brac, misty etchings, antique silver pieces, caviar, and rococo jewelry. And his most treasured possession was an onyx ring, the size of a robin's egg, which he wore on his right index finger. (22)

Artificial, vain, and superficial, with his secondhand manners and "bizarre" aesthetic costume, Eustace takes dandyism into the realm of the cliché. Like those fin-de-siècle dandies who sought to revive the style of the Regency era, Eustace seeks to embody the gracefulness, youthfulness, and elegance of a lost, aristocratic era. His passion for rococo is a fitting emblem of his affinity for Old Regime France and the superficial elegance and ornamentation that constitute his fantasy of whiteness.[18] Despite his almost desperate pursuit of an aristocratic, "civilizing" ideal, Eustace's dandyism does not ultimately rise beyond vulgar imitation; his comb-over is the perfect example of how his embrace of artifice and illusion moves toward vulgarization.

I would argue that Eustace's dandyism is depicted as debased because it is a form of cross-cultural aspiration that aims to displace blackness through an identification with a fetishized rendering of white identity. Although the text never directly disparages Eustace for his androgynous blurring of masculinity and femininity, I do think that Thurman uses Eustace's effeminacy as a sign for the weakness of the black man who is ashamed of his color and yet continually "wails" about "his lack of opportunity" because of it (104)—an artist who, because he cannot reconcile his black skin with his desire to be white, threatens to corrupt his own talent and the project of the Renaissance itself. Nowhere is Eustace's opposition to the Harlem arts movement more evident than in his refusal to sing black spirituals. Describing the contemporary craze for spirituals, he asks, "Aren't there enough people already spurting those bastard bits of doggerel? Must every Negro singer dedicate his life to the crooning of slave songs?" (107). Thurman suggests that Eustace's problem is not that he prefers Schubert or Beethoven to spirituals, but that he refuses to recognize African American artistic innovations that emerge from slave culture as legitimate expressive forms in their own right.

Eustace's ashamed suppression of folk forms is contrary to the very essence of the New Negro movement's commitment to cultivating race consciousness, race pride, and racial solidarity (Locke, "Introduction," *The New Negro* 7). Alain Locke's essay "The Negro Spirituals" challenges such "neglect and disdain" (199) of this uniquely American folk song, making the spiritual an emblem for the great past and future of African American art. Building on the groundbreaking work done by Du Bois on the "sorrow songs,"[19] Locke emphasizes the slave songs' thematic and rhythmic richness and argues that the epic spirituality of this black musical idiom achieves a universality that, as he puts it, "transcends the level of its origin" (199); in other words, for Locke as for Du Bois, African American sorrow songs are "the articulate message of the slave to the world" (Du Bois 179). Eustace, however, rejects this interpretation of the spiritual as a triumph over the experience of bondage, degradation, and racial terror. As he declares, "I'm no slave and I will not sing slave music if I never have a concert" (108). Eustace may appear to be shaking off the model of the Old Negro—who willingly accommodates a white racial fantasy of the servile black man—but Thurman suggests that, in reality, this move signals Eustace's adherence to a Eurocentric, rationalized racism that not only denies the creative black self, but also banishes the slave experience from modern Western artistic and cultural production.[20] Raymond, who finds Eustace's objections to singing spirituals "unintelligent" and "indefensible," makes explicit the ideology of racial inferiority implicit in the singer's position:

> He had no sympathy whatsoever with Negroes like Eustace, who contended that should their art be Negroid, they, the artist, must be considered inferior. As if a poem or a song or a novel by and about Negroes could not reach the same heights as a poem or a song or a novel by or about any other race. Eustace did not realize that by adhering to such a belief, he also subscribed to the theory of Nordic superiority. (108–9)

Eustace's retreat from his own ethnicity and traditions is problematic not because Thurman thinks that every black artist must focus on race (to the contrary, as we have already seen); instead, the problem is that Eustace's preference for European classicism over African American expressive culture is grounded in his refusal to recognize the contributions of black art and folk culture. The literary and artistic merit of black folk and oral traditions and the cultural work that these traditions perform are of course important and much-discussed topics. For the purposes of this argument, I want to emphasize that what is at stake in Thurman's treatment of this theme is the foundation of modern African American identity itself—how it had been defined historically and the battle over its redefinition by Renaissance artists and writers. Eustace objects to the notion that black cultural identity is primarily rooted in rural, southern folk traditions, but in trying to escape the image of the Old Negro, he ultimately takes on an impersonation of whiteness that bears a close resemblance to minstrelsy. For example, Eustace's trademark "spoonerisms" ("mad to gleet you!") are similar to the linguistic games of the blackface minstrel, transforming the gentility to which he aspires into the minstrel's "spectacle of vulgarity." Eustace's reiteration of this iconographic representation of racial meaning suggests that an ambivalence between "making" and "being" the joke may be definitionally built into minstrel conventions.

Capital, we might say, wins in the end. Eustace eventually does relent and is hired to sing spirituals, a move that brings about his physical and spiritual ruin. Thurman suggests the social and personal costs of Eustace's desire to "pass" are devastating, but so are the results of his effort to embody the stereotypical form of blackness that white people will pay to see performed. As his racial disavowal turns against the self and he succumbs to the unbearable weight of his own "physical and mental apathy" (272), Eustace is transformed into a hollow shell: "True, he still retained in some measure his aristocratic bearing, but he was by no means as jaunty as he had been in the past. He seemed to be shriveling up, to be the victim of some inner dessication, which had left his exterior self without color or vitality" (264–65). We should remember that the hollowness of inner life that Thurman describes is a defining feature of capitalism's capacity to reify consciousness. Taking on the inert and withered appearance that symbolizes his utter commodification, Eustace is propelled toward personal and social disintegration:

> Eustace did not exist any longer. Even the shell had begun to shrivel to a mere shadow of its former self. He had no spirit left, no vitality, no part of life. . . . He lived mechanically, animated only by a frugal stream of blood which his weary heart worked manfully to keep in action. . . . Eustace had been forcibly carried to the city hospital, forcibly because he had no desire to live, and resented any artificial attempts to delay the end. (272)

Like a true decadent, Eustace is overtaken by a fatalistic ennui that has literally infused his being with death, turning him into the archetypal hollowed-out object: the commodity. In his slide into fragmentation and commodification, Eustace lives the "social death" of the slave (Gilroy 63). Here, Thurman suggests a kinship between the black dandy and J. K. Huysmans's classic decadent hero, des Esseintes (*Against Nature*); in both cases, decadence is linked with disease as the dandy's act of repudiation ultimately becomes a form of slow suicide—the living death of an increasingly inert and reified subjectivity.

I have discussed Eustace and his transformation into an alienated object at some length because I believe that Thurman's dramatic rendering of Paul's suicide, which concludes the novel, needs to be read alongside the spiritual death of Eustace. In my view, Thurman describes the black dandy as "suspended between nightmares"—I have borrowed this phrase from Rosalind Willliams (151)—that is, between the living death of Eustace, whose hollowing out signals his transformation into fetishized commodity, and the actual suicide of Paul, whose withdrawal from social reality is a symbol of the black dandy's exclusion from history. I contend that Paul's suicide is in keeping with his deployment of dandyism as a gesture of renunciation and repudiation—what the critic Sharon P. Holland in her study of death and black subjectivity names "a disidentification with life" (179). Discussing the conclusion of *Infants*, David Blackmore has asserted that the text represents queer African American artists as "at least partially responsible for the downfall of the Harlem Renaissance" (528). Similarly, Michael Cobb claims that Thurman's novel scapegoats the queer: "What makes this ending of the novel extraordinary is that the queer character, who dares to violate Harlem and wander free of a particular formation of a conservative race consciousness and expression, not only perishes, but that he is the literal author of and artist of the New Negroes' representational death" (342). I agree with Cobb that the thematics of death in Thurman's novel are a solution to a fundamentally political problem regarding the relation between queerness and blackness, but Paul's theatrical sunset (especially when compared with Eustace's spiritual death) seems to me to represent not only the dandy's self-conscious rebellion against commodification but also his profound sense of cultural displacement.

As Thurman presents it, Paul's suicide is described as a highly ritualized spectacle of racialized difference, the ultimate aestheticizing strategy in the face of reification and fetishization:

> No one had been prepared for the gruesome yet fascinating spectacle which met their eyes. Paul had evidently come home before the end of the party. On arriving, he had locked himself in the bathroom, donned a crimson mandarin robe, wrapped his head in a batik scarf of his own designing, hung a group of his spirit portraits on the dingy calcimined wall, and carpeted the floor with sheets of paper detached from the notebook in which he had been writing his novel. He had then, it seemed, placed scented joss-sticks in the four corners of the room, lit them, climbed into the bathtub, turned on the water, then slashed his wrists with a highly ornamented Chinese dirk. When they found him, the bathtub had overflowed, and Paul lay crumpled at the bottom, a colorful, inanimate corpse in a crimson streaked tub. (283)

It is worth noting the voyeuristic pleasure in looking at the exoticized corpse of the black dandy that this passage conveys. Following the all too real cultural logic that links homosexuality with death, Thurman's funereal aesthetics conceptualizes the black dandy as most "seen" at the moment of his disappearance.[21] But if Paul achieves a new public visibility in death, he nonetheless remains, finally, as enigmatic as the pages of his novel that "had been rendered illegible" by the overflow of water (283). Simultaneously primitive and artificial, savage and civilized, Paul is a spectacle of contradiction. Thurman uses the tropes of Orientalized decadence to construct queer identity as a secret, much in the way that Wilde does in *The Picture of Dorian Gray*, but he does not position the black dandy's rebellion as fundamentally murderous. Thurman himself undercuts a tragic reading of the queer aesthete with a wry and darkly comic inversion, which suggests that Paul manufactured his death as the ultimate publicity stunt for his novel, *Wu Sing: The Geisha Man*. Upon seeing Paul's corpse for the first time, Raymond declares, "What delightful publicity to precede the posthumous publication of his novel" (283). However, all that remains of the novel is Paul's drawing of a crumbling image of Niggeratti Manor surrounded by "blindingly white beams of light" and the dedication: "To/Huysmans' Des Esseintes and Oscar Wilde's Oscar Wilde/Ecstatic Spirits with whom I Cohabitate/And whose golden spores of decadent pollen/I shall broadcast and fertilize/It is written" (284). For all its debt to the European tradition of dandyism and decadent aestheticism, *Infants of the Spring* does not conclude with the typical decadent thematic of a diminished sun and a conquering night. To the contrary, the rays of light and luminous sky suggest that, although the project of Niggeratti Manor has ended, the black dandy's "golden spores of decadent pollen" will take root in the new dialectical consciousness engendered by the culture of modernity.

5

GUTTER DANDYISM

The Queer Junkie in Cold War America

> Look down at my filthy trousers, haven't been changed in months. . . . The days glide by strung on a syringe with a long thread of blood. . . . I am forgetting sex and all sharp pleasures of the body—a grey, junk-bound ghost. The Spanish boys call me *El Hombre Invisible*—the Invisible Man.
>
> —William S. Burroughs, *Naked Lunch*

William S. Burroughs is America's most famous gutter dandy. An unrepentant junkie and unapologetic queer (his preferred term[1]), Burroughs consolidated in the 1950s the persona that would become his enduring image: a gray, funereal figure wearing a three-piece suit, tie, fedora, and overcoat with a velvet collar. Whether brandishing a shotgun or a cane, the indelible image of "Mr. B." is one of weary detachment, cool danger, and gentlemanly morbidity (Figure 5.1). Burroughs himself seems to be an incarnation of a central contradiction shared by the queer and the junkie: both figures become overwhelmed by a physical need so intense that it overtakes them, rendering the subject—paradoxically enough—ghostlike, invisible, and disembodied. The tension between spectral anonymity and a pronounced and abject physicality (the addict is transformed by the indelible mark of junk, the queer is ravaged by desire) is one facet of the contradiction

FIGURE 5.1. William S. Burroughs with shotgun standing in front of his "shotgun painting" (1987). Photo by Mario Ruiz. Time & Life Pictures/Getty Images.

between invisibility and hypervisibility that permeates all of Burroughs's early work. In texts such as *Junky* (1953), *Queer* (written in 1952), *Yage Letters* (1963), and *Naked Lunch* (1959), the iconic Burroughs hero is a subject on the verge of disappearing and a subject whose decay and corruption turn him into a spectacle of bodily excess—an exorbitance that dismantles the boundaries of the body itself.[2] Burroughs's life and work considerably complicate the one-dimensional view of him as "*El Hombre Invisible*," revealing instead a complex, ongoing engagement with the problem of being simultaneously "seen" and "unseen."

This chapter seeks to account for the paradox of visibility at the heart of a new postwar logic that links homosexuality and addiction in the figure of the queer junkie. This paradox of visibility makes Burroughs's form of gutter dandyism a privileged emblem for the contradictions that define gay and lesbian identity in cold war America. An incarnation of the open secret, queer identity during this period is an object of surveillance that eludes containment, making it both invisible (very much like the undetectable "red" menace of communism) and hypervisible (a ubiquitous threat to national security). My goal is to show how this contradictory logic of visibility is embedded in the logic of capitalism—specifically, the imperatives of postwar Fordism and its crisis of masculinity. During the cold war era, widespread anxieties about the influence of domesticated, passive, and conformist models of manhood—such as "the organization man" and the suburban dad—reflected an ambivalence about the contradictory imperatives of Fordist ideologies, which called on American men to both resist and affirm postwar commodity culture. Like other outlaw masculinities of the Beat movement, Burroughs's queer junkie reinforces and mobilizes postwar anxieties about feminization; he is in rebellion against the penetration of male subjectivity by the commodity form even as he is represented as a perverse, feminized subject in the gender ideology of the cold war consensus.[3]

My reading departs from a critical tendency to separate the logic of capital from the logic of the queer in Burroughs's novels. The critic Jamie Russell, for example, tends to assume that Marxist readings of Burroughs's "schizophrenic fragmentation"—such as those offered by Timothy S. Murphy and David Savran—are necessarily opposed to a queer critique that would recognize such fragmentation as specific to gay identity in heteronormative society (Russell 13). Russell's move is symptomatic of assumptions that ground the very best Burroughs criticism. For example, Timothy Murphy's work highlights a critical propensity to read junk as an emblem for capitalist social control and then to separate the themes of addiction, commodification, and power from Burroughs's focus on the social regulation of sexuality and gender. As Oliver Harris astutely points out, Murphy downplays sexuality as a site of social control in order to privilege the addict as an emblem of cold war hysteria and state regulation. Nevertheless, Harris unintentionally falls into a similar trap; arguing that there is a "fundamental difference between Burroughs's first two novels," he sharply distinguishes between the "textual politics" of *Junky* and *Queer* (77–78). He reads the author's first novel as "straight"—and therefore associated with a disembodied self-mastery that purports to be objective, rational, authoritative, and factual. *Queer*, on the other hand, is figured in the long-standing trope of gay identity as secret, enigmatic, and unknowable; it is precisely for this reason that it becomes the site of emotions, desire, and indeterminacy for Harris. This tendency to separate capitalism and sexuality—the politics of *Junky* from those of *Queer*—results in a dangerous polarization of rationalization and erotics. It is this polarization that my framing of the queer junkie seeks to disrupt.

Far from being a marginal figure in fifties culture, the queer junky or gutter dandy embodies two central cultural contradictions of the postwar era. First, he inhabits a contradiction between the reification and dehumanization of everyday life and modernity's promise of liberation (through an aesthetics of perception and transgressive eroticism). According to Herbert Marcuse, the contradiction between freedom and oppression constitutes "the syndrome of late capitalism: namely, the apparently inseparable unity—inseparable for the system—of productivity and destruction, of satisfaction of needs and repression, of liberty within a system of servitude" ("Liberation" 280). An emblem of this dialectic of liberation, the queer junkie embodies his two constituent identities through a paradoxical union of artifice (decadence) and authenticity (the primitive), which facilitates his insertion in a specifically American colonial formulation of sexual subjectivity and modernity. Second, the opposition between invisibility and hypervisibility that defines this Burroughsian icon is an extension of the appearance/essence split that (as I have argued in chapter 1) is at once paradigmatic of the queer and the commodity. As I argued at the outset, the Wildean dandy inaugurates queer identity as a contradiction between the visibility of outward appearances and the invisibility of inner relations—a disjunction between exteriors and interiors that characterizes modern industrial capitalism. However, the twin imperatives of secrecy and disclosure acquire a new form in cold war America due to the porousness and instability of the boundaries between public and private in postwar society. As a result, the logic of the open secret is remade into what Gilles Deleuze and Félix Guattari call a more ubiquitous, "infinite form of secrecy" (288). In other words, in the cold war culture of surveillance and containment, the secret takes on a more undefined and paranoid form, making queer identity imperceptible and nonetheless hypervisible. This produces a new dialectic in the figure of the queer junkie. Preexisting gender paradigms of addiction enter a new arena of social contest—namely, as I will explain later, the field of pulp fiction. Here, Burroughs intervenes in the contemporary, intertwined nexus of opiate addiction, femininity, and decadence, simultaneously reinscribing and subverting cultural logics of the cold war consensus. However, Burroughs arrives at his incarnation of the gutter dandy through a jettisoning of the feminizing elements of hypervisibility that would otherwise hinder his claims to a truly radical disruption of postwar models of wounded masculinity. As I will explain, the residual contradiction is that this strategic claim to masculinity is caught in a racialized and gendered logic of colonialism, ultimately producing a figure who inoculates himself with and against modernity.

BEAT REBELLION, GUTTER DANDYISM, AND THE EMPIRE OF OPIUM

> The new bohème, the beatniks and hipsters . . .—all these "decadents" now have become what decadence probably always was: poor refuge of a defamed humanity.
>
> —Herbert Marcuse, "Political Preface," *Eros and Civilization*

> Techniques now being used for control of thought could be used, instead, for liberation.
>
> —William S. Burroughs, *Burroughs Live*

Despite the obvious differences among the early work of Burroughs, Kerouac, and Ginsberg, these three principle Beat writers all promoted a sexual openness and antibourgeois attitude that distinguished them sharply from the dominant culture they variously sought to oppose. Emphasizing their queer aesthetics and politics, Regina Marler points out that "it isn't the gay content alone that made the work of Ginsberg and Burroughs and Kerouac controversial, but rather its unapologetic outsider status: its rejection of literary conventions and cold-war hysteria, its celebration of low life, its spiritual searching, its sexual explicitness" (xxviii). One might note that at a time when the "affluent society" promoted materialistic values and heartless conformity, the Beats were brave enough to propose a poetics based on the freedom of mind, desire, and imagination even when their own work was censored and attacked. However, their effort to "leave a record of combat against the native fascist militarization of the U.S. soul" had its limitations, particularly around the politics of race, colonialism, and gender (Ginsberg, *Deliberate Prose* 253). Unlike other Beats (such as Ginsberg) who tend to downplay their implication within power relations, Burroughs's work reflects a complex understanding of the queer subject's contradictory relationship to systems of domination. As Ann

Douglas states, "he believed that nothing happens without our consent; we are always complicit in what we take to be our God-given circumstances. 'To speak is to lie—to live is to collaborate'" (xvii). Nevertheless, like many avant-garde artists of the postwar era, Burroughs has a fundamentally individualistic notion of liberation that fails to engage with those systems of domination his work so powerfully exposes. Like other forms of Beat rebellion, Burroughs's gutter dandyism itself reproduces the contradictions of capitalism.

The queer junkie becomes the perfect emblem for the contradictions of capital, since he is at once the embodiment of reification and modernity's promise of utopia. This modern icon offers a decadent vision that takes pleasure into negation; the queer junkie is a hollow or empty body, overtaken by death and decay. He embodies a liberatory potential, but "instead of making a body without organs sufficiently rich or full for the passage of intensities," queer junkies—like other drug addicts—"erect a vitrified or emptied body, or a cancerous one: the causal line, creative line, or line of flight immediately turns into a line of death and abolition" (Deleuze and Guattari 285). Burroughs is very specific about this fatalistic dimension of opiate addiction; in *Naked Lunch*, for example, junk is linked to the parasitism of the virus, which inhabits and overtakes its host (201). This is perhaps why in Burroughs's early work the queer junkie strongly critiques the alienation, dehumanization, and violence that have made modern U.S. society a "renunciation of life itself" (NL 113). Emphasizing America's institutionalized racism and imperialism, Burroughs draws our attention to alarming concentrations of wealth and power in a supposedly "classless" society, as well as the injustices of U.S. social policies both at home and abroad. However, Burroughs's gutter dandy is fascinated and seduced by those aspects of modern life he would appear to despise. As Deleuze and Guattari remind us, "drug addicts continually fall back into what they wanted to escape" (285). For the queer junkie, the dehumanizing effects of capitalist modernity have a certain appeal, akin to the sex appeal of the inorganic. Burroughs shares with the nineteenth-century dandy or decadent aesthete a fascination with the ugliness of the modern world, with decay and death-in-life, as well as with a critique of instrumental reason and its myth of progress.

At the same time, the persistent and surprising yearning for a feminized authenticity in Burroughs's early work distinguishes the gutter dandy from his nineteenth-century predecessor and inscribes the author's postwar writing with a specifically American, colonial conception of Orientalist difference and primitive authenticity. This aspect of Burroughs's work is easily missed or misunderstood, but I want to emphasize that the queer junkie is a distinctly modern icon precisely because his drug use and eroticism are always modes of repression and rebellion; gutter dandyism emerges, then, as an experiment of liberation from capitalist control that is limited by the global horizon of capital itself. Kerouac's representation of people of color as exotic/erotic Others is one well-known example of the Beats' tendency to privilege marginalized, "authentic" identities/spaces as an antidote to the artificiality of fifties culture. This comes through in Ginsberg's journals from the early 1950s, especially in one electric description of the "bestial brilliance" of an urban Latin passerby, who seemed to the poet to look too wild and free "to live in society" (*Journals* 19). Although this impulse takes a more complex and less romantic form in Burroughs's writing, his yearning for freedom and authenticity is most powerfully represented in his search for the South American plant yage or ayahuasca, a hallucinogen that he believed offered its users telepathic powers, thought control, and out-of-body migrations. (In 1953, Burroughs traveled to the Amazon in South America to find the drug; his experience is recounted in *The Yage Letters*.) I want to emphasize that the authentic, "uncut" high of yage is always figured in relation to the reification of heroin. Burroughs makes this explicit in the conclusion to *Junky*, when the narrator declares his plan to leave for Columbia to "score" for yage: "I am ready to move on south and look for the uncut kick that opens out instead of narrowing down like junk. . . . Maybe I will find in yage what I was looking for in junk and weed and coke. Yage may be the final fix" (J 127–28). As I will demonstrate, junk (as a form of chemical technology) and yage express a dialectic of liberation in Burroughs's early work, which figures gutter dandyism as both authentic and artificial, primitive and decadent—an incarnation of liberatory potential and social relations overtaken by reification.

This contradictory aspect of the queer junkie is clearly apparent in Burroughs's relationship to the South and the East. In *The Yage Letters* and *Queer*, he critiques U.S. cultural imperialism, but is nevertheless seduced and intrigued by the "ruined" cultures it produces in places like Mexico, South America, and Tangier. Although his work offers a decidedly unromantic image of these locations, his writing nonetheless tends toward a primitivizing and Orientalist view of Southern and Eastern cultures. Noting Burroughs's interest in Spengler's *Decline of the West*, critic Manuel Luis Martinez points out that this text generated a "Beat historiographical understanding" grounded in Spengler's notion that "the West was on the verge of decline, but the southern climes had already fallen into decay" (62). In *Queer*, Lee has an attitude that is at best resigned toward his enmeshment in the hierarchies of a colonialist global order. Lee's quest for the elusive drug locates it as an authentic fetish, and himself as a colonial adventurer determined to wrench it from its native land. Of course, there are moments in the text when Burroughs is clearly satirizing Lee's imbrication in the web of colonial power, especially in regard to his relationship to the boys he lusts after and/or pays for sex: "A blond Mexican boy went by pushing a cart. 'Jesus Christ!' Lee said, his mouth dropping open. 'One of them blond-headed Mexicans! 'Tain't as if it was being queer, Allerton. After all, they's only Mexicans" (Q 77). At the same time, Burroughs's early work demonstrates that his ideology of privacy as freedom—the right to be left alone—is constructed via a fantasy of erotic authenticity beyond the borders of the United States. In "The Search for Yage" (1953), the author states that the "average *non queer* Peruvian boy" (Burroughs's emphasis) has "no inhibitions":

> If they do go to bed with another male, and they all will for money, they seem to enjoy it. Homosexuality is simply a human potential as is shown by almost unanimous incidents in prisons—and nothing human is foreign or shocking to a South American. I am speaking of the South American at best, a special race part Indian, part white, part god knows what. He is not, as one is apt to think at first fundamentally an Oriental nor does he belong to the West. He is something special unlike anything else. He has been blocked from expression by the Spanish and the Catholic Church. (YL 33–34)

This is an extraordinary passage not only because Burroughs was writing at a time when homosexuality was overwhelmingly seen as a pathology or mental illness, but also because he arrives at this insight by way of a primitivizing and feminizing colonialist logic. I am struck by his own failure to register how the structuring relationship of the commodity and the inequalities of global capitalism mediate his encounters with young boys, hustlers, and other men he pays for sex. Furthermore, there is more than a little Orientalism in the Western sexual tourist's romanticizing of South Americans as a sexually fluid, "special race." In *Queer*, Lee comments to Allerton that "I saw some beautiful boys on the waterfront. The real uncut boy stuff. Such teeth, such smiles. Young boys vibrating with life" (98). Here, as in *Yage*, we see the gutter dandy's imperialist nostalgia for a hidden, primitive world of "uncut" pleasures that are simultaneously sexual and herbal/chemical.[4] As the critic Greg A. Mullins notes in his discussion of *Queer*, "Junk enforced isolation from other people, but Lee hopes yage can help him connect with others, possibly bringing sexual experience and drug experience together in a harmony of plentitude" (56–57). However, since this dream of connection is dependent on individualistic ideologies of unfettered access, anonymity, and privacy, Burroughs's queer junkie ultimately yearns to live outside of modern society. Invoking an unwitting ahistoricism, the author therefore imagines non-Western spaces as "sanctuaries of noninterference" beyond social context.[5]

Like the nineteenth-century dandy, for whom "modern urban life is virtually intolerable," Burroughs and other Beats seek to retreat from a hostile, ugly world (*Burroughs Live* 149). However, the dandy or decadent aesthete seeks to create an utterly artificial world; although his "alternate reality" is equally constructed, the male Beat more often imagines that his counterreality is a free, spontaneous, and authentic world. This is why his retreat is enacted primarily through an individualistic notion of privacy as freedom, made available through drugs or travel to non-Western lands. For Burroughs, what drugs—especially junk and other painkillers—offer is the ability to "drop out." His early work constantly invokes and extols the right of the individual "to mind one's own business." Although *Naked Lunch* declares that junk imposes contact, more often Burroughs figures the queer junkie as a fundamentally separate and solitary subject—or, even better, an object:

> I lived in one room in the Native Quarter of Tangier. . . . I did absolutely nothing. I could look at the end of my shoe for eight hours. If a friend came to visit—and they rarely did since who or what was left to visit—I sat there not caring that he had entered my field of vision—a grey screen, always blanker and fainter—and not caring when he walked out of it. If he had died on the spot I would have sat there looking at my shoe waiting to go through his pockets. Wouldn't you? (NL 203)

In this well-known passage, Burroughs emphasizes that, for the addict, there is no participation in the social; even "the world network of junkies" (7) is shrouded by junk and its endless cellular thirst, which washes away "human lines" (9) and transforms the addict into a spectral figure, inhabiting a borderland between the living and the dead. In contrast with early twentieth-century depictions of opium dens as degenerate spectacles of racial and gender promiscuity, the network of drug circulation seems to fall into the background for Burroughs's modern urban addict.[6] Like the nineteenth-century dandy, the queer junkie seeks to transcend embodiment and nature, hopelessly searching for "momentary freedom from the claims of the aging, cautious, nagging, frightened flesh" (J 128). In this way he aspires to the nonattachment of the Baudelairean dandy, a transcendent state attained by Ginsberg through Buddhism. Whereas nirvana for Ginsberg is the selfless I, the sense of being one with the universe, for the figure of the gutter dandy, nirvana represents a complete extinction of phenomena; it is not bacchanalian joy, but rather nothingness—the extinction of all attachment and desire.

With this context in mind, I want to complicate the by-now fairly typical reading of junk as an emblem of social control.[7] My point is not primarily that critics are wrong when they make the argument that heroin becomes an emblem for the reification of capitalist modernity; rather, I strongly believe this reading flattens out the complexity of the thematics of junk and drug use in Burroughs's work. Of course, any reader confronted with the brutality of *Naked Lunch*'s images of junkies must conclude that Burroughs finds heroin addiction utterly devoid of joy, beauty, and pleasure. Furthermore, he departs from the Beat sensibility of Ginsberg and Kerouac since he suggests that the queer junkie and other male hipsters suffer from a lack not an excess of joie de vivre:

> The young hipsters seem lacking in energy and spontaneous enjoyment of life. The mention of pot or junk will galvanize them like a shot of coke. They jump around and say, "Too much! Crazy! Man, let's pick up! Let's get loaded." But after a shot, they slump into a chair like a resigned baby waiting for life to bring the bottle again. (J 123–24)

Here, Burroughs is not only interested in showing how junk drains young people of life and libidinal energy; in suggesting that junkies are reduced to the passivity of an infantile state, he emphasizes that junk narrows consciousness and incapacitates the subject in ways far more dangerous than its physical effects. The political and social effects of such an immobilization are hardly countercultural, as Burroughs himself conveys in a 1970 interview: "Heroin is a drug that is much more to the advantage of the Establishment than grass. I don't want to exaggerate the matter, but it does incapacitate people so they are solely concerned with heroin. This is certainly dangerous from a revolutionary point of view" (*Burroughs Live* 152).

But Burroughs never sees drugs, even heroin, as merely something negative; they are seductive and horrifying because they are both repressive and liberatory in his work. I want to emphasize that by "liberatory" I mean to invoke the sense of nirvana I referred to earlier; drugs are not euphoric or a Dionysian mode of excess and pleasure, but rather a method of release, a way out—a means of spacetime travel, disassociation, abstraction, escape from the body, or escape into animal or vegetative states. This is what Baudelaire calls the "absolute bodily quiescence" of opium (*Artificial Paradises* 60); similarly, in *The Yage Letters* Burroughs elaborates on a "junk reduced to pure habit offering precarious vegetable serenity" (46). For Burroughs, this "precarious vegetable serenity" is one aspect of a process of desubjectification that uses travel, technology, and drugs to shift frontiers, deterritorialize the body, and liberate the subject from his "identity habit." But this is not Baudelaire's "artificial paradise"; unlike the dandies, decadents, and aesthetes who tend to seek to discover an artificial paradise, for the Beats drugs do not offer an artificial paradise but rather something approaching "supreme reality," one that is posited as both outside and only accessible through modernity. Although this is particularly true for Ginsburg, Burroughs's quest for the "uncut kick" of yage is an identifiably utopian moment in his work.

I am not aware of any studies that link Aldous Huxley and Burroughs, but it is worth noting that some of the ideas Burroughs developed were anticipated by Huxley, who remained fascinated by the paradoxical role that drug taking plays in society both as a mode of social control and a method for spiritual enlightenment. This tension takes a different form in Burroughs's work, but it is there in his sense that what drugs offer is "supreme reality." What Huxley's novel *Brave New World* (1932) points to is a major insight of Marcuse and the Frankfurt school: that in modern society domination takes pleasurable forms. This is exemplified by the high-tech, sterile pleasures of Huxley's "soma," which produces a mindless chemical euphoria that anestheticizes the individual and thus reconciles her to her social conditions. The example of Huxley's soma helps us to see that Burroughs does not represent junk as only or primarily an instrument of control. Although he is careful to state that "consciousness expansion is certainly not dependent on drugs," he also sees them as one way to interrupt massified forms of thought control (*Burroughs Live* 143). "Yage is space time travel" (Y 44) and offers "telepathic sensitivity" (46). Drugs make available a rebellious mode of becoming—like Alice in Wonderland, the drug user experiences an unfixing of identity and temporality that allows her to elude the present. For Deleuze and Guattari, drug experience offers the potential to erect a body without organs through the disorienting of perception: "Nothing left but the world of speeds and slownesses without form, without subject, without a face. Nothing left but the zigzag of a line, like 'the lash of the whip of an enraged cart driver' shredding faces and landscapes. A whole rhizomatic labor of perception, the moment when desire and perception meld" (*A Thousand Plateaus* 283).

However, I do not wish to become rhapsodic here; the melding of desire and perception may facilitate seductive anonymity, simultaneity, and a stripping away of the self, but "the empire of opium" is not a mode of liberation (Baudelaire, *Artificial Paradises* 130). For Deleuze and Guattari, as for Burroughs, drug addiction forecloses its potential to access the plane of the infinite. In this respect, Burroughs distinguishes heroin from hallucinogens, which are typically considered sacred by users. As he points out in "Deposition: Testimony Concerning a Sickness":

> no one ever suggested that junk is sacred. There are no opium cults. Opium is profane and quantitative like money. I have heard that there was once a beneficent non-habit-forming junk in India. It was called *soma* and is pictured as a beautiful blue tide. If *soma* ever existed the Pusher was there to bottle it and monopolize it and sell it and it turned into plain old-time JUNK. (NL 201)

In this passage there is a very cynical sense of junk as reification, as the ultimate commodity; it produces desire with a mathematical precision that is quantitative (the algebra of need), seeking—like capital—to conquer new markets because of its endless drive to expand. (This vision makes sense considering, in the postwar era, Burroughs was writing at a time of unprecedented expansion of capital.) The "junk virus" is a commodified form of desire, which is why it cannot partake of the sacred. And yet there is for Burroughs the persistent attraction of an exotic, mythic "uncut high," which he imagines in India because, for him, the East fundamentally exists outside social context and commodity relations.

THE POST-MALE JUNKIE

> Burroughs is the chief prophet of the post-male post-heroic world.
> —Leslie Fiedler, "The New Mutants"

The connection between addiction, perversity, and homosexuality is a long-standing one in modernism—this link is made in various ways in Baudelaire, Renée Vivien, Arthur Rimbaud, Jean Cocteau, and Oscar Wilde's *The Picture of Dorian Gray*. In his essay "The Name Is Burroughs," the writer recounts an early memory:

> As a young child I wanted to be a writer because writers were rich and famous. They lounged around Singapore and Rangoon smoking opium in a yellow pongee silk suit. They sniffed cocaine in Mayfair and they penetrated forbidden swamps with a faithful native boy and lived in the native quarter of Tangier smoking hashish and languidly caressing a pet gazelle. (*Adding Machine* 2)

Burroughs's tendency to combine drug use (opium, cocaine, and hashish) with the dandyish, decadent sensibility of the queer artist is a fascinating example of how he draws upon European and English traditions of the decadent homosexual artist/writer, even as he refashions its vision to reflect the Beat movement's U.S. imperialist fantasy of the masculine, individualistic adventurer.

However, as I argued at the outset of this chapter, the exigencies of the postwar era result in the particular force with which the identities of the queer and the junkie fuse in Burroughs's work. Cold war culture causes homosexuality and addiction to be linked by a new logic of the "epidemic" that sees both the junkie and the queer as embodiments of a particularly threatening form of identity: the secret agent of social decay, who is an invisible (and yet ubiquitous), degenerate Other who preys upon and/or seduces the innocent. This notion of the queer as insatiable and vampiric, requiring more and younger "victims" (Miller 110), is especially evident in *Queer*, which describes Lee as a predatory degenerate corrupting the childlike Allerton (24). Due to the postwar focus on supposed threats to the family, homosexuality, drugs, and delinquency all become constructed as social illnesses. The widespread medicalization of deviance in postwar culture and the new power of psychiatry produced a pathologizing and criminalizing of both homosexuality and drug taking as deviant identities, not simply acts of excess. It should be noted that this confluence in the postwar era is symptomatic of a cultural legacy that dates back to the nineteenth century. In an extraordinary conjunction, opiate addiction and homosexuality shift from practices to identities at the same time. Before 1870, "the prevailing view of opiate addiction was as a vice, a bad habit indulged in by weak-willed and sinful but otherwise normal persons" (Cartwright 123). Similarly, as Michel Foucault and other historians of sexuality have demonstrated, modern forms of sexuality, including homosexuality, were transformed in the late nineteenth century from practices to identities grounded in biology. In 1870, as Foucault famously states, "the homosexual was now a species" (43). The rise of nonmedical addicts and accompanying shifts in class, social status, and eventually race (the addict moves from the core to the periphery) seems to have played a part in the shift from addiction as vice or sin to personality disorder. This trend continues in the early twentieth century as nonmedical addicts gradually overtake medical ones to become the majority of the addict population. By the 1920s and 1930s, the reigning psychiatric view of addicts as mentally disturbed or psychopathic was firmly in place. Like the queer or sexual pervert, the junkie suffered from a personality disorder that made him fundamentally sick, deviant—his perverted/deviant acts or "morbid cravings" are merely symptoms of his inner pathology. It is not until the dramatic postwar shifts in addiction patterns (the new addicts tended to be young African American men from poor, urban communities) that this psychiatric model was discredited by sociological ones (Cartwright 152).[8] That Burroughs published *Junky* at a transitional moment is reflected in the text, since it draws on both psychiatric and sociological models of addiction.

In *Junky* in particular, the figure of the queer junkie is linked to degeneracy and criminality. When Lee comes into possession of some morphine and tries to sell it, it immediately takes him into a sinister underworld whose entrance is announced by a "large flabby middle-aged queer, with tattooing on his forearms and even on the backs of his hands" (J 4). The submerged world of the novel is populated with strange creatures—decaying and barely human junkies such as Mary, who is like a "deep-sea creature" with "cold, fish eyes"; as the narrator states, "I could see those eyes in a shapeless, protoplasmic mass undulating over the dark sea floor" (J 11). Or, to cite another example, we might consider Subway Mike, who, with his pale face and long teeth, is like "an underground animal that preys on animals of the surface" (J 9). But this is not to suggest that Burroughs simply accedes to dominant models of the degenerate junkie. He pointedly references the postwar stereotype of the psychopath, but distinguishes this figure from Lee, thereby offering a subtle critique of those psychiatrists and others who would see opiate addiction as evidence of a psychopathic personality disorder. Jack, who is not a junkie, casually tells a story about beating a guy to death with a pipe:

> "You could see the brain there and the blood coming out of it." Jack began to laugh uncontrollably. "My girl was waiting out in the car. She called me—ha-ha-ha!—she called me—ha-ha-ha!—a cold-blooded killer."
>
> He laughed until his face was purple. (J 6)

Writing against the cultural logic of his day, Burroughs does not pathologize the addict as a "cold-blooded killer" or deranged, antisocial animal. In his original introduction to the first edition of the novel (which was replaced with the biographical introduction demanded by the publisher), the author explicitly refutes the stereotype of the crazed, sociopathic junkie. He rejects as "official propaganda" the "myth" that "*there is a connection between junk and insanity. Addicts turn into maniacs when they cannot get junk* [original ital.]." "Actually," Burroughs dryly states, "I have never seen or heard of an insane addict. For some reason, the two conditions do not occur together" (J 142). This theme continues throughout *Naked Lunch*, when none other than Dr. Benway declares: "I have never seen a schizophrenic junkie" (NL 29). From this perspective, Burroughs both contests and reproduces the postwar tendency to depict queers and junkies as subcultural deviants. On the one hand, he is invested in the outsider status of queers and junkies and seeks to establish their difference from and rebellion against the world of "straights." On the other hand, he seems to anticipate the normalization of previously deviant practices and identities by presenting crime, homosexuality, and drug use as merely one facet of the hipster's rebellious and risky life. Burroughs is determinedly agnostic on the question of the etiology of addiction and homosexuality. The radicalness of his refusal to theorize a "cause" for drug use or homosexuality (or heterosexuality for that matter) cannot be overemphasized. With this in mind, I want to stress that the cross-pollination of deviance that links homosexuality and addiction cannot be explained by the fact that both were underground and criminal identities in the 1950s; as I have been arguing, it is a product of the fundamental contradictions that define these tropes and their imbrication in the logic of cold war culture.

As historian David T. Cartwright has shown, by 1940, opiate addiction in the United States had transformed from a nineteenth-century condition of primarily respectable, bourgeois, and wealthy white women (who were administered opium and morphine by physicians for a wide range of diseases and symptoms) to the stereotype of the lower-class, hustling male junkie who is "on the needle." We might speculate that it was because this stereotype cohered in the mid-twentieth-century—a time of cultural anxieties about the fluidity of gender and changing definitions of masculinity and femininity—that it was haunted by the previous era's image of the feminized user. By the 1950s, the figure of the heroin addict was linked with an urban underworld of crime, gambling, prostitution, and gangs and, at the same time, the outlaw status of the junkie was becoming increasingly seen as a betrayal of traditional masculinity and linked in the popular imagination to feminization, passivity, and sexual fluidity.

In Nelson Algren's *The Man with the Golden Arm* (1949), Frankie Machine is a hustler and stud-poker dealer who is fundamentally too weak to overcome his addiction, telling himself to "tough it out, kid, tough it out" (305), and succumbing again and again to "God's medicine" and the feminine pleasure of the needle. As Leslie Fielder asks "what could be more womanly, as Elémire Zolla was already pointing out some years ago, than permitting the penetration of the body by a foreign object which not only stirs delight but even (possibly) creates new life?" (*Essays* Vol. 2, 397). Although both Burroughs and Algren are interested in the ways in which junk comes to replace sex, in Burroughs's *Junky* the fix is ultimately presented as a hollow pleasure and an enslavement to need—a paradoxical union of sex and death that strips pleasure of libidinal energy. In contrast, Algren's novel presents the fix as the ultimate orgasm—a surrender so complete and violent that it resembles the self-shattering pleasures experienced by "womenish men" (288) who allow themselves to be penetrated, and thus (in this cultural logic) punished by pleasure. The critic Stephen Perrin points out this aspect of Algren's work, arguing that the author "sees a strong vein of homosexual masochism running through the addict personality" (25). Perhaps even more important, there is the sense that Frankie—like all junkies—has abdicated his gender role as father, worker, and breadwinner. One narcotics cop, Sergeant Dugan, knew that addicts "liked to be treated like children," which enabled him "to pick them up like a father taking a wayward child home" (292). And when Molly tries to help Frankie, he is described as a disobedient child and she becomes "an outraged mother" who scolds and punishes him (320). In short, Algren suggests that the junkie flees his manly, earthly duties and chooses instead to reside in "Cloudland."

Although there are echoes of this impulse in *Junkie*, Burroughs is invested in presenting the queer junkie's outlaw masculinity as a form of rebellion that is dangerous and butch. He has more in common with gangsters, adventurers, thieves, killers, bootleggers, "commies," and spies than he does with the post-war era's figure of the abject, limp-wristed fag. In the 1950s, the street robber, petty criminal, "vice-merchant," or pimp was nothing more than "a predatory parasite pure and simple with little political or economic power and little or no public support or tolerance" (Lea 88). However, for Burroughs, the queer junkie is an urban pirate who dares to overcome great obstacles and do the hard work it takes to be a thief, keep up a habit, endure withdrawal sickness, and stay a step ahead of the law. Burroughs's own phobic reaction to male femininity is especially fascinating because he himself came to represent a particularly threatening form of nontraditional, perverse, and feminized masculinity in the popular imagination. In "The New Mutants" first published in *The Partisan Review* in 1965, Leslie Fielder points to Burroughs as "the chief prophet of the post-male post-heroic world" (Fielder, *Essays* Vol. 2, 392). Elsewhere, he describes both Ginsberg and Kerouac as emblematic of the hipster's arrested development and yearning for boyhood (Fielder, *Essays* Vol. 1, 492); however, he reserves his greatest admonition for the Burroughsian queer junkie, perhaps because this figure combines two different but related forms of rebellion against white masculinity, which cohere to produce a profoundly threatening, "radical metamorphosis of the Western male" (Fielder, *Essays* Vol. 2, 394).

THE QUEER DECADENCE OF PULP FICTION

Published by pulp house Ace Books in 1953, Burroughs's *Junkie: Confessions of an Unredeemed Drug Addict* features "a magnificently lurid cover painting of a man wrestling a packet of heroin from the hand of a sumptuous blonde" (Server 74; Figure 5.2).[9] Like many pulp covers, the illustration presents for the voyeuristic pleasure of readers a tabloid-like snapshot of frozen yet feverish desire. The sensational tableau depicts a beautiful woman who is arrested from fulfilling her desire by an emblem of masculine restraint. Although this image (like the book jackets of many postwar paperbacks) did not actually represent Burroughs's narrative, the cover painting resonates with the gendered logic of addiction that—as we have already seen—was so pervasive in the postwar era. I do not want to minimize the clearly commercial impulse behind Ace's decision to depict a voluptuous blonde caught in a shocking and compromising position—her "works" are on display and she is about to "cook up" the junk in her hand. At the same time, I want to insist that the feminization of the addict was so historically entrenched that even a novel as "hard-boiled" as *Junky* could not escape being positioned within the nexus of opiate addiction, femininity, and decadence. Considering this historical context, the wrestling figures on the cover of the text would seem to illustrate the supposed sexual ambiguity of the heroin addict, who is a split subject doomed to battle his feminine yearning for the passive pleasures of the needle.

In arguing that there is something "queer" about *Junky*'s cover illustration, I deliberately mean to suggest a connection between this novel and *Queer*. The latter text was written in 1952 while Burroughs was working on the *Junk* manuscript, and conceptualized as an extension of this first novel. It therefore

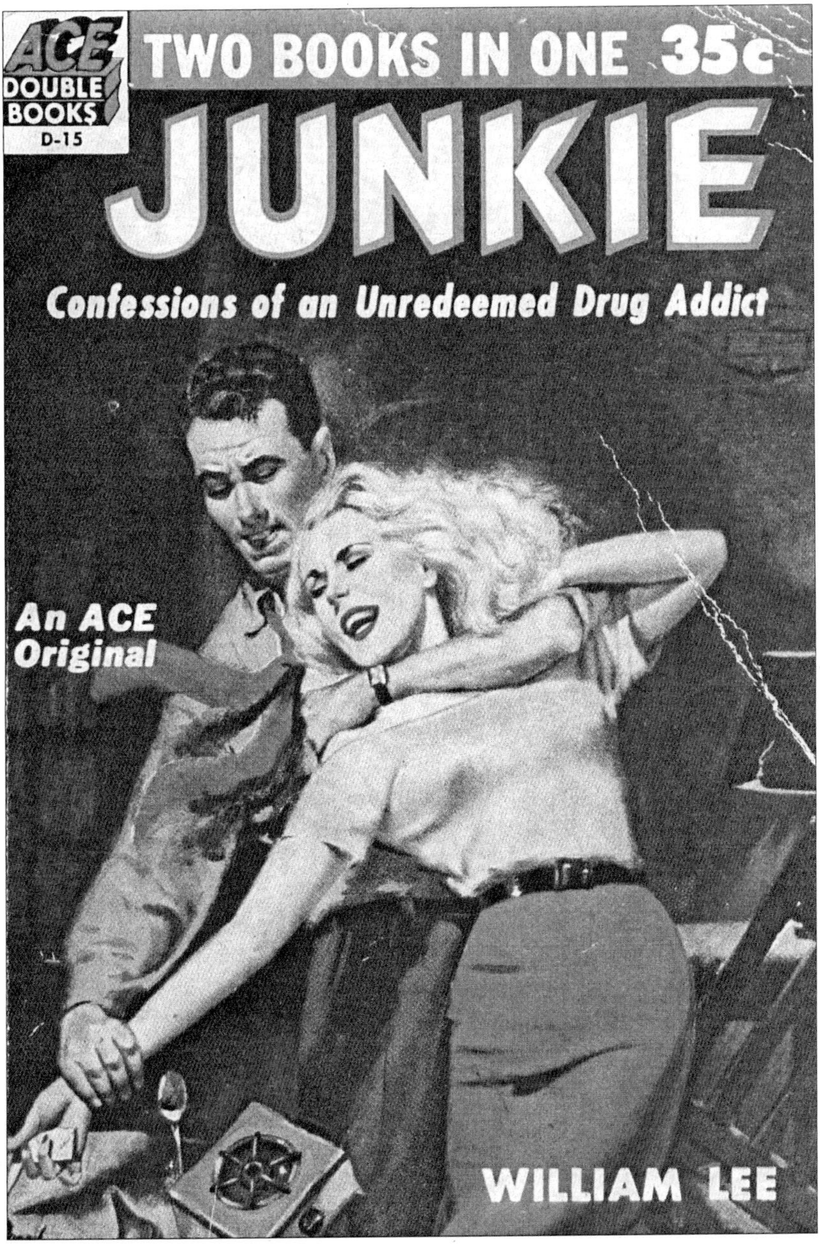

FIGURE 5.2. Cover illustration for *Junkie: Confessions of an Unredeemed Drug Addict*, Ace Books (1953). Courtesy of the Charles E. Young Research Library, Department of Special Collections, UCLA University Library.

makes sense to ask how postwar paperback publishing trends may have influenced these texts. Significantly, Ace Books rejected the *Queer* manuscript because its controversial content made it unpublishable in the early 1950s. In a 1984 interview, Burroughs explains, "the head at Ace Books, Carl Solomon, which was my entrée into Ace Books where *Junky* was published, said, 'Well, if I published this I'd go to jail'" (*Burroughs Live* 597). In fact, what historian Susan Stryker calls the "golden age" of queer pulps was primarily Sapphic. During this era, presses found it safer to publish lesbian pulps that were geared primarily to a straight male readership. Contrasting the commercial success of lesbian pulps with novels about gay men, Michael Bronski states, "it is reasonable to assume that no gay male titles sold the tremendous quantities attained by the most successful of the lesbian pulps" (*Pulp Friction* 4). Burroughs's decision to downplay or even obscure Lee's sexuality in his first novel needs to be understood in this context. Not only did the original version of the novel delete references to the author's homosexuality, but, in order to make the novel more publishable, Burroughs gave his narrator a wife, although she is a spectral figure in the text, barely present, in fact, before she disappears entirely from the narrative. In short, I want to argue that the author's strategic privileging of the junkie in his first novel should not prevent us from recognizing that this figure is, for him, always and already queer.

In considering the pulp context of Burroughs's early work, I do not mean to suggest that these novels reproduced the conventions of the genre. Burroughs was not the only Beat writer to gravitate toward pulp; it is worth noting that Kerouac wrote a book in this genre, a mass-market paperback called *Tristessa*, based on the author's own relationship with a beautiful, morphine-addicted Mexican prostitute. Published by Avon in 1960, Kerouac's more typically Beat treatment of his material infuses this "ravishing, ravished junky lady" (to quote Ginsberg) with an exotic beauty that is at once tragic and transcendent. Published much earlier than Kerouac's novel and with a sensibility that often seems more noir than Beat, *Junky* is unusual for pulps of the fifties because it pushes against the boundaries of the genre. Striking in its antisensationalism and existentialist indifference to questions of meaning, the novel has no "moral" congruent with postwar expectations. Unlike other narratives more typical of the genre, Lee is not punished at the end of *Junky* and does not regret his drug use; in fact, although Burroughs looks unblinkingly at the horror of addiction, he refuses to demonize the "dopefiend" or any drug, including heroin.[10] Furthermore, he boldly states in his prologue: "I never regretted my experience with drugs. I think I am in better health now as a result of using junk at intervals than I would be if I had never been an addict" (J xxxviii). Although his publishers clearly believed that the author's refusal to be "redeemed" was a selling point (they chose the subtitle, *Confessions of an Unredeemed Drug Addict*), Ace Books felt obliged to assure their audience of their moralistic position on drugs. As a result, they paired Burroughs's book with Maurice Helbrant's more conventional novel, *Narcotic Agent: Gripping True Adventures of a T-Man's War against the Dope Menace*. Ace Books was the creator of the "Ace Double"—two complete novels, each with their own cover, that were printed back-to-back, or in Ginsberg's memorable turn of phrase, "69'd" (*Deliberate Prose* 385). When readers finished the first novel, they simply turned the book upside down and started the other one.

Despite the fact that his work challenges many of the tropes pulp put into play, the rise of the paperback industry in postwar America provided a unique forum for Burroughs to synthesize oppositional and commercial responses to mass cultural production. In his study of masculinity in cold war poetics, Michael Davidson argues that "far from rejecting the cultural mainstream, the Beats embraced many of its more oppositional features" (51). Surprisingly, Davidson never considers pulp fiction as one such oppositional force, and never mentions Burroughs as an artist with a relationship to mass culture. However, like Andy Warhol, Burroughs negotiates the problem of the avant-garde's relationship to commodity culture by actually refusing the fraught opposition between high and low culture. What distinguishes his writing in texts like *Junky* is his capacity for transforming mass cultural production into a mode of cultural critique. His trenchant critique of American culture suggests that it is not only junkies, hustlers, or other marginalized figures who are overtaken by decay and degeneration; in *Junky*, for example, the Valley is symptomatic of a rottenness in America: "All the worst features of America have drained down into the Valley and concentrated there" (90). As a modernist incarnation of the decadent hero, Burroughs's queer junkie reflects a shift within modernism from a focus on the decadent as abstract individual to locating the decadent within a decaying society. I want to emphasize that it is pulp as a paperback genre that facilitates this decadent critique of modern mass culture.

Frankly erotic and frankly commercial, mass-market paperback books were a "gloriously subversive" voice of dissent in the cold war culture of consensus (Server 9). Precipitated by the birth of the PBO or Paperback Original, the booming paperback industry of the late 1940s and early 1950s created a space in American popular culture where marginalized voices could be heard and "deviant" and dangerous identities were not only represented but—according to some cultural observers—even promoted.[11] What had begun primarily as a source of portable, cheap, and disposable reading for the U.S. Armed Services during World War II emerged as a symptom of widespread cultural ambivalence; pulp fiction mobilized anxieties around the new domestication of the American man, the return of women to traditional roles after the war, and cold war society's focus on the nuclear family, now reorganized as a specular site of mass consumption. In the bright, optimistic postwar culture, these paperback books were a place where one encountered a more cynical vision of America. As Stryker asserts, they were "harboring the brooding content that lingered beneath the bright, false, chrome-plated surfaces covering much of postwar American life" (7). Of course, the Fordist welfare state of this era also brought tremendous reforms: expansion of schools, housing, and health care as well as an increase in income, particularly from factory jobs that provided higher wages for some segments of the working class. But the so-called social problems of the 1950s foregrounded by pulp—drugs and delinquency in particular—need to be understood as a rebellion against the unequal distribution of wealth masked by an ideological vision of a prosperous, secure, and conflict-free America. With its focus on gangs, violence, poverty, and the hopelessness of the "urban jungle," the pulp genre of juvenile delinquent fiction in particular was "a devastating indictment of American society" (Server 84).

While the decadent critique of pulp fiction was a disruptive force in cold war culture, the genre's representations of deviant pleasures were by no means a queer utopia. In fact, pulp saturated its subjects in the paradox of visibility that, as we shall see, defines the strategic contradictions of the queer junkie. With their lurid, colorful, and outrageous covers, the pulps themselves embodied an opposition between excessive visibility and secret or hidden content. They were meant to catch the reader's attention but also point to unspeakable and tantalizing secrets. Of course, the world of paperbacks itself was founded on an opposition between straights and queers. However, although it circulated the cold war cliché of gays and lesbians as tormented and tragic souls (who often had to be punished for violating social taboos), it also presented unashamed and scandalous pleasure-seekers who got their "kicks" in a twilight underworld of drugs, prostitution, booze, and perversity. In this way, the pulps "supplied a porous, emotionally charged, two-way boundary between the hidden and the seen" (Stryker 8).

DEVIANCE, DESIRE, AND CAPITAL'S PARADOX OF VISIBILITY

Gays and lesbians of the 1950s were ideologically constituted as excessively visible, deviant Others who nevertheless remained secret and unseen, rendering them simultaneously everywhere and nowhere in U.S. society. This contradictory representation of queer identity is reflected in scholarship on gays and lesbians in the cold war era. Certainly, our most widely circulated images of postwar gays and lesbians are grounded in motifs of secrecy, invisibility, criminality, and perversion. As a wide range of historical and cultural critics have demonstrated, the 1950s were a time of repression and surveillance for queer people, a time when anticommunist ideology linked sexual perversion with political subversion in the popular imagination, and gay and lesbians became the targets of police persecution and governmental and military witch hunts.[12] An invisible "enemy within," the queer subject is represented as a deviant and dangerous figure who secretes his (essential) identity in order to infiltrate American political, social, and cultural institutions. These anxieties may have been partly provoked by the Kinsey report of 1948, which suggested that queer desires and experiences among men were much more common than Americans realized, with over a third of U.S. men reporting some "homosexual experience" (D'Emilio and Freedman 286). Such findings not only called into question the reification of sexuality into the categories of hetero and homo, but also suggested to many cultural observers (ranging from journalists to FBI Director J. Edgar Hoover) that "sexual perverts," like Communists, were secretly disseminated throughout the American society they threatened to subvert.[13]

In fact, the state repression, scapegoating, and surveillance of the McCarthy era might be best understood as a backlash against the unprecedented visibility gays and lesbians achieved after World War II. As historian K. A. Cuordileone states, "despite the deserved reputation of the 1940s and 1950s as a repressive era for gay Americans, homosexuality may have been more visible in American life than ever before" (71). The postwar period saw the development of the first urban gay and lesbian communities, which brought a new visibility to social arrangements organized outside the heterosexual nuclear family.[14] Although typically depicted as furtive outcasts who lived in fear and loved in secret (this pulp cliché is epitomized by the shadowy and often seedy world of the era's gay bar), working-class queers in particular formed what the historians Madeline Davis and Elizabeth Kennedy have called a "culture of resistance." For example, lesbian working-class communities grounded in the bold markers of butch and femme genders provided a significant contrast to the "discreet" lives of many white, bourgeois lesbians, who often led "double lives."[15] The cold war era also saw the formation of the first gay and lesbian political organizations in the United States such as the Mattachine Society and the Daughters of Bilitis (DOB). I do not want to overemphasize the scope of this small but determined "homophile" movement. Nevertheless, it is clear that their new politicization of queer identity had a significant cultural impact. In 1958, Leslie Fielder could write disparagingly of "the homosexuals" as "the staunchest party of all": "Indeed, one feels sometimes that homosexuality is the purest and truest protest of the latest generation, not a burden merely, an affliction to be borne, but a politics to be flaunted" (Fielder, *Essays* Vol. 1, 405). Fielder's claim actually points to the degree to which queer identity was already being "flaunted" in American society. Consider, for example, the mainstream success of writers like Gore Vidal, Tennessee Williams, James Baldwin, and Truman Capote. At the level of popular culture, as I have mentioned, the boom in pulp fiction publishing "were signs and symptoms of the newfound visibility that sexuality in all its myriad forms achieved in America during the tumultuous years around World War II" (Stryker 5). But, as I have been arguing, this visibility is always mediated by the oppressive logic of the open secret. I wish to emphasize that the contradictions of the cold war era made gay identity the privileged emblem for a logic of containment that was fixated on invisible yet ubiquitous Others.

Since in his work the tropes of hypervisibility and anonymity travel beyond any particular abject bodies, Burroughs's figuration of the queer junkie simultaneously reinscribes (gender and racial) ideologies of difference and challenges them by deconstructing the distinction between outward appearance and inner essence. With this framework in mind, I want to foreground the gendered dimensions of the themes of hypervisibility and invisibility in Burroughs's early work. In general, Burroughs associates hypervisibility with femininity, the figure of the fag/queen, racialized difference, the feminization and degeneration of the Orient (the ruined, conquered exotic), and the excessive visibility of decadence and decay. Invisibility, on the other hand, is linked in his early work to masculinity, the figure of the queer, the freedom of anonymity but also modern Western society's control mechanism through which subjects are disembodied and personalities are dissolved. Burroughs's refusal of the feminine drives his effort to separate the supposedly virile and vigorous "queer" from the ineffectual, limp-wristed "fag."[16] When Carl Solomon of Ace Books wanted to entitle his second novel *Fag*, Burroughs instructed Allen Ginsberg—who was acting as his friend's literary agent—to lay down the law:

> Now look you tell Solomon I don't mind being called a queer. T. E. Lawrence and all manner of right Joes (boy can I turn a phrase) was queer. But I'll see him castrated before I'll be called a Fag. That's just what I been trying to put down uh I mean *over*, is the distinction between us strong, manly, noble types and the leaping, jumping, window dressing, cock-sucker. Furthechrissakes a girl's gotta draw the line somewheres or publishers will swarm all over her sticking their nasty old biographical prefaces up her ass. (Burroughs, *Letters* 119–20)

There are a number of very striking things about this passage. First of course is Burroughs's abjection of the feminine and his attempt to elevate and masculinize the queer by invoking cold war culture's cruel cliché of the fag as horrifyingly effeminate, perverse, and sexually unrestrained. In this way, he seeks to (paradoxically enough) claim a normative, and even heroic status for himself and other "manly" queers who are "right Joes." The "window dressing" fag, on the other hand, shamelessly delights in the commercialism of mass culture, the aesthetics of display, and the feminized pleasures of commodity culture. We also can see how the fag for Burroughs is figured as a grotesque spectacle, "leaping" and "jumping" in an appalling display of womanly hypervisibility. Perhaps most interesting of all, though, is how Burroughs ends the passage with a campy bit of gender inversion, imagining himself as a "girl" whose ass is vulnerable to penetration by "nasty" publishers. As we have seen, the author's ambivalent relationship to femininity is revealed in the contradictions of the queer junkie, whose gutter dandyism bears more than a passing resemblance to the figure of the nineteenth-century European dandy. Ginsberg and others who knew Burroughs well clearly saw their friend in this light. For example, in his introduction to Burroughs's *Letters to Allen Ginsberg* (1982), the poet claims that his friend has "given himself away" in this epistolary self-portrait, revealing "the strange Burroughs that Kerouac and I knew, the gentle melancholy Blue Boy, the proud elegant sissy, the old charmer, the intelligent dear" (*Deliberate Prose* 388). With his reference to Thomas Gainsborough's well-known portrait *The Blue Boy* (1770), Ginsberg creates an image of Burroughs as an effete, costumed dandy whose hyperrefinement is the very antithesis of his image as cool and cantankerous tough guy.

Because of Burroughs's complex relationship to femininity, one feels that his gritty, hard-boiled style aims to purge the queer junky from dandyism, aestheticism, and the taint of femininity. At the same time, in his early work he is constantly thinking about how homosexuality and addiction are coded as problems of visibility, which facilitates their insertion into the gendered logic of Fordism and cold war culture. In *Junky*, addiction is described as invisible and its effects are elusive: "The actual changes are difficult to specify and they do not show up in a mirror" (19). This is akin to the homosexual for Burroughs: in *Queer*, Lee is often described in the familiar tropes of the predatory, degenerate queer but since he does not possess "some degree of overt effeminacy" (Q 27), he emerges as oddly disembodied and "curiously spectral, as though you could see through his face" (Q 13). And yet Lee's queerness and addiction have left their indelible mark. As Burroughs notes, "a user may be ten years off junk, but you can still make him for a junkie. The mark of junk is indelible" (J 95–96). Even after Lee has been off junk for a while, when he meets Pat in a bar in New Orleans, the latter "looked at me with a special recognition, like one queer looks at another" (J 61). In a few hours, the reader is not surprised to learn that Lee has a needle in his arm again, if only because we recognize that junk has already taken him over, filling him with "the lack, vague and persistent, a pale ghost of junk sickness" (J 93). When Lee goes to visit Ike in jail, he observes that both fags and junkies have telltale ways of holding their bodies that communicate their identity: "The junkies were grouped together, talking and passing the junkie gesture back and forth, the arm swinging out from the elbow palm up, a gesture of separateness and special communion like the limp wrist of the fag" (J 101). Obviously, Burroughs has an ambivalent relationship to this hypervisibility. On the one hand, he clearly delights in the codes and signs that mark queer, junkie, and criminal subcultures; on the other hand, his refusal of femininity leads him to see the fag as a grotesque figure engulfed by death and degeneration. At a queer bar in New Orleans, Lee observes:

> A room full of fags gives me the horrors. They jerk around like puppets on invisible strings, galvanized into hideous activity that is the negation of everything living and spontaneous. The live human being has moved out of these bodies long ago. But something moved in when the original tenant moved out. Fags are ventriloquists' dummies who have moved in and taken over the ventriloquist. The dummy sits in a queer bar nursing his beer, and uncontrollably yapping out of a rigid doll face. (60)

Like Bradley the Buyer in *Naked Lunch*, who has "lost his human citizenship" and become a creature without species, Burroughs's dehumanizing vision of the fag is the final, horrifying incarnation of spectacular difference (17). For the author, the fag resembles abject figures of old, hollowed-out junkies who have been swallowed up by the parasitism of the junk virus, leaving their bodies and minds behind. What I am most interested in here is the way in which Burroughs's refusal of the feminine and effeminacy does not result in a productive tension in his work, but halts and stalls the figure of the queer junkie. It is only after Burroughs has divorced hypervisibility from femininity—and its attendant apparatus of medical intervention that I have earlier noted he particularly eschews—that he can claim its radical force for the gutter dandy.

This is apparent in *Queer* when Burroughs uses the link between addiction and homosexuality to present Lee's gutter dandyism as a mode of decadent rebellion. During his travels in Ecuador, Lee's lustful pursuit of Allerton leads him to ask for sex more than their "contract" requires, which is twice a week. The fact that their sexual relationship is conceptualized in the vocabulary of law and commerce links it to the many paid sexual encounters Lee has with "boys" throughout the text. Although Lee critiques the crushing oppression of bourgeois society, clearly he has an opportunistic attitude toward the reification of sexuality it produces. This is why, like a nineteenth-century decadent aesthete, he is irresistibly tempted by the modern world's artificial, commodified, and unhealthy pleasures—of which homosexuality and narcotics are privileged, intertwined emblems. Immediately after his apology to Allerton for seeking sex "so soon after the last time," Lee inverts the terms of the debate:

> Lee said, "Really, Gene, aren't you taking an unfair advantage? Like someone was junk sick and I don't use junk. I say, 'Sick, really? I don't know

> why you tell about your disgusting condition. You might at least have the decency to keep it to yourself if you are sick. I hate sick people. You must realize how distasteful it is to see you sneezing and yawning and retching. Why don't you go someplace where I won't have to look at you? You've no idea how tiresome you are, or how disgusting. Have you no pride?'"
>
> Allerton said, "That isn't fair at all."
>
> "It isn't supposed to be fair. Just a routine for your amusement, containing a modicum of truth." (Q 103)

In this complex and layered routine, Burroughs invokes the similar ideological constructions of homosexuality and addiction as "sick" and "disgusting" morbid cravings that cannot be controlled or hidden. Lee satirizes the cultural logic that assigns an excessive visibility to the addict and the queer, turning them into abject Others who are made monstrous by their corruption and lack of "pride."[17] In a fascinating move, Burroughs represents the queer junkie as a sickly decadent who insists on claiming decay, perversion, and illness as antinatural reversals of bourgeois values. This distinguishes him sharply from the hollow, feminized decadence of the fag, who—as we have already seen—Burroughs strips of his rebellious attitude. Like Huysmans's decadent hero Des Esseintes, Lee finds that his passion for pleasure has turned into decay and corruption, and his body becomes the site of an alarming disintegration. Although Burroughs's gutter dandyism contains no pretense to self-mastery and so departs from earlier models of dandyism, both the gutter dandy and the nineteenth-century dandy employ perversion to position themselves "outside the domination of the performance principle" (Marcuse, *Eros* 50).

Although the critical tendency has been to see Lee's pursuit of Allerton as rather pathetic (and this is certainly true to some extent), a textual moment such as this suggests that there is something subversive in Burroughs's project to defend the decadent, antinatural pleasures of the queer junkie. Lee embraces his hypervisibility/excess, but resists the tragic presentation haunting the wounded models of masculinity that were circulating in the postwar era.[18] As I have argued, Burroughs's contemporaries tended to represent junkies and queers as emblem for a newly wounded and/or passive masculinity; however, the motifs of decadence (particularly excess and the grotesque) enable Burroughs to frame his conception of the gutter dandy in more complicated terms. The queer junkie is abject, sick, and deviant, but the mirror he dares to hold up to mainstream society exposes the hypocrisy and sickness at the center of modernity and its relations. Despite its highly politicized agenda, the routine has a light, comedic sensibility. For example, the passage's repeated references to fairness are a comic touch: here Lee invokes the principle of equity, which is defined by *Black's Law Dictionary* as "the spirit and habit of fairness, justness, and right dealing which would regulate the intercourse of men with men." Finally, Lee's claim that the routine is "for [Allerton's] amusement, containing a modicum of truth" is a gentlemanly flourish, a bit of refinement that contrasts with the biting social critique that precedes it. Since it reflects "decadence's paradoxical double essence," this tension between refinement and brutality gives a distinctly decadent sensibility to the whole routine while also daring Allerton—and the reader—to recognize its truths (Weir xviii).

If in the twenty-first century Burroughs strikes us as prophetic, this is because his work epitomizes the polarized oppositions that continue to define our lives today. As Marcuse states, "this society turns everything it touches into a potential source of progress *and* of exploitation, of drudgery *and* satisfaction, of freedom *and* of oppression. Sexuality is no exception" (*One-Dimensional Man* 78). The argument I have presented here demonstrates how the logic of the queer and its paradox of visibility is embedded in the dialectic of liberation that modern industrial capitalism puts into play. For precisely this reason, Burroughs's iconic figure of the gutter dandy is a queer hero of modern life whose mode of rebellion is a privileged emblem for the contradictions of cold war America. Despite the force of the gutter dandy's decadent critique of U.S. society, Burroughs's negative relationship to femininity ultimately limits his response to the imperatives of postwar capitalism. As we have seen, the booming paperback industry in postwar America provided a unique forum for Burroughs to synthesize oppositional and commercial responses to mass cultural production; ultimately, however, the gutter dandy's refusal of femininity infuses his aesthetic with an avant-gardist and adversarial relationship toward commodity culture. Burroughs's relationship to modern culture always tends toward negation, due to his decadent attitude toward the reified social relations that make American society sick, poisoned, and empty. In the next chapter, we shall see how the move from the gutter dandy to the Pop dandy, from a decadent rebellion against reification to an erotics of reification, is enabled by Warhol's more complex and positive relationship to feminization—thus giving birth to a new, frankly commodified queer aesthetic.

6

THE DANDY GOES POP

Andy Warhol's Queer Commodity Aesthetics

Reporter: What is the meaning of your art?
Warhol: It's decorative.

—Andy Warhol

In 1968, only a few years after creating works such as his Death and Disasters series (which contained images of car crashes, electric chairs, and police violence against African American civil rights protestors), Andy Warhol declared: "I don't get involved with politics. I believe in everything."[1] With his iconic silver wig and impermeable blankness, Warhol carefully cultivated the nonjudgmental, naive, and apolitical image for which he is most widely known today.[2] In fact, although he seemed to find everything interesting, he relished being "a sphinx without a riddle," as Truman Capote memorably called him.[3] By the late 1960s, he had developed a reputation for baffling and thwarting interviewers with his three favorite replies to questions: "yes," "no," and "I don't know." Other favorite stock responses used with abandon by Warhol were "wow" and "great" (Bourdon, *Warhol* 51).[4] Like those interviewers who tended to conclude that the artist's vacuous, "know-nothing" public persona meant that he had nothing to say, a surprising range of commentators have taken Warhol at his word (Geldzahler 42). Many critics who draw on traditional approaches to art history have concluded that the artist's work must compel us not because of its typically banal and seemingly unexamined subject matter but, instead, because of its formal elements and material production—most crucially, Warhol's formal innovations such as his use of repetition, grid patterns, and silkscreen technology.[5] Grounded in the realm of high art, such critics see Warhol's work as a mysterious aesthetics of the surface that dazzles us with what Carter Ratcliff calls "the allure of absolute nothingness" (23).[6] Because, from this perspective, his work possesses no point of view beyond its yearning for blankness, "there is nothing redemptive about his art. He appropriates an image not to improve it but to leave it blunter, starker, more aggressively itself than before" (Ratcliff 103). Warhol, one imagines, would agree; like other Pop artists, his work is a radical departure from earlier movements (e.g., Surrealism, Cubism, and Abstract Expressionism) that sought to transform and therefore complicate the content of the image (Morphet 12).[7]

Warhol's disinterest in transforming the content of the image—his literalism, in other words—became for many commentators evidence that the artist's work was not really about anything at all. Furthermore, his embrace of countercultural practices and identities in his 1960s Factory—including drug taking, homosexuality, drag queens, and hustling—perhaps helped to cement the public association of the artist with antibourgeois, "amoral transparency" (Hughes 83). The perception of Warhol as a decadent, gum-chewing nihilist with an "aesthetic of noninvolvement" (Hughes 80) was presented with icy brilliance by art historian Robert Hughes, whose 1971 review essay for *Time* magazine, "Man for the Machine," was saved by the artist himself in *Time Capsule 7*. This short essay contains many (if not all) of the key elements that have defined the public reception of Warhol's life and work for the past three decades: his passivity; his "gee-whiz obsession with glamour and stardom"; the "artist-as-celebrity"; the "use of multiple and serial images, of mechanical reproduction, of systemic banality as an absolute"; his impersonality and "strategy of self-effacement"; his amoral disengagement. For Hughes, these various aspects of the vacant Warholian personality cohere in one unifying image: the artist as machine. As Hughes writes, "Says Andy with utter sincerity: 'I want to be a machine'—which to him means never to make choices" (80).

Warhol *seemed* to refuse aesthetic selection, but he made choices, lots of them.[8] By noting the gap between his performed, public identity and private one, a very different view of Warhol emerges from many who were close to the artist, such as art critic David Bourdon and Henry Geldzahler, the former curator of contemporary art at the Metropolitan Museum of Art in New York City, who describes himself as "best friends" with Warhol during the 1960s (Shore 130). As Geldzahler notes, "What holds together in both media [paintings and film] is the absolute control Andy Warhol has over his own sensibility—a sensibility as sweet and tough, as childish and commercial, as innocent and chic as anything in our culture" (34). Geldzahler's emphasis on Warhol's affect and artistic control points the way toward an approach that dares to take the artist's aesthetic choices and social commitments seriously. In my view, Warhol himself invited this engagé reading as much as he invited the cliché of Warholian blankness. In *Time Capsule 7*, along with Hughes's essay, "Man for the Machine," Warhol also enclosed an article by Gregory Battcock, "The Andy Warhol Generation" (c. 1971), that perfectly explains this approach:

> It will seem strange to some that Warhol, high priest of camp, prima donna of the art world, should be even aware of The Third World, the revolution in perception and the future of socialist society. That's simply because, like so many really good artists, Warhol is a fraud. He is not what he pretends to be. Warhol is not supremely aloof and indifferent but, rather, deeply committed and surprisingly sophisticated concerning repressive society. . . . Warhol is not socially uninterested and politically ambivalent but has some understanding as well as sympathy for the causes of protest and revolt in American society. Nor is he asexual and anti-sensual but most encouraging of people who overtly display their sexuality. (Battcock n.p.)

Not the affectless and vapid "tycoon of passivity" (Koch 23), Battcock's Warhol is empathic, politically committed, thoughtful, and sex positive. Approximately twenty years later, Battcock's view was institutionalized in the Andy Warhol Museum (which opened in Pittsburgh in 1994); the availability of archival materials has made it increasingly difficult to argue that Warhol was as naive and unselfconscious as he pretended to be. Seeking to give scholars, artists, and the public a fuller picture of the artist, his sources, intentions, and processes, the Warhol Museum set out to debunk museological and art historical canonizations of the artist as the cold and detached Prince of Pop. Instead, the museum rightfully presents him as deeply engaged in a wide range of commitments—a multimedia artist, entrepreneur, and documentary chronicler of his times who was emotional, campy, daring, nostalgic, political, collaborative and communal, and audaciously sexual.[9] Warhol himself reminds us that one of his primary legacies is his relentless and inspired interrogation of the very notion of art and its commercial underpinnings—in other words, its inextricability from relations of production and consumption. Knowing that "good business is the best art," the artist himself declared in *The Philosophy of Andy Warhol* that "business art is the step that comes after Art. I started as a commercial artist, and I want to finish as a business artist" (92).

As the literature on the artist reflects, it is a critical commonplace to state that Warhol's work is about consumer capitalism—or, as Juan Suárez puts it in his original book on mass culture and queer underground cinema of the 1960s, "Warhol's art has been taken as a symptom of the penetration of the imagery of consumer culture into the avant-garde" (214). From this perspective, Marxist interpretations of the artist may seem not so much to be arguments but observations about Warhol's art and its relationship to the culture of capitalism. From the Brillo boxes of the 1960s to the Dollar Sign series of the 1980s, issues of value, consumerism, and standardization seem to be obviously present in Warhol's life and work. It is perhaps for this reason that such critics often focus their attention on the question of whether or not Warhol's work is subversive of the capitalist world it depicts. As Steven Shaviro succinctly puts it:

> We're usually asked to choose between two readings of Warhol's work: one that praises him for exposing the institutional structures of commodity capitalism and the art world, and one that condemns him for being in complicity with these same institutional structures. But aren't both of these readings beside the point? After all, "if a mirror looks into a mirror, what is there to see?" Of course Warhol is in complicity, and of course he is always calling attention to that complicity. But the real interest of his work lies elsewhere. (93)[10]

I agree that the real interest of Warhol's work lies elsewhere, but how do we define and theorize its aesthetic and conceptual force? Unfortunately, Shaviro's reading ultimately returns to familiar territory, concluding that "it all comes down to images, and nothing but images. Warhol's art really *is* about fashion and style. It couldn't care less about what's beneath the surface" (94). Claims such as this one—which are cited so often that they have almost become truisms—seem to me to skirt the complexities of the artist's body of work. I believe Warhol's art fascinates precisely because it critiques commodified relations and self-consciously inhabits them—a point my use of the term "queer commodity aesthetics" aims to encapsulate. Warhol captures the aesthetic abstraction, seriality, and reification engendered by Fordist production, even as he lays bare postwar commodity culture's new and seductive forms of beauty, pleasure, and desire.[11]

My argument turns on the concept of "Pop dandyism," a term I use to convey the democratic and empathic side of Warhol's approach to dandyism. No longer burdened by the nineteenth-century dandy's ambivalence about the commodity and modern life, Pop dandyism unhesitatingly embraces the pleasures of mass culture, flaunting its passion for what is ordinary while nevertheless maintaining an aura of avant-garde distinction.[12] As I will demonstrate, Fordist rationalization and postwar America's mass-produced pleasures created the context for Warhol's daring articulation of this new, frankly commodified form of dandyism. Contesting the critical tendency to isolate analysis of the artist's sexuality from his engagement with questions of production and consumption, my argument situates his queer aesthetic within both gay subcultural styles and the reorganization of masculinity that was central to American society as it shifted to Fordist models of mass production and consumption.[13] I take up this project by focusing on Warhol's two stylistic strategies for addressing the different but related problems of masculine identity and artmaking in commodity culture: "camp" and a sensibility I call "outlaw masculinity."[14] These two gendered aesthetics constitute a dialectic between artifice and authenticity that has played a pivotal role in defining queer identity as a privileged emblem for the modern. However, as I hope to show, in the era of contemporary (post-1945) capitalism, artifice and authenticity are bound together by an emergent queer sensibility—epitomized by the new figure of the Pop dandy—that integrates the rationalizing force of the economic with the libidinal energy of the sensuous/aesthetic by embracing the positive implications of an "erotics of reification."[15] If, for so many commentators, Warhol's work has been seen as emblematic of the contemporary world, I would argue that this is because it thematizes many of the central cultural contradictions of capitalism—in particular, the interpenetration of postmodern flexibility and Fordist modernity.[16] In other words, Warhol's artistic production stages those fundamental, inseparable, and opposed tendencies we have come to recognize as constitutive of the modern world: contradictions between the ephemeral and the eternal; surface and depth; fragmentation and standardization; and avant-gardism and commercialism. I would like to stress that the dialectic between camp and outlaw masculinity presents gay identity in these very terms, demonstrating that the artist's gendered aesthetics and commodity aesthetics are characterized by the same set of complex contradictions.

There is still a persistent critical tendency to separate Warhol's Pop paintings from the full range of his artistic production, which includes films, videotapes, photographs, writings, collections, sculpture, commercial art, drawings, commissioned portraits, audiotapes, and time capsules. While my own study cannot possibly engage with all of this material, I do wish to emphasize the continuities and cross-references between Warhol's aesthetic practices. I have therefore resisted a chronological organization of this material, connecting, for example, the artist's male nudes of the 1950s and 1970s. This is not to impose a false sense of artistic unity on Warhol's production, which is composed of multiple, complicated gestures that resist unitary arrangements and approaches. There are significant and striking differences between and within his aesthetic sensibilities and artmaking, as my study will demonstrate. What I mean to highlight here is the relational quality of Warhol's art—an element that has been underemphasized in much critical commentary. Examining his aesthetic practices together reveals his striking insistence on seeing sameness and continuities across public and private divisions. This is the expansive, democratic aspect of Warhol's Pop dandyism, which delights in highlighting those dualisms that it then proceeds to take apart. My point, then, is that the "real interest" of his work lies in its rebellion against the oppositions of art/industry and erotics/economics. Warhol's "queer" desire to disobey and disregard the central oppositions of modern culture—itself a provocative critique of the imperatives of industrial capitalism—points to the radical possibilities embedded in the artist's way of looking.

COMMODITY AESTHETICS; OR, THE IMAGE OF DESIRE

> In terms of industrial capital, sexual sensuality is valorizable only in abstracted form.
>
> —Wolfgang Haug

> Sex is so abstract.
>
> —Andy Warhol

Warhol's Brillo box sculptures—silkscreened plywood boxes created by the artist and his assistant Gerard Malanga to duplicate the originals delivered to supermarkets—have been widely regarded as thought experiments about the very nature and meaning of art.[17] Their 1964 exhibition literally transformed the gallery space into a warehouse, "answering" a question Marcel Duchamp had posed in 1913: "Can one make works which are not works of 'art'?" (Tomkins 5). In *Brillo Box*, Warhol takes his attempt "to paint nothing"[18]—as he described his Campbell's soup can—to its logical conclusion by handcrafting an assembly line of industrial boxes that thematize the negation of the art object under modern industrial capitalism. Like his most famous Pop work from 1962 to 1964, the Brillo box sculptures are not just about the artificiality and massification of contemporary society, as many critics have asserted, nor do they simply mirror what Baudrillard calls "the sublime and repetitive world of the commodity" (*For a Critique* 208). Instead, as Peter Wollen suggests, Warhol points to a new aestheticization of everyday life:

> Rather than producing images of commodities, he was repackaging packaging as a commodity in itself. In this process it was the element of display that fascinated Warhol, the transfer to a new space (the art gallery) of images whose display was already familiar in different spaces (the supermarkets, the daily newspaper, the fan magazine). It was precisely the proliferation of 'spectacle', of the 'to-be-looked-at', the saturation of everyday life by a new scopic regime, that Warhol chose to replicate in a further gesture of theatricality. (Wollen 164)

Wollen rightly emphasizes the importance of abstraction and spectacle for Warhol, whose avant-garde cinema revolts against Fordist imperatives but is also seduced by the voyeuristic possibilities of Fordism's new scopic regime. *Brillo Box* captures the complexity of this contradictory aspect of Warhol's vision, registering a democratic embrace of the inextricability of art and commerce, a key principle of the Bauhaus school whose teachings dominated his art education at the Carnegie Institute of Technology. Perhaps because of this early training and his experience as a commercial artist in the 1950s, Warhol's take on contemporary consumer society is never infused with the arrogant disdain that sometimes marked the nineteenth-century dandy; he seeks not an art of transcendence but immanence. This is a crucial point I want to stress; Warhol positions his work both inside and outside the intoxications of commodity culture.

Warhol's Pop dandyism materializes the contradiction between avant-gardism and commercialism inherent in the cultural logic of modernity and proposes a new queer relation to commodity aesthetics. According to Wolfgang Haug, the aesthetic language of commodities emerges from the contradiction between use-value and exchange-value and the need for value to be realized as money. "The problem of realization" in the political economy of the postwar era requires the total integration of aesthetics into the production and exchange of commodities. With the rise of Fordism, commodity aesthetics—or, to put it another way, the image of desire and its promised satisfaction as "use-value" (147)—detaches itself from the commodity-form. This produces a culture dominated by appearances, aesthetic abstraction, and mediated and mass-produced pleasures (i.e., "sexual semblance"). For Haug, these developments are not (simply) ideological relations but cultural practices; he points to "the intervention of commodity aesthetics in the presentation of identity" and the modes in which individuals experience their bodies, desires, and lives (123). As we will see, Warhol's work uses queer subcultural expressions both to illuminate and contest the cultural effects of this aesthetic reorganization of everyday life.

Warhol's most radical and productive insight was perhaps how he reshaped sexuality into a cultural effect of commodity aesthetics. As he often declared, "sex is so abstract"—an observation that is echoed in Haug's claim: "in terms of industrial capital, sexual sensuality is valorizable only in abstracted form" (119). From this perspective, we can understand what is at stake in a work such as the 1962 painting *Marilyn Monroe's Lips*, which Warhol produced soon after Monroe's death. Repeating her lips 162 times in 49 square feet, the image invokes an assembly-line sexuality rather than the actress' heartbreaking beauty. It does not nostalgically mourn her tragic death (as some of his other Monroe paintings seem to) but instead documents the commodification of her body while invoking the great Warholian themes of profit, death, and fame. Warhol brilliantly abstracts and desexualizes the "essence" of Marilyn as object of exchange, subject to endless repetition and fetishistic fragmentation.[19] As he says in *The Philosophy*, "Marilyn's lips weren't kissable, but they were very photographable" (54). Here, Warhol slyly hints at the productive possibilities of repetition and standardization, an insight that becomes part of the more positive (even redemptive) treatment of reified eroticism that characterizes his work on the male body. This complexity is not, in my view, generally realized in Warhol's engagement with tropes of femininity; for this reason, it is no accident that he makes use of the figure of the female sex symbol to offer one of his most pessimistic visions of desire, devoid of sensuality and haunted by the refusal of satisfaction. Although my focus in this chapter is on gay masculinity and dandyism, it should be noted that the inability of the female body to transcend social constraints (here, those imposed by dictates of Fordism) is certainly a familiar motif, one that returns us to the hierarchies and strategies of the nineteenth-century dandy.

OUTLAW MASCULINITY AND WARHOLIAN AUTHENTICITY

I want to begin my discussion of outlaw masculinity in an unlikely place and discuss a largely overlooked aspect of Warhol's artistic production in the 1950s: his collection of Americana. Almost as soon as he began to make money from his commercial art, Warhol began collecting American folk art. By the mid-1950s, he established himself as a major folk art collector, assembling a range of objects that included quilts, weathervanes, cigar store Indians, and other carved wood figures from the nineteenth century (Smith 17). Warhol continued to collect folk art for over twenty years. In 1978, his collection—memorably entitled *Folk and Funk*—was exhibited at New York's Museum of American Folk Art. Famous for epitomizing his cultural and historical moment, Warhol draws our attention to the role of authenticity and nostalgia in the cultural logic of the 1950s. Due to the pressures of postwar overproduction and intensive accumulation, artists and intellectuals became increasingly ambivalent about the reorganization of American society by a Fordist model of mass production and consumption. Despite their avant-garde affinities, both Abstract Expressionism and the Beat movement share this ambivalence about the massification and commodification of American society with a "commercial" artist such as Warhol; although this ambivalence takes different forms in Warhol and, say, Jackson Pollock, what we see in both artists is the way in which authenticity is privileged as an antidote to the artificiality of 1950s American culture.[20]

This may seem like a counterintuitive claim to make about Warhol, even the Warhol of the 1950s. After all, Andy loved technology, television, and what was modern and new. However, he was equally passionate about vernacular traditions, including Native American art and various folk art forms. He therefore gives us insight into the complexities and contradictions of Pop dandyism, since his collecting joins populist and elitist consumption. Departing from the narrowly aristocratic passions of the nineteenth-century dandy, Pop dandyism revels in both the ordinary and the extraordinary, creating a paradoxical elitism—a not-quite-populism that simultaneously aggrandizes and levels. (This impulse takes its most campy form in Warhol's collection of kitsch.) Always eager to embrace contradiction, Warhol's collecting begins to look more familiar when we consider the elitist dimensions of his interest in craft; for example, his exquisite collection of early nineteenth-century American Empire furniture. In the 1950s, however, Warhol was a folk art collector. Although what these folk art objects meant to Warhol is difficult (if not impossible) to discern, I would argue that the folk collection as a whole articulates a distinct logic of the Fordist era—a nostalgia not simply for the "artifacts of yesteryear" but for a simpler America, free from the rationalization and instrumentality of a modern, mechanized world (Bourdon, "Andy's Dish" 18). I have discussed this aspect of the dandy's nostalgia in chapter 1, "The Dialectics of Dandyism." As quite a few observers have noted, nostalgia is a theme that runs throughout all of Warhol's work, including his thirty-year obsession with collecting; his thirteen-year art piece, *Time Capsules*; and even his most famous images, such as those of Marilyn Monroe, whom he first painted the day after her tragic death. Interestingly enough, Warhol's interest in folk art forms that are separate from the sterility and repetitions of the mass market departs from the aesthetic of mechanical reproduction for which he is most well known. Like his collection of Americana, Warhol's artmaking in the 1950s privileges a "naive" style and the imperfections and detail of hand labor over the uniformity of the machine.[21]

We can see how the handmade look of Warhol's signature commercial style in the 1950s conveys a sensibility that would appear to have more in common with the late nineteenth-century Arts and Crafts movement than his own industrial, mass-produced aesthetic from the 1960s. In postwar commercial advertising, ambivalence about consumerism and mass culture helped to propel the sudden (and ironic) popularity of hand-drawn illustration. Capitalizing on this trend, Warhol's distinctive "blotted-line" technique transferred or blotted ink from one sheet of paper to another, creating the outline of an image. An example of this technique is found in the 1950s illustration, *Shoe and Leg* (Figure 6.1), which beautifully combines elegance and simplicity of line with the sentimental emotion and unfinished idiosyncrasies of the handcrafted look. A similar aesthetic is at work in Warhol's 1956 book, *In the Bottom of My Garden*, which was inspired by the song, "There Are Fairies at the Bottom of Our Garden" (Bourdon, *Warhol* 56). Suggesting an implicit link between "fairies" and queers, Warhol's mischievous, winged figures often strike sexual poses amid butterflies, flowers, and exotic animals. In one frankly sexual illustration (*In the Bottom of My Garden*; Figure 6.2), the artist presents

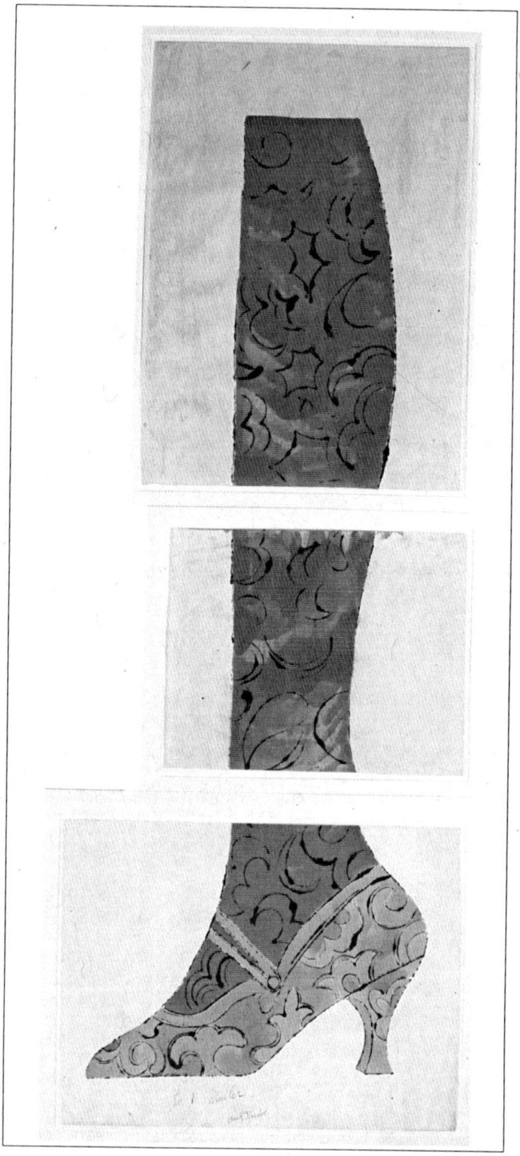

FIGURE 6.1. Andy Warhol, *Shoe and Leg (1950s)*. Ink and Dr. Martin's Aniline dye on Strathmore paper. a: 15 x 20 in. (38.1 x 50.8 cm.). b: 11 7/8 x 15 in. (30.2 x 38.1 cm.). c: 22 x 16 in. (55.9 x 40.6 cm.). Founding Collection, the Andy Warhol Museum, Pittsburgh. © The Andy Warhol Foundation for the Visual Arts/ARS, New York. Courtesy of the Andy Warhol Museum.

'IGURE 6.2. Andy Warhol, *In the Bottom of my Garden* (c. 1956). Graphite, ballpoint ink, newspa-
)er, and magazine collage on illustration board ink and Dr. Martin's Aniline dye on Strathmore
)aper. 13 3/4 x 16 3/4 in. (34.9 x 42.5 cm.). Founding Collection, the Andy Warhol Museum, Pitts-
)urgh. © The Andy Warhol Foundation for the Visual Arts/ARS, New York. Courtesy of the Andy
Varhol Museum.

erotic groupings of androgynous and polymorphously perverse cherubs, who self-consciously celebrate the repetition of their own couplings in a queer Garden of Eden. In much of this early work, Warhol cultivates a perverse but childlike sensibility that engages the repetitive world of the commodity it ultimately seeks to replace; in his advertising and other imagery, one senses that the consumer is being recalled to a lost world of uncommodified pleasures and enchanting objects. Most crucially, the appeal of his handmade aesthetic signals a nostalgic yearning for authenticity that reverberates where we would least expect it: in his work on masculinity, homoeroticism, and the male nude.

A Gold Book (self-published in 1957; Figure 6.4) contained, among other drawings, striking and explicitly homoerotic images of male nudes, many of them printed on gold paper.[22] *Golden Boy* is an example of the ideal Warhol often evokes in his early male nudes—boyish, effeminate, delicate, smooth-skinned or hairless, with slim waists, chests, and limbs. In short, he presents the iconic image of the homosexual in postwar visual representation, including pornography, which began to be mass-produced for gay men in the late 1950s.[23] It is worth noting that the *Time Capsules* contain a wide variety of images of the male nude, from gay porn to physique and art magazines.[24] As Warhol explains in *POPism*:

> Personally, I loved porno and I bought lots of it all the time—the really dirty, exciting stuff. All you had to do was figure out what turned you on, and then just buy the dirty magazines and movie prints that are right for you, the way you'd go for the right pills or the right cans of food. (I was so avid for porno that on my first time out of the house after the shooting I went straight to 42nd Street and checked out the peep shows with Vera Cruise and restocked on dirty magazines.) (294)

Warhol's unabashed appreciation for commodity culture's reified eroticism becomes central to his films of the 1960s, in which he sought to fuse avant-garde cinema with the objectification of beefcake imagery and gay porn, as well as the voyeurism of 42nd Street peep shows. Thomas Waugh has argued along these lines in his examination of Warhol's late films in the context of the "burgeoning homo marketplace" for pornographic imagery (71). We may speculate that, to date, primarily Warhol's films and paintings from the 1970s have been linked to pornography because of their cruisy and impersonal gaze. In her illuminating essay on Warhol's nudes, Linda Nochlin argues that it is "the rich tradition of male erotica provided by photography that offers the closest analogy to what Warhol is up to in his nude images of the mid-seventies." However, Warhol's early work can also be productively linked to the commodification of the gay male body by the porn industry. As I will show, the artist's work from the 1950s and early 1960s not only insists upon the visibility of the gay male body in postwar America, but also renegotiates the terms of its representation.

Beginning in the 1950s, Warhol created a number of drawings and paintings that reveal his persistent fascination with the gendered rebellion and/or sexual ambiguity of the figure of the outlaw. Andy's identification with the theatrically macho outlaw is enormously important to his work of the early 60s, when he produced images of James Cagney brandishing guns in both hands, and a leather-jacketed Marlon Brando on a motorcycle as the biker gang leader of the 1954 film, *The Wild One*. In the 1970s, Warhol's *Mick Jagger* (1975) expresses a similar aesthetic; as David Bourdon notes, "Jagger was an ideal subject for Warhol: like Marlon Brando, James Dean and Elvis Presley, he was not just another pretty face, but sullen, brooding, and turbulent" (*Warhol* 350). In the 1980s, Warhol infused his own image with a new rebelliousness when he embarked upon a friendship and collaboration with the notoriously wild Outsider Art star, Jean-Michel Basquiat. In his art and life, Warhol sought to build danger into his representations of masculinity and, by extension, his queer aesthetic. Michael Bronski points to the importance of the dangerously eroticized male body for the postwar era, arguing that "the young white male 'outlaw' became the symbolic antithesis to the stifling security of institutionalized heterosexuality" (*The Pleasure Principle* 91). Warhol's famous, almost life-size paintings of Elvis are especially interesting in this context because they portray what we might call the frontier Elvis, transformed from rock 'n' roll musician to theatrically macho cowboy equipped with knife and gun and ready to shoot. Interestingly enough, the source for *Double Elvis [Ferus Type]* (1963; Figure 6.3) was a publicity photo for Presley's 1960 western with the campy title *Flaming Star*. In my view, Warhol's fascination with the aestheticized masculinity of these icons reveals a distinct set of political investments that shape the outlaw sensibility as it emerges in his own work and takes hold in gay male culture.

In the well-known image of James Dean that Warhol used to introduce *A Gold Book* (Figure 6.4), we can see how the artist articulates a specifically queer identification with Dean's incarnation of the youthful outlaw or rebel.[25] (The artist's source for this portrait was a publicity photo for Dean's film *Rebel Without a Cause*.) Discussing the star's "gay-specific appeal" to postwar queers, cinema scholar Roy Grundmann points out that Dean "combined elements of the volatile outlaw with those of the sensitive, misunderstood, and insecure youth" (136–38). This helps to explain why Dean (and his perceived sexual ambiguity in particular) could serve as a kind of transitional figure in the redefinition of the gay male image—an early, distinctly queer form of rebellion, we might say, against the stereotype of the gay man as narcissistic weakling. We can locate a variation on this theme in Warhol's 1960 painting, *Strong Arms and Broads*. Here, the artist's source material was a Charles Atlas ad promising hetero

FIGURE 6.3. Andy Warhol, *Double Elvis [Ferus Type]* (1963). Silkscreen ink and silver paint on linen. 84 3/16 x 53 in. (213.9 x 134.6 cm.). Founding Collection, the Andy Warhol Museum, Pittsburgh. © The Andy Warhol Foundation for the Visual Arts/ARS, New York. Courtesy of the Andy Warhol Museum.

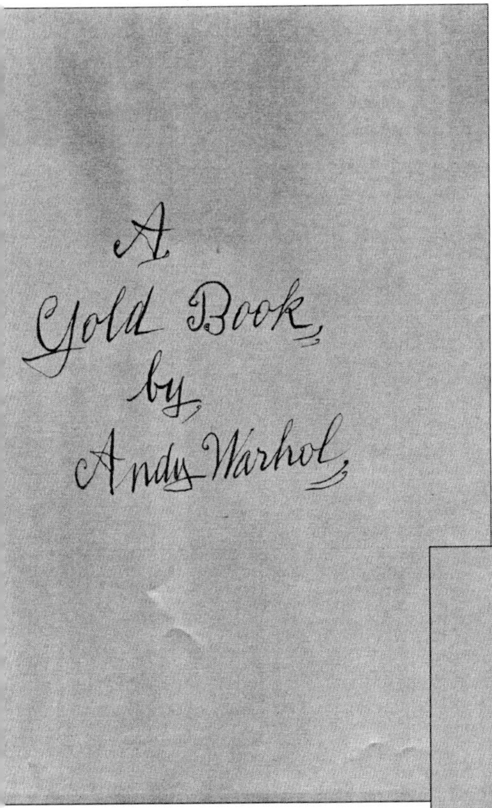

FIGURE 6.4. Andy Warhol, *A Gold Book* (1957). Offset lithograph and Dr. Martin's Aniline dye on paper and coated metallic paper, with board cover. Book: 15 1/16 x 11 3/4 x 1/2 in. (38.3 x 29.8 x 1.3 cm.). Plates (each): 14 1/4 x 11 1/4 in. (36.2 x 28.6 cm.). Founding Collection, the Andy Warhol Museum, Pittsburgh. © The Andy Warhol Foundation for the Visual Arts/ ARS, New York. Courtesy of the Andy Warhol Museum.

hypermasculinity to "ninety-seven pound weaklings" who take Atlas's 50-cent bodybuilding course (Bourdon, *Warhol* 72–73). Much like the countercultural masculinities of rock 'n' roll and the Beat movement, the queer attraction to outlaw masculinity expresses an opposition to the postwar rise of the "organization man" (which stressed corporate conformity) and the new domestication of masculinity through consumer imperatives and suburban fatherhood. However, this opposition often took a deeply nostalgic form, as in Warhol's depiction of Dean as a defiantly sensitive "urban cowboy" (Grundmann 143), forever frozen in the popular imagination as the teenage rebel who colonizes the public sphere with his passionate yet "cool" pose. (We can also locate Warhol's 1950s pantheon of ageless "boys" in this context.) As the historian Robert Corber argues in his important study of homosexuality in cold war America, "underlying this nostalgia[26] was a desire to return to an earlier stage of capitalism before the rise of mass culture, when male subjectivity had supposedly not yet been penetrated by the commodity form" (14).

The notion of a theatrically masculine aesthetic as a rebellion against domesticated, middle-class values is crucial to Warhol's film *Blow Job* (Figure 6.5), one of the artist's early experimental, black and white films from 1964. *Blow Job* is a silent, cinematic portrait that Warhol projected at a slow-motion speed, requiring the viewer to come closer, to linger on images, lighting, and subtle movements. In contrast to the artist's explicit 1950s drawing of a young man enthusiastically performing a blow job (Archives of the Andy Warhol Museum), the film of the same title is a classic Warholian tease; it offers us not the sex act itself but a 30-minute close-up of a handsome young man's face while he receives a blow job, comes, and—of course—smokes a cigarette. All the while, the strong lighting of the film creates a play of light and dark across the nameless man's face and the brick wall behind him. Like the other minimalist works from this era—films such as *Sleep* and *Couch*—*Blow Job* demonstrates Warhol's insight about the seductive power of frozen and reified forms of desire. However, despite the portrait quality invoked by *Blow Job*, this work modifies "the purity of the original eventless film," as Parker Tyler notes in his 1967 essay, "Dragtime and Drugtime; Or Film a la Warhol." With this in mind, we might properly name the film a celebration of "post-dynamic sensuousness," to borrow Lucy R. Lippard's turn of phrase. As Lippard points out, the languid temporality of minimalism (what Tyler calls "dragtime") edges toward a liberation of the erotic that refuses emotional expressivity and becomes, ironically enough, more personal and intimate in its sensuous abstraction: "The rhythms of erotic experience can be slowed to a near standstill and convey all the more effectively a languorous sensuality" (Lippard 217). I want to argue that Warhol's slowing down of time needs to be understood in the context of the "speed-up" of Fordist production—an acceleration of temporal processes produced by the assembly line's new "organizing and

FIGURE 6.5. Andy Warhol, *Blow Job* (1964). 16 mm film, black and white, silent, 41 minutes. Film still courtesy of the Andy Warhol Museum.

fragmenting of the spatial order of production" (Harvey 266). The culture of Warhol's 1960s Factory, which revolved around widespread amphetamine use, eagerly accommodated this Fordist spatialization of time. Warhol, who wrote that he "only slept two or three hours a night from '65 through '67," explained that he decided to make a movie of a person sleeping (*Sleep*; 1963) because "seeing everybody so up all the time made me think that sleep was becoming pretty obsolete" (*POPism* 33). Like *Sleep*, *Blow Job*'s "dragtime" is in my view both a rebellion against the imperative to "speed-up" and a nostalgic effort to capture an earlier temporality.

Eroticizing stillness and passivity, the outlaw sensibility of Warhol's cinema continues the voyeuristic gaze of his early "boy drawings" from the 1950s. In both cases, there is a sense of lingering on a face or a body part until it gives up its meaning. One might be tempted to locate in such an aesthetic not only the democratic promise that Warhol and his coterie saw in Pop, but also its promise of redemption as even the most banal and trivial detail is infused with meaning. This is what Battcock points to when he asserts that Warhol "seems to be determined to discover a way of bestowing significance upon utterly insignificant detail" (n.p.). Minimalism is, at heart, an aesthetic of subtraction, but it is a particular achievement of Warhol's cinema to accomplish this pursuit of essential meaning while also "giganticizing with time," as Tyler puts it. Exaggeration and excess—key elements of Warhol's camp aesthetic—here work to counteract the modern spatialization of time. However, in its tendency to use the camera to impose a form of spatial rationality, *Blow Job* enacts a long-standing modernist tension between a sense of time and a focus on place (Harvey 271). How one experiences desire in space and time is further complicated by the contradictions of post-1945 commodity aesthetics, which the film reinforces by leaving the viewer simultaneously wanting more and less. Seduced and stimulated by the desire-to-watch, one yearns to see what Warhol's static camera refuses to reveal, and yet the unwatchable boredom of "dragtime" and the unvarying quality of the film make it a test of endurance without the visual pleasure of a cinematic payoff, thereby invoking a world of mass-produced and "amputated" pleasures (Haug 120).[27]

Although *Blow Job* offers a visualization of the mind-body split, Warhol does not efface the body, but instead makes it central yet absent, reeroticizing it through the tease of its absent presence. In its reference to the anonymity and iconography of porn, the film also points to the fetishistic depiction of the male body in pieces—a crucial element that links Warhol's work in the 1950s to his mostly male nudes of the 1970s, such as the faceless and fragmented *Sex Parts* and *Torso*. Works such as *Torso* (1977), which Warhol exhibited upside down, are not interested in investigating personhood (Hainley 5), but deconstructing it. As in muscle magazines, physique culture and gay porn—all source material for the artist—the reification and objectification of the male body are exploited and even celebrated for their democratic pleasures and anonymity. In *Blow Job* and elsewhere, the outlaw sensibility is less concerned with inversion (of gender, for example) and more with perversion as art and social rebellion. In its allusion to the iconic image of James Dean in a leather jacket, leaning against a brick wall, *Blow Job*'s queer aesthetic combines Warhol's fascination with the doomed eroticism of Dean with the raw sexual power of the hustler/john dyad, which—to quote film curator Callie Angell—"recurs as a kind of motif in a number of Warhol films" (33). Here, Warhol's famous aesthetic detachment is also a form of (camp) earnestness.[28] The outlaw sensibility finds sensuality and beauty in unexpected places—in forms of male subjectivity and embodiment that refuse to conform to social norms, in street hustlers and bike boys, in drug addicts, in public sex, and even in gangsters and criminals.

Warhol's interest in criminality took center stage in 1964, when he was commissioned by the architect Philip Johnson to produce a large mural for the New York State Pavilion at the World's Fair in New York. As in his Death and Disaster series, he was interested in portraying the dark side of American society (one thinks here of Warhol's cruelly beautiful Electric Chair paintings); he used "wanted" posters from the FBI and produced a mural of mug shots to represent the American dream gone wrong—a far cry from the intended celebration of "man's achievements" set forth by the World's Fair publicity literature. Perhaps for this reason, Warhol's *Thirteen Most Wanted Men* was censored, painted over by silver house paint only a few days after its installation. The architect Johnson claimed that the mural was suppressed by Governor Rockefeller because the men featured were all Italian and many had since been exonerated. However, as the art historian Richard Meyer notes, Warhol's choice of outdated mug shots implicitly asks viewers, "If the police is no longer pursuing the outlaws pictured here, by whom are these men most wanted now?" (*Outlaw Representation* 137). The answer, Meyer persuasively argues, is Warhol himself. The point I wish to stress here is not simply the homoerotic subtext of the work, but rather Warhol's identification with the figure of the criminal and the impersonal allure he locates in the mug shot's frozen and immobilized features. Of course, the motif of artist as thief has a long history in modernism. Warhol explicitly cites Duchamp's previous use of the mug shot to stage an artistic identification with the figure of the "Most Wanted Man;" in *Wanted/$2,000 Reward* (1923; assisted readymade), Duchamp inserted photos of himself in a fake wanted poster. Warhol makes his own identifications explicit in his discussion of *Thirteen Most Wanted Men* in *POPism*, in which he writes that he was at least in part glad that the mural was destroyed: "Now I wouldn't have to feel responsible if one of the criminals ever got turned in to the FBI because someone had recognized him from my pictures" (72). Disrupting the hierarchical relationship between normative and outsider masculinities and framing the outlaw as an object of desire, Warhol produced an intersection of homosexuality, fame, and criminality so lethal to bourgeois American values that it provoked state suppression.

I have been arguing that the outlaw aesthetic represents a rebellion, often nostalgic, against the reorganization of masculinity that characterized the postwar culture of Fordism—a form of oppositional and supposedly authentic masculinity that rejects domestication, privileges illicit pleasures, and refuses the "feminizing" influence of consumer culture. In the final part of my discussion, I aim to demonstrate that Warhol is equally interested in debunking the cultural logic that links masculinity to authenticity, cultivating a camp aesthetic that embraces the very seductions of the commodity that the outlaw sensibility opposes. As I have already suggested, the dialectic between camp and outlaw masculinity not only defines Warhol's queer aesthetic but also suggests why both he and his art are privileged emblems for modern masculinity in commodity culture.

THE CAMP ARTIFICE OF POP DANDYISM

> Camp is the modern dandyism. Camp is the answer to the problem: how to be a dandy in the age of mass culture.
>
> —Susan Sontag

Although memorably named "the tycoon of passivity, the last dandy" by Stephen Koch (22), Andy Warhol might be more usefully conceptualized as America's first great Pop dandy. Of course, he has much in common with earlier incarnations of the queer aesthete or dandy, such as Oscar Wilde. This connection was not lost on Warhol's contemporaries, as Geldzahler reminds us: "I've written about Andy that only Oscar Wilde, as far as I know, was able to the same extent to invent a way of behaving with people who were at the margin of society. That whole aesthetic, *Yellow Book*, Aubrey Beardsley, Ronald Firbank, was invented by the esthete Wilde. Andy in the sixties did something like that also, that lifestyle" (Shore 130).[29] Like his predecessor, Warhol used his effeminacy, aesthetic costume, intimacy with objects, and celebrity connections to advertise himself as a highly polished, aesthetic surface. From this perspective, camp might be understood as an effort to aestheticize the experience of living within (and in fact embodying) a central contraction of modernity. For this reason, the concept of camp expresses many of the defining features of Warhol's work, as a great deal of scholarship has demonstrated. In his artistic production, we find a cultivation of pleasure and play, an embrace of mass culture, a privileging of the perverse, and a refusal of sincerity. The camp sensibility is famously difficult to pin down, but I will hazard a brief definition here: camp is a mode of passionate extravagance. It celebrates a theatrical and self-conscious reversal or mocking of conventions, rules, or standards (of good taste, for example).[30] As Esther Newton points out in her classic study, *Mother Camp* (1972), camp "depends on the perception or creation of incongruous juxtapositions" (Newton 103). From this perspective, Andy's most famous images, such as his spectacular paintings of the lowly Campbell's soup can, are quite possibly the campiest contributions to modern art. Delighting in artifice, banality, stylization, and mistakes (something Warhol adored), camp relentlessly deflates seriousness, but it requires us to be mindful in order to get the joke.

As Peter Wollen has persuasively argued, it is one of Warhol's "key achievements" that he successfully combines the over-the-top excesses of camp with the minimalist impulse toward repetition, neutrality, and impersonality (158). Wollen's dialectical framework is an important effort to complicate the high-art reading, which, as we have already seen, has had tremendous appeal for commentators from a range of critical perspectives. In 1971, Robert Hughes claimed that the artist's work is the ultimate act of minimalism: it is "one long strategy of self-effacement, a disappearing act behind the gaudy colors and aggressively banal subject matter. Hence is the paradox of his enormous fame. He is 'a personality' with no personality, transparent as air" (80). This erasure of camp extravagance (and its queer associations) in order to present Warhol and his work as "a disappearing act" has not exclusively been the providence of commentators who downplay or disengage with the artist's sexuality. In an early essay from *Time Capsule 15*, entitled "'Prince of Boredom': The Repetitions and Passivities of Andy Warhol" (1968), William Wilson presents Warhol and films such as *Blow Job* in the now familiar tropes of mechanical repetition, numbness, mindlessness, and inaction. Very much like Huysmans' classic incarnation of the nineteenth-century dandy as "sterile sensualist" (Moers), Koch's and Wilson's readings seem to present Warhol as the last gasp of dandyism because his passivity moves beyond idleness, threatening to neutralize pleasure and aesthetic distinction. Despite Warhol's well-known assertion about liking—really liking—boring things,[31] critics like Koch and Wilson promote a vision of the artist as exhausted by sensuality and pleasure and overcome by ennui.

Extending this line of inquiry in his 2001 biography, Koestenbaum presents Warhol's focus on passivity in a positive light by framing his embrace of boredom as a spiritual exercise in "saintly patience" that relinquishes control and instead waits and watches for an appearance of "the miraculous core of the material world" (Koestenbaum 9–10). However, Warhol's decidedly undandified and famously ceaseless work ethic and his ongoing effort to aestheticize his life and body—through wigs, cosmetics, fashion, plastic surgery, collagen injections, and other skin treatments—all would suggest that the sort of passivity Koestenbaum describes was actually an unlikely fusion of minimalist discipline and control with the exaggerated sensibility of camp performance, such as his well-known "swish" affectation.[32]

Victor Brockis points out the performative dimensions of Warhol's persona in an illuminating passage from *Warhol: The Biography* (2003):

> Everything was work to Andy. "He would pick me up in a taxi to go out at night and say, 'OK, this is work,'" recalled Maura Moynihan. "Then he'd pull out his camera and tape recorder and put on his blank personality. . . ." But he was showing signs of tiring. When Debbie Harry broke up her rock group Blondie . . . he asked a friend why she had stopped being Blondie.
>
> "Because Debbie's too intelligent to remain in the role of a cartoon character every day," the friend replied.
>
> "What do you think I've been doing for the last twenty-five years?" Warhol snapped.
>
> "Sometimes," he said, "it's just so great to get home and take off my Andy suit." (456)

For the artist, "being" Andy was clearly a job, so it is not surprisingly that, after "work," he was eager to take off his "Andy suit." Although I have been arguing that Warhol's persona needs to be understood as a form of camp artifice, I want to emphasize that his stylized subjectivity complicates any easy divisions between an authentic Andy and an artificial one.[33] In fact, as Wilde sought to demonstrate, the notion of living one's life as art and performing one's identity calls into question the relationship between essence and appearance, as well as reality and its representation. Warhol seems to suggest this himself in *The Philosophy* when he uses television as a metaphor to make a very postmodernist point about the "unreal" quality of real life, insisting he has always suspected that, instead of living life, he has been watching television (91). This sense of experiencing life through the mediation and aesthetic distancing of the image (a characteristic of our post-Fordist society of the spectacle) also points to the ways in which Warhol's quest for fame and reified experience ultimately moves him toward the depersonalized abstractions of Pop dandyism.

The dandy's well-known "cult of the self" (Baudelaire, *The Painter of Modern Life* 27) is pushed to the brink of extinction by Warhol. Much like the Warholian Pop dandy, the nineteenth-century dandy turns himself into a work of art and empathizes with commodities. Demonstrating an affinity for the world of objects, Baudelaire's dandies regularly vaporize into the crowd, losing their humanist figuration or identity. Warhol exaggerates and extends this modernist tradition by deconstructing personhood through a reification of the erotic; in this way, his art reconceptualizes categories such as pleasure, identity, and the aesthetic as cultural effects of postwar consumerism's aesthetic abstraction and standardization. With this in mind, let me return to Warhol's famous 1964 declaration: "I want to be a machine." This is an enormously rich gesture that puts into play the modern contradictions I have been examining while also bridging the gap between the industrial/economic and the aesthetic/erotic. Demonstrating how to be a dandy in the age of mass culture, Warhol's identification with the machine turns its back on the myths of heroic individualism by calling for the extinction of the humanist tradition in art. The artist's expressed desire to transform himself into an instrument of production also highlights the degree to which, despite the privileging of expressivity by the art world of the 1950s, artistic production in the postwar world had become (increasingly) a form of dehumanizing and alienating labor. Warhol's embrace of the inorganic uniformity of the machine takes on ghostly associations, reminding us that, for Marx, the machine is a form of "dead labor." This is perhaps why Warhol's identification with the machine signals the death of humanism for many commentators of the 1960s and 1970s.[34] Ironically, what such critics overlook is that the aspiration to be a machine must ultimately fail and therefore reveal what is inescapably human. Because he is not capable of a machine's "endless and perfect repetitions," Warhol "can only succeed in showing that when repetition is an ideal, it is unattainable" (Wilson 14). This insight suggests that Warhol's dream of mechanization is not simply a wish to accommodate himself to the dehumanization and alienation of Fordist production. In fact, his affectless persona and desire to mechanize the artist's body simultaneously enact and satirize the notion that, under capitalism, the artist must separate himself from life in order to depict it (Wolff 6). He takes this myth to its logical extreme by presenting himself as a kind of machine or alien, or as someone "more half-there than all-there" (*Philosophy* 91), or, after the 1968 shooting by Valerie Solanas, as someone "back from the dead" (Hackett *Diary* x).

Despite his avowed love for "the now," Warhol's industrial aesthetic was also in part a nostalgic effort to return to pre-Taylorist forms of work—not the division of labor characteristic of Fordism but rather the collective labor of the Warholian Factory. His sense of the liberatory possibilities of automation ("everyone should be machines"), his romantic treatment of mechanization and standardization, and the futuristic, space-age quality of his Silver Factory, all express a yearning for "the technological sublime": a search for sublimity through technology that, according to art historian Caroline Jones, characterized much of 1960s art and culture (54–55). A particularly ebullient and playfully queer form of Warhol's techno-utopianism is memorably expressed in the artist's legendary installation, *Silver Clouds* (1966). Among its many witty references, Warhol's piece responds to sculptors like David Smith, who used welding to produce a strongly masculine, machine-age aesthetic. Warhol declared that he too would create a metal sculpture—"except mine will float."[35] In 1964, he worked with engineer Billy Klüver to create the helium-filled clouds, which are made out of shiny Scotchpak and designed to resemble oversized bed pillows. The clouds float on air currents and respond to the touch of viewers, who are encouraged to interact with them. Being inside the clouds and interacting with them gives the viewer the sense of being surrounded by multiple mirrored universes—a microcosm, if you will, of our society of the spectacle; we feel a loss of self as we surrender to the pleasures of an utterly artificial environment, itself an emblem of the glittery seductions of commodity aesthetics. At the same time, we experience the sense of being reflected, magnified, like a star surrounded by the bright flash of cameras snapping one's picture. A form of "disposable art for people who felt burdened by too many possessions," as well as an effort to "queer" contemporary sculpture and denaturalize modern masculinity, *Silver Clouds* presents Warholian performance as both campy spectacle and ultraminimalist disappearing act (Bourdon, *Warhol* 230).[36]

In a similar vein, when the art world was heralding a return to painterly expressivity and technique, Warhol produced a series of works that playfully mocked neo-expressionism and the art world's investment in the figure of the masculine artist as inventor, while articulating a queer relation to the logic of capital. These 1970s paintings—*Oxidations*, *Piss Paintings*, *Sex Parts*, and *Torsos*—are all part of Warhol's long-standing passion for abstracting sex, deconstructing high art's humanistic treatment of the nude through fragmentation and depersonalization. For his Oxidation paintings, Andy and his assistants coated canvases with copper paint and urinated on them, joking that their penises were "paint brushes." The uric acid and copper sulfate combined to produce a green patina, visible in works such as *Oxidation Painting* (1978). Here, Warhol's postmodernist trash aesthetic subverts the laws of exchange under capitalism by recycling a waste product (urine) and transforming it into something valuable, beautiful—and funny. As he states in *The Philosophy*: "I always like to work on leftovers, doing the leftover things. Things that were discarded, that everybody knew were no good, I always thought had a great potential to be funny"(93).[37] The paintings allude both to Duchamp's revolutionary *Fountain* (a readymade urinal; 1917) and Jackson Pollock's famous "drip" paintings, offering a witty critique of Abstract Expressionism, phallic masculinity, and the macho, avant-garde pretensions of Pollock himself.[38]

Warhol's concern with questions of value and desire and his swish critique of machismo can be traced to his early artistic production, which often humorously exploits his own identification with objects and uses the iconography of fashion to present art itself as a commodity. His delightfully campy rendering of Zsa Zsa Gabor as a shoe is an emblem for the artist's joyful surrender to the seductions of the commodity, a decidedly feminized position in postwar American society. "Za Za Gabor Shoe" appeared as part of the artist's

1956 exhibition entitled "The Golden Slipper Show" (the show featured fantastic and ornate designs for celebrity footwear). It demonstrates Warhol's fascination with shiny, glittery and metallic objects, which, as we have seen, often suggest the beckoning world of consumer artifice. It also conveys not only the beauty but also the sexual charge he locates in the commodity, here depicted as cherished fetish. Viewing these works, one thinks of Warhol's foot fetishism and his erotic relationship to shoes, both of which are associated with sensuality and pleasure in his life and work. In this respect, I diverge from Wendy Steiner's rather puzzling claim that Warhol's shoes suggest "the extreme ambivalence we now feel toward beauty both within and outside art. We distrust it; we fear its power; we associate it with the compulsion and uncontrollable desire of a sexual fetish. Embarrassed by our yearning for beauty, we demean it as something tawdry, self-indulgent, or sentimental" (32). What Steiner seems to miss in Warhol is the element of camp, which is, as Susan Sontag points out in her classic essay, a mode of appreciative and generous enjoyment "that identifies with what it is enjoying" (291). But this sensibility nonetheless revels in contradiction; in Warhol's "golden slipper" drawings and flamboyant 1955 book, *A la Recherche du Shoe Perdu*, camp irony mocks and celebrates the very obsessions it dramatically encodes. In this way, his ornate shoes and "shoe poems" enact a witty critique of the masculine pieties of the established art world, while articulating a queer sensibility that speaks in the language of commodity aesthetics.

Warhol's campy subversion of phallic masculinity is unmistakably expressed in his "boy drawings" of the 1950s, images such as *Golden Boy*. During this time, the artist also did hundreds of "cock" and foot drawings, asking acquaintances if he could draw their genitals or feet for a future *Cock Book* or *Foot Book*. Warhol made many of these sketches public in his Valentine's Day exhibition in 1956, entitled "Drawings for a Boy-Book," which included rapturous and reclining male nudes, and a stylized image of the penis as beckoning commodity. Decorated with tiny flowers and hearts and gift-wrapped with a ribbon, the penis becomes a sensuously enjoyable effect of commodity aesthetics (*Male Genitals*; Figure 6.6). Despite the obvious humor in much of this work, these drawings boldly contest postwar sex/gender ideology by articulating a queer commodity aesthetic that reeroticizes the gay male body, while simultaneously insisting that both art and manhood are best understood as exercises in what Sontag has memorably called "failed seriousness" (287).

As I have argued, Warhol's effort to denaturalize modern masculinity through camp artifice and the subversive reversals of Pop dandyism is always linked to a nostalgic yearning for an authentic masculinity that would transcend the imperatives of Fordist production. The inextricability of camp artifice and the authenticity of the outlaw sensibility is beautifully illustrated by *Barne "Boy with USN Tattoo"* (ca. 1957; Figure 6.7). This image refers to the

FIGURE 6.6. Andy Warhol, *Male Genitals* (1950s). Ballpoint ink on Manila paper. 17 x 14 in. (43.2 x 35.6 cm.). Founding Collection, the Andy Warhol Museum, Pittsburgh. Courtesy of the Andy Warhol Museum.

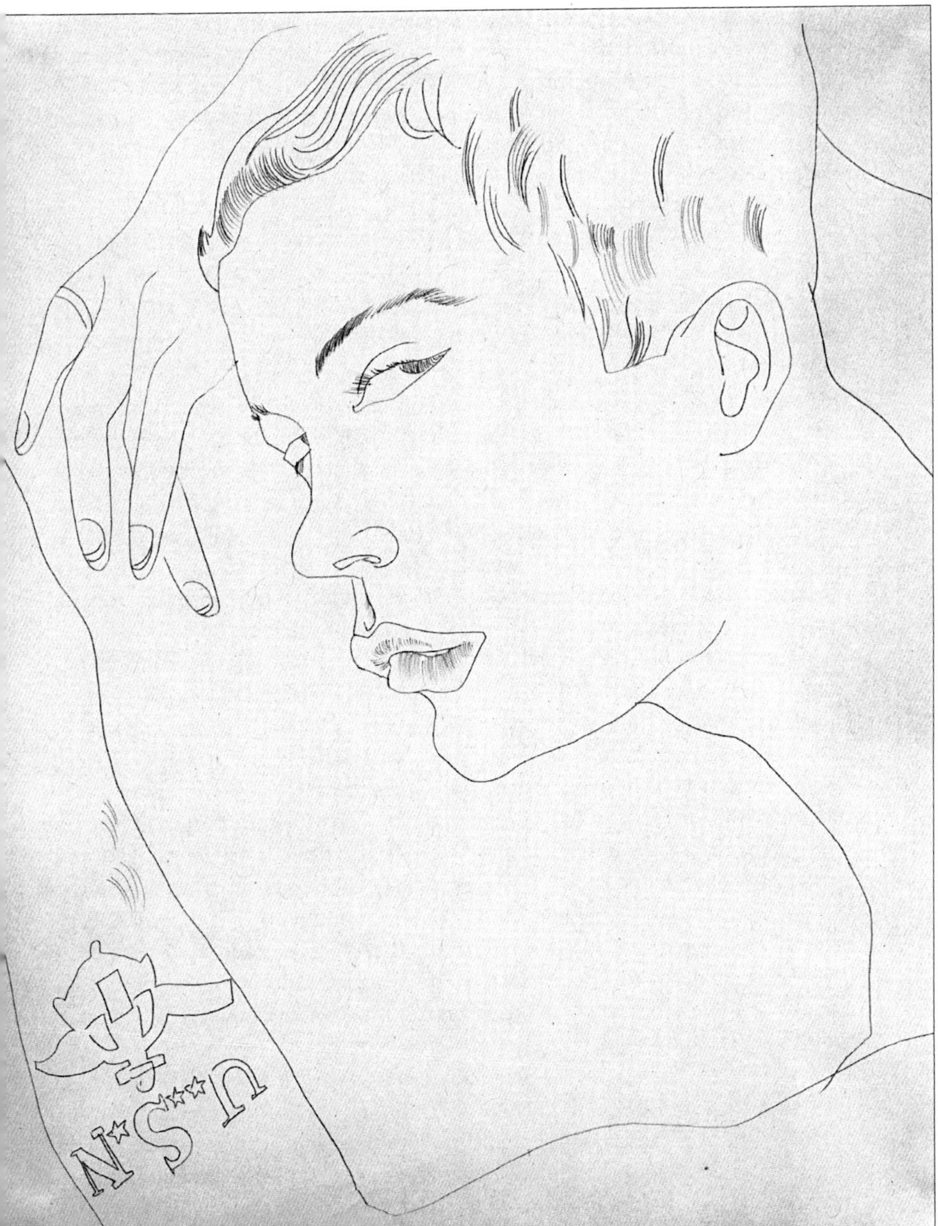

FIGURE 6.7. Andy Warhol, *Barne "Boy with USN Tattoo"* (c. 1957). Ballpoint ink on tan paper. 16 3/4 x 14 in. (42.5 x 35.6 cm.). Founding Collection, the Andy Warhol Museum, Pittsburgh. © The Andy Warhol Foundation for the Visual Arts/ARS, New York. Courtesy of the Andy Warhol Museum.

centrality of sailors in queer iconography—a long-standing tradition of gay visual representation that includes pornography, Tom of Finland, beefcake photos, and American painters such as Charles Demuth and Paul Cadmus. What I find intriguing about Warhol's drawing is that he subverts the norms encoded in these representations by presenting the sailor not as heterosexualized, butch "trade," but rather as an openly queer erotic archetype. Recruiting the tattooed marker of virile masculinity for gay male subject construction, he offers a campy comment on the cold war logic that divided the morbid, narcissistic, and effeminate image of the homosexual from the virile, athletic, and heroic image of heteromasculinity. As I have been arguing, Warhol's engagement with tropes of masculinity is characterized by complex and unresolved tensions. In contrast to works such as *Torso*, which offers a more fetishistic treatment of the male body in pieces, *Barne* does not impersonalize its abstraction of the male body as object of exchange. The body's representation as an instrument of pleasure (its objectification) becomes a thoroughly dialectical image of sexual reification and liberation. With his long slender fingers, dainty pinky ring, sexy bee-stung lips, and sleepy bedroom eyes, this sailor (like the subject of *Blow Job*) seems to tempt us to consider what remains unseen—a nude torso and buttocks perhaps?—and to celebrate his transformation into an erotic object.

The tension between "the seen" and "the unseen" in Warhol's representations of gay masculinity returns us to one of the foundational assertions of this study: the logic of queer identity installs a logic particular to the commodity and its contradictions. Oscar Wilde and Andy Warhol are perhaps our most famous examples of how queer icons of modernism use tropes of dandyism to reconfigure their relation to the "open secret"—that is, the commodity's paradoxical culture of visibility. Despite such continuities in queer subject construction, I have argued that Warhol's stylistic strategies of camp and outlaw masculinity propose a new relation to the commodity-form that combines the rationalizing force of the economic with the libidinal energy of the sensuous/aesthetic. For precisely this reason, his work inhabits an opposition; it critiques the increasing penetration of capital into American society while also mobilizing the liberatory potential of a queer commodity aesthetics. Certainly, Warhol is well-known for his consumer imagery and frankly commodified aesthetic; however, I have stressed that this is not due to his art's "transparency" or "blankness," but because his Pop dandyism aims to put questions of value and desire into relief by deconstructing the oppositions that have been my abiding focus: economic/erotic, production/consumption, work/play, and appearance/essence. Cultivating a queer style that embraces the erotics and aesthetics of the commodity, Warhol defiantly presents gay men as both subjects and objects of modernization.

AFTERWORD

THE NEW DANDYISM?

Strive toward a state of peculiarity. Never approach the world in a perpendicular manner, but always at the queerest of angles.

—Lord Whimsy

In his 1962 essay "Dandyism and Fashion," Roland Barthes argues that fashion's industrialized extermination of singularity from clothing has killed dandyism: "Once limited to the freedom to buy (but not to create), dandyism could not but suffocate and die" (68). Despite Barthes' claim about the fatal power of standardization to extinguish the dandy's rebellion, the twenty-first century is experiencing a striking and, some might say, unexpected renaissance of dandyism across a wide range of international locales. In "A New Dandyism Takes Shape" (which appeared in *The International Herald Tribune* in 2005), Rebecca Voight reported on a new dandyist sensibility in menswear collections that were, in sum, eclectic, luxurious, decadent, and utopian.[1] Tom Notte and Bart Vandebosch of Les Hommes offered a similarly provocative reading of dandyism as both "street" and urbane, civilized and decadent, in their Milan Menswear Show for Spring 2007.[2] Alice Cicolini's book *The New English Dandy* (2005)—based on the British Council touring exhibition "21st Century Dandy"—testifies not only to the durability of the dandy as a modern icon but also his potential to incorporate contemporary notions of cultural fusion and hybridization, street style, and subcultural styles such as punk (one thinks immediately of Vivienne Westwood, who "fused elements of the suit, worker's clothes, the straitjacket and tartans into punk's aggressive tribal attire").[3] Furthermore, the contemporary dandyist sensibility is not an exclusively male phenomenon. Exhibiting the wide-ranging appeal of a stylized androgyny that disrupts oppositions, female dandies have not only had an important influence in defining lesbian subcultural styles but have also emerged as a powerful fashion presence in recent years. (Think, for example, of Chloë Sevigny, actress and fashion icon, on the December 2004 cover of *L'Uomo Vogue*.) Hip-hop dandies such as Diddy (Sean Combs) and André 3000 inject a cool edge into a sartorial style that once connoted fussiness by combining urban, street elements with rakish, impeccable tailoring.

Dandyism's revival and reinvention extends beyond celebrity culture and the runways of Paris and Milan.[4] In 2006, Lord Breaulove Swells Whimsy (the fictional alter ego of Allen Crawford, made a—dignified, of course—splash in literary circles with the release of his witty book, *The Affected Provincial's Companion, Volume I*, which aspires to teach readers how to become "self-willed aristocrat[s] of the soul." Whimsy is an especially fascinating figure because his dandyism is an unlikely synthesis of aristocratic refinement and provincial vulgarity, decadent artifice and folksy naturalism (Figure A.1). An artist "not fit for civilian life," he makes his home in rural New Jersey with his wife, the dandyish Lady Pinkwater, where they live surrounded by Victorian curios and specimens of butterflies and carnivorous plants ("Preface"). Further testifying to a resurgence of popular interest in dandyism, the New York Public Library's exhibition "A Rakish History of Men's Wear" (September 8, 2006–May 6, 2007) focused on the social aspects of fashion history and the importance of the dandy in defining the streamlined, understated style of the modern suit (this, of course, is the primary legacy of Beau Brummell). In its February 2007 issue, *Domino* (a home décor magazine targeted to "style-conscious" female shoppers) celebrates the dandy as a source of fanciful inspiration for women and men of style.

Having sketched in broad strokes some indices of dandyism's contemporary revival, I'm sure it is clear to the reader that this trend is not only or primarily a gay subcultural style. Although in some of its varieties the new dandyism *is* a mode of queer identification, desire, and/or performance (which I explore next), here I want to emphasize the significance of a more mainstream cultural trend that both invites and disavows queer specificity. In the United States, the new dandyism has emerged as one response to a redefinition of gay identity in the popular imagination. To cite a few prominent examples: the rise of a new gay and lesbian niche market in the 1990s; the new "cultural visibility" of queers in public life; the cultural fascination with the figure of the "metrosexual"; the recycling and mainstreaming of lesbian sartorial styles, ranging from the campiness of drag king culture to the refined and sexy androgyny of the L.A. lesbian look (popularized by the *The L Word*); and the neutralization of "queer" through shows such as *Queer Eye for the Straight Guy*, which cemented the association of homosexual aestheticism with a particularly vapid and rationalized notion of lifestyle. Although the new dandyism may be

FIGURE A.1. Lord Whimsy the Affected Provincial. Photo by Adam Wallacavage for *Swindle* magazine (2006). Courtesy of Adam Wallacavage.

approached from different angles, I want to emphasize the phenomenon's relationship to my argument about the paradigmatic and contradictory place of the queer subject in modern culture. As it relates to the American context in particular, this framework helps us to see how the new dandyism (as enacted by men and women of various erotic affiliations) can be productively interpreted as both a symptom of and rebellion against the increasing commodification of queer identities, desires and styles that has proliferated in recent years.[5]

In other words, the "new" dandyism may not be as new as we have been led to believe. It is still too early to make any definitive declarations about these matters, but I would speculate that the new dandyism may soon be recognizable as the working out of dandyism's constitutive contradictions in the wake of meterosexual conformity and "mass-brand fetishization" (Whimsy, *The Affected Provincial* 119). Conjuring the Baudelairean dandy, Lord Whimsy declares unapologetically that "to set out to live as beautifully as one's circumstances will allow may be the most radical thing a person can do in a contemporary culture mired in an ethic of ruthless utility" (*Men of the Cloth* 150). Like his predecessors, contemporary dandies occupy a contradictory place in modern life, functioning as both privileged emblems of modernity and as dissidents in rebellion against modern society. As I have argued, Oscar Wilde's *The Picture of Dorian Gray* is a particularly prescient example of how the queer dandy's paradox of visibility embodies the structural contradictions of capitalism; a fatally fractured and divided subject, he is radically split between appearance and essence, outside and inside.

This model of queer dandyism as a doubling of identity and a mode of world-weary decadence—a paradoxical synthesis of visibility and invisibility—is deployed to great effect by British dandy-popstar-flâneur Dickon Edwards, who combines the decadent tradition of Huysmans and Wilde with the Pop dandyism of Warhol. His unique synthesis of aesthetic modernism and mass culture is most notable on his website, where his blog serves as an archive of and tribute to a new practice of what we might call virtual dandyism (in the decadent sense of virtuality as artifice). Just as his blog continues the dandyist impulse to be an artist-in-life, he explicitly articulates his continuation of the dandy tradition in his own public representations. One particularly striking photographic portrait of Edwards reading *The Philosophy of Andy Warhol* (Figure A.2) contains within it three different images of Edwards himself—two photographs (one of which appears on the computer monitor) and a painting. Together, they suggest not only an echo of Wilde's *The Picture of Dorian Gray* but also a "new dandyism" in which identity is not divided (as it is for Wilde) but multiplied and serialized (as it is for Warhol). Furthermore, a copy of Jerome K. Jerome's *Idle*

FIGURE A.2. Dickon Edwards in his London bedsit. Sarah Kate Watson, *Dickon Edwards—for the series New Muses* (2003). Photo by and courtesy of Sarah Kate Watson.

Thoughts of an Idle Fellow (1884) propped up against the painting reminds us of the dandy's revolt against industriousness and assertion of the freedom to be idle—a protest I find especially meaningful in today's world, when the concept of freedom itself has been degraded to the "right" of free enterprise (Harvey, *Neoliberalism* 183). Across the Atlantic, professional dandy Patrick McDonald—who describes himself as "dandy to fashionistas everywhere" on his MySpace profile—also demonstrates the ongoing relevance of aestheticism and dandyism for contemporary gay male subject formation. With his signature, Elizabeth Taylor-inspired eyebrows, McDonald has a dramatic, highly individualized style that makes him an immediately recognizable, unabashedly spectacular celebrity dandy (Figure A.3). His inspired vision is a unique combination of camp extravagance (e.g., his famous collection of hats that function as plumage, his equally famous penciled brows and beauty mark) with a highly disciplined, ascetic attention to what Roland Barthes names the hallmark of dandyism: the vestimentary detail. Indeed, McDonald embraces the aesthetics of the commodity and feminized techniques to perfect his appearance, thereby continuing and extending the Wildean project of self-cultivation and pursuit of originality. That he accomplishes this triumph of singularity in the realm of twenty-first-century high fashion is worth noting, particularly in light of Barthes's opposition of fashion and dandyism. With the exception of early dandies such as Brummell, the desire to remove oneself from the marketplace has never been more than a utopian wish—however powerful—for the modern dandy. Like other dandies of the nineteenth and twentieth centuries, today's dandies must inevitably participate in and critique the increased democraticization of dandyism. This is a structural contradiction I have tried to illuminate, rather than smooth away.

According to critic Rhoda K. Garelick, dandyism is a conflation of "textual and human seduction" that produces a "contagion" of style: "critics writing about dandies or their texts fall easily into dandyist style and succumb to its charms" (11). By examining queer heroes of modern life "immanently," my project has been to uncover the traces of desire and the commodity-form in queer cultural production, while remaining within the logic of dandyism itself. I have sought to embody the contraditions of dandyism by refusing to choose between commodification and seduction—that is, between the reification of the commodity, industry, and instrumental reason, on the one hand, and the utopian promise found in the cultivation of beauty, art, and pleasure, on the other. If the book's constellation of dialectical images can be said to have a singular force, I have no doubt that its motor resides in queer dandyism's playful subversion of the oppositions that define modern culture. Succumbing to the charms of the dandy, then, has never been more essential.

FIGURE A.3. Patrick McDonald at Mercedes-Benz Fashion Week (Fall 2007). Photo by Katy Winn/Getty Images for IMG.

NOTES

INTRODUCTION

1. While all dandies do not pursue "queer" or "perverse" modes of pleasure, sensation, and affect, the figure of the dandy has had a gay specificity since about the turn of the century, as I will discuss.

2. I use the term "relation" here to convey a connection between capital (itself a social relation) and queer identity, as well as to emphasize the dialectical or relational approach that informs this study.

3. On the emergence of consumer culture see Auslander; Clarke et al.; de Grazia; Leach; Richards; Roberts; Scalon; Slater.

4. In chapter 1, I take up the Marxist opposition between essence and appearance and the question of essentialism in feminist and queer studies. I therefore refer readers to that chapter for a more detailed discussion of these concepts and their theoretical and political implications.

5. In this respect, my reading follows Jameson's eloquent defense of Lukács's ideological critique. Jameson's reading avoids the pitfalls of nondialectial thinking (e.g., "true" vs. "false") by conceptualizing ideology in terms of "structural limitation" or "strategies of containment."

6. In addition to the Frankfurt school thinkers I draw upon throughout this study, my thinking about the concepts of mediation, totality, and dialectics has benefited greatly from the work of Maurice Cornforth, István Mészáros, and Bertell Ollman. See in particular Ollman's discussion of abstraction in Marx's dialectical method, especially with regard to the relation of identity/difference—that is, the interpenetration of opposites that produces identity in difference (*Dance of the Dialectic* 15–16; *Dialectical Investigations* 43).

7. While there are pessimistic moments in the work of Frankfurt school thinkers such as Theodor Adorno, I would argue that critical theory is fundamentally motivated

by an ethical and moral vision of liberation that is far from fatalistic. It is this vision of social transformation that has motivated my own engagement with theorists such as Adorno, Benjamin, and Marcuse.

8. Marcuse argues for the emancipatory promise of art—its *promesse de bonheur*—in his discussion of beauty, pleasure, and happiness under capitalism in "The Affirmative Character of Culture" (*Negations* 115).

9. For useful discussions of the formula "dialectics at a standstill," see Adorno; Benjamin; Buck-Morss; Helmling; Martin Jay; Jennings.

10. In his project to conceptualize a "Red Queer Theory," Donald Morton offers a "revolutionary Marxist" critique of the "pro-capitalist queer left." See Morton; Ebert; Field.

CHAPTER 1

1. Sedgwick argues that gay people confront cultural, institutional, and judicial formations that make the disclosure of one's sexuality both compulsory and forbidden (*Epistemology of the Closet* 70).

2. I refer readers to the introduction for an analysis of the relationship between dandyism and homosexuality.

3. There is a vast literature that links the dandy to artifice, aestheticism, and style. For example, see Stephen Calloway's "Wilde and the Dandyism of the Senses," which traces Wilde's cultivation of "aesthetic response" and "heightened sensibility" in the context of the aesthetic and decadent movements of the 1880s and 1890s (34, 36). Recent cultural criticism that depicts dandyism as a transgression of gender boundaries shares with Calloway a notion of the dandy as the triumph of style over substance. Exemplified by the literary critic Jessica Feldman, this scholarship claims that the dandy is an "icon of modernism" because he must be conceptualized as "neither wholly man nor wholly woman, but as the figure who blurs these distinctions" (11). Appropriating Judith Butler's influential theory of gender as performative, critics such as Feldman and Marjorie Garber join gender with aesthetics and, in so doing, define the gay male dandy's disruption of gender norms in terms that resemble Sontag's model of homosexuality as aestheticism, or Calloway's model of dandyism as a cult of aesthetic response. On camp's strategy of integration, which "renders gender a question of aesthetics," see Dollimore (311).

4. Literary and cultural critics such as Bristow, Felski, Gagnier, and Sinfield are among our most compelling contemporary scholars on this subject precisely because they unite the model of dandyism as style with the model of dandyism as political rebellion. Similarly, Nunokawa and Waldrep join these models in their works on the Wildean dandy. Despite the differences in their projects, both critics demonstrate the ways in which Wilde's dandy-aesthete sets the stage for modern culture's reorganization of subjectivity and sexuality. "Wilde's aestheticism, therefore, is not just an escape from commercialism or the tyrannny of the middle class but also an

attempt at rewriting aesthetics by working through the body from a materialist standpoint" (Waldrep xvii).

5. For discussions of essentialism in gay/lesbian studies and queer theory and politics, see Abelove et al.; Duggan; Fuss; Warner.

6. Marcuse's "The Concept of Essence" in *Negations* addresses the materialist concept of essence and its difference from idealist philosophy's notion of essence. Larrain examines essence and appearance as part of a broader discussion about the Marxist concept of ideology in *The Concept of Ideology* (55–63) and *Marxism and Ideology* (122–68). In a similar vein, see Mepham (148–53) and Geras. Finally, for a rereading of the Marxist opposition between essence and appearance using the concepts of "overdetermination" and "structural causality," see Althusser and Balibar (182–93).

7. In her account of the novel as a bourgeois form, Terry Lovell (15–16) asserts that capitalism requires this split subject due to the opposition between production and consumption, a topic I address later.

8. The terms "public" and "private" require explanation. As Nancy Fraser points out, contemporary feminist theorists often problematically use the term "private" as a synonym for intimate personal or family life and the term "public" to refer to "everything that is outside the domestic or familial sphere" (110). Fraser is right that such a conception of the public fails to distinguish between the multiple components of the public sphere: state apparatuses, economic markets, and the arenas of public discourse. But with respect to the definition of the private, the feminist theorists Fraser critiques are correct to the extent that twentieth-century society is characterized by a "shrinking" of the private sphere to the family (Habermas, *Structural Transformation of the Public Sphere* 159). Nevertheless, since this chapter focuses on nineteenth-century cultural formations, I use the title of the "private" in the classical bourgeois sense—it refers both to the intimate sphere of personal life (including emotional, sexual, and familial relations) and to the concept of private property, with its attendant notion of privacy as freedom from state authority (Habermas, *Structural Transformation of the Public Sphere* 74).

9. My argument employs Larrain's definitions of appearance and essence: "Appearances are not mere illusions nor is the essence more real than the appearance. Both essence and appearance are real. In other words, reality itself is the unity of essence and appearance" (*The Concept of Ideology*, 57).

10. The classical oppositions of form/content and appearance/essence—both reconceptualized by Marx in dialectical and materialist terms—are not strictly analogous, but I have aligned these terms in the present discussion since Marx's analysis of commodity fetishism sets up parallels between them. See "The Fetishism of the Commodity and Its Secret" in *Capital* (163–77).

11. On the duality of thought and existence as an antinomy of bourgeois thought, see Lukács's reading of Kant in "Reification and the Consciousness of the Proletariat," *History and Class Consciousness* (especially 110–209).

12. For examples of recent scholarship on transparency and manhood in the context of the French Revolution, see Lynn Hunt's work. On the union of body and soul

as a cornerstone of modern masculinity, see Dean's "The Making of Gay Male Sexuality" in *The Frail Social Body* and Mosse, *The Image of Man.*

13. The trope of the disguise is crucial to Wilde's description of Dorian's secret pleasures "in the sordid room of the little ill-famed tavern near the Docks, which, under an assumed name, and in disguise, it was his [Dorian's] habit to frequent" (112). Basil also tells Dorian that there are "stories that you have been seen creeping at dawn out of dreadful houses and slinking in disguise into the foulest dens in London" (132). On the centrality of the mask and its relationship to "reinvention of the self" in Wilde's work, see Waldrep (7, 17–19, 59).

14. As Buck-Morss argues in *The Dialectics of Seeing*, the notion of mass culture as a commodified dreamworld is key to Benjamin's vision of modernity. Williams also uses this concept to frame her history of consumption in late nineteenth-century France, *Dream Worlds*.

15. See Baudrillard's "The System of Objects" (10–28) and "Consumer Society" (29–56) in his *Selected Writings*.

16. This quote is taken from Benjamin's essay "Louis-Philippe or the Interior" in *Charles Baudelaire*. The essay also appears in the collection *Reflections* (154–56).

17. My argument draws on Baudrillard's analysis of the production of needs in "The Ideological Genesis of Needs" (*For a Critique* 63–87).

18. In her account of the Victorian aesthetic movement, Linda Dowling interprets Wilde's personal originality in relation to an opposing impulse toward aesthetic democracy. In so doing, Dowling locates a tension between Wilde's "intense individuality," which cultivates aristocratic elitism, and his affirmation of "the democratic scope and generous utopian dimensions of art" (*The Vulgarization of Art* 90). Although I follow Bourdieu in reading aestheticism mainly as a mode of aristocratic distinction, I am indebted to Dowling's critique of the prevalent notion that aesthetes like Wilde simply retreated from politics or history into a separate world of art and beauty. On "the sense of distinction" as it relates to economic and cultural capital, see Bourdieu (260–317). Finally, James Eli Adams argues that bourgeois self-presentation is designed to efface originality in *Dandies and Desert Saints* (193).

19. The brothers Goncourt mourned the fact that they were born too late to take part in the aristocratic world of eighteenth-century leisure, style, and privilege. In 1869, they sought to escape modern city life by installing their extensive collection of eighteenth-century artifacts in a mansion in Auteuil, which they fashioned into an authentic recreation of Old Regime France. See Silverman (20).

20. Renato Rosaldo uses the term "imperialist nostalgia" to describe the nostalgia of colonizers for the native cultures they themselves destroy. For an analysis of "exotic nostalgia," which seeks to "salvage values and a way of life that had vanished, without hope of restoration," see Chris Bongie's article on Joseph Conrad and the politics of imperialism (270).

21. Said's *Orientalism* remains the classic text on European fantasies that made the Orient "Oriental" through cultural discourse and institutional authority.

22. On this point, Felski (107) cites A. E. Carter, *The Idea of Decadence in French Literature: 1830–1900* (Toronto: University of Toronto Press, 1958).

23. Other lives are required for the aestheticization of Dorian's life: Basil Hallward, Sibyl Vane, James Vane, Alan Campbell, and others (Wilde 131). For a reading of *Dorian Gray* based on the metaphor of the vampire, see Twitchell's *The Living Dead* (171–78). In *Skin Shows*, Halberstam also reads Dorian as a vampiric, Gothic monster, but she makes this claim as part of a broader argument about the relationship between identity, art, and homoerotic desire (53–85).

24. On the transformation of the commodity into spectacle see Debord; Felski; Richards; Silverman; and Williams.

25. For a discussion of dandyism as a retreat to the interior see Felski (91–114) and Williams (127–49).

26. Williams analyzes the conjunction between consumption and the civilizing ideal in her discussion of "courtly consumption" (19–57).

27. There is a tremendous amount of literary criticism that views *Dorian Gray* as a moral fable about the relationship between art and life. Although different from these critics in many respects, Sedgwick also focuses on Wilde's "moralizing" optic (*Epistemology of the Closet* 131) as part of her analysis of the sentimental/antisentimental relations that structure the novel's "framing and hanging of the beautiful male body" (*Epistemology of the Closet* 148).

CHAPTER 2

1. In his *Les Fleurs du mal* [*Flowers of Evil*], Baudelaire uses this language of artifice and death to describe the lesbian in poems such as "Femmes damnées: Delphine et Hippolyte." For Faderman as well as more sympathetic readers such as Sandra Gilbert and Susan Gubar, the morbid aspects of Vivien's life—particularly her early death from alcohol, laudanum, and self-starvation—are reductively explained as the result of the poet's identification with and internalization of the poisonous image of the lesbian *femme damnée* (Faderman, *Surpassing the Love of Men* 268; Gilbert and Gubar 227).

2. On the importance of the decadent tradition for lesbian modernists, see also Laity; Rea.

3. The intersection of decadent and Sapphic aesthetics is variously addressed by a number of female modernists, including H.D., Natalie Barney, and Colette.

4. The poem in "Douceur de mes chants . . ." appears with the title "Let Us Go to Mytilène" in *The Muse of Violets* (1977).

5. We can see a similar impulse toward reformulating the vocabulary of the decadent French tradition in the work of Djuna Barnes. In Barnes's *Nightwood*, the much-discussed duality of lesbian identity in the novel does more than reproduce the kind of nineteenth-century images of lesbian narcissism associated with a writer like Pierre

Louÿs. As the critic Julie Abraham has asserted, Djuna Barnes's Robin Vote is caught in the contradiction between what Barnes calls "love and anonymity" (55); in other words, she is caught in the contradiction between the private experience of lesbianism and the public record of history that makes the lesbian anonymous and invisible (Abraham 136).

6. On the "dual negation" of decadence, Rita Felski (107) cites A. E. Carter, *The Idea of Decadence in French Literature: 1830–1900* (Toronto: University of Toronto Press, 1958).

7. Vivien's 1904 trip to Mytilène was the first of many visits to the island, where she maintained a villa and returned "almost every year until her death in 1909" (Blankley 59).

8. Vivien's poem "La Soif impérieuse" ("The Insatiable Thirst") begins with the declaration, "Yesterday I was a solitary voyager"—"J'étais hier la voyageuse solitaire" (*Poèmes de Renée Vivien* 1).

9. Because Vivien does not oppose art and nature in the manner characteristic of male French writers working in the decadent tradition, Vivien departs from the fin-de-siècle dandy who uses artificiality as the basis for an escape from the commodification of modern culture. It is worth noting that, in this quote, Vivien ultimately longs for "a fresh green silence between living water and forests," a naturalized antidote to the ugliness of modern life. I will take up Vivien's relationship to the artificial in the next section, "So Blonde, So Pale."

10. In "Paroles à l'Amie" ("Words to a Lover") Vivien declares, "Et l'on a dit: 'Quelle est cette femme damnée/Que ronge sourdement la flamme de l'enfer?'" (*Poèmes de Renée Vivien* 39–40).

11. From this perspective, Vivien's morbid epitaph begins to make sense:

> My ravished soul, from mortal breath
> Appeased, forgets all former strife,
> Having, from its great love of Death,
> Pardoned the crime of crimes—called Life.
> (Faderman, *Suprassing the Love of Men* 363)
>
> Voici donc mon âme ravie,
> Car elle s'apaise et s'endort
> Ayant, pour l'amour de la Mort,
> Pardonné ce crime: la Vie.
> ("Épitaphe sur une Pierre tombale," *Poèmes de Renée Vivien* 5–8)

12.

> Je ne sais, présageant les mortelles douleurs,
> Si, dans la nuit lointaine où l'aurore succombe,
> Ton souffle n'a pas fui comme un souffle de fleurs,
> Sans effort d'agonie et sans râle et sans pleurs,
> et si ton lit d'amour n'est pas déjà la tombe.
> ("Sommeil," *Poèmes de Renée Vivien* 6–10)

13. The language I am using here echoes Vivien's in "D'après Swinburne" ("After Swinburne"):

It is sweet, for a little while, before death,
O *chère!* To tremble, to hope, to fear,
It is sweet, having drunk the ecstasy, to extinguish
Myself slowly, in autumnal agreement.
(Vivien, *Sweet Hour* 22)

Il est doux, pour un peu de temps, avant la mort,
O chère! de trembler, d'espérer et de craindre;
Il est doux, ayant bu l'extase, de s'éteindre
Avec lenteur, ainsi qu'un automnal accord. . . ."
(*Poèmes de Renée Vivien* 29–32)

14. Benjamin (*Charles Baudelaire* 55) quotes from Baudelaire's *Oeuvres*, ed. Yves-Gérard Le Dantec, vol. 1 (Paris, 1931–32) 420ff.

15. La nuit vient assombrir tes cheveux d'asphodèle,
Et les chauves-souris ont frappé de leur aile

Bleue et longue ma porte où l'ombre vient pleuvoir . . .
J'ai fait taire mon cœur que l'angoisse martèle,

Car la Mer et la Mort me rappellent, ce soir. . . .
("Départ," *Poèmes de Renée Vivien* 6–10)

16. Vivien explores her the attraction to Lesbos's "silvery" spell in her story, "Sappho Enchants the Sirens" (93).

17. For a treatment of Sappho's influence on lesbian modernists, see Benstock, *Women of the Left Bank*; Blankley; DeJean; Gilbert and Gubar; Marks; Prins.

18. Continuing for sixty years after its founding in 1909, Natalie Barney's salon at 20 rue Jacob has been extensively treated in biographies and literary studies, including Benstock; Chalon; DeJean; Jay; Weiss; Wickes. For a satiric depiction of Barney's coterie by one of its most distinguished members, see Barnes's *Ladies Almanack*. *Adventures of the Mind* offers valuable portraits of this literary and artistic circle by Barney herself.

19. My thinking here is indebted to Susan Buck-Morss, whose study of Benjamin's *Arcades Project* seeks to make visible "the difference between the repetition of the past and its redemption," locating a desire for utopia in the latter's "anticipatory images" (Buck-Morss 147).

20. Many of Vivien's poems that invoke Sappho and Lesbos are introduced with Sappho's poems or fragments (Sappho's fragments appear in small type and are positioned near the right margin). For examples of this technique, see Vivien's collection, *Sapho*, in *Poèmes de Renée Vivien*, from which the following poem is taken:

The stars around the beautiful moon
veil their clear faces when, in her
full, she illumines the earth with
gleams of silver.

All is white where the moon pours her shower.
At her feet groans the tormented sea.

Serene, she sees solitude flower
In the night, and chastity.

Before divine Selene the stars
Have veiled their shining faces, and the white,
Snowing from the candid sky, scars
The earth with silver light.
("All is white . . . ," *Muse*)

Les étoiles autour de la belle lune voilent aussitôt leur clair visage lorsque, dans son plein, elle illumine la terre de lueurs d'argent.

Tout est blanc, la lune ouvre sa plénitude,
A ses pieds gémit l'Océan tourmenté:
Sereine, elle voit fleurir la solitude
Et la chasteté.

Les astres, devant la Séléné divine,
Ont voilé leur face, et la clarté, neigeant
Du ciel virginal et candide, illumine
La terre d'argent.
("Tout est blanc . . . ," *Poèmes de Renée Vivien*)

21. Buck-Morss (291) is quoting Benjamin here. See *Gesammelte Schriften*, eds. Rolf Tiedemann and Hermann Schweppenhäuser, vol. 5 (Frankfurt am Main: Suhrkamp Verlag, 1972–) 588 (N7a, 3).

22. Although she represents the savagery within civilization, the prostitute is also the emblem for a particularly modern sensibility that Baudelaire valorizes: "What people call love is a very small, restricted feeble thing compared to this ineffable orgy, this holy prostitution of the soul that gives itself entire, poetry and charity, to the unexpected that appears, to the unknown that passes." This sacred form of surrender is an "unanchored empathetic capacity" that, in Baudelaire's formulation, the prostitute shares with the flâneur (Bernheimer 73).

23. "Lesbos, terre des nuits chaudes et langoureuses,/Qui font qu'à leurs miroirs, stérile volupté!/Les filles aux yeux creux, de leurs corps amoureuses" (Baudelaire, "Lesbos," *Les Fleurs du mal* 17–18).

24. On the connection between lesbianism and prostitution in France see Blankley; Corbin; Dean; Faderman; Hunt.

25. This tendency to represent whores as lesbians and lesbians as whores persists during the twentieth century, as Dean demonstrates in her work on the construction of lesbian sexuality in interwar France.

26. Tes cheveux irréels, aux reflects clairs et froids,
Ont de pâles lueurs et des matités blondes;
Tes regards ont l'azur des éthers et des ondes;
Ta robe a le frisson des brises et des bois.

Je brûle de baisers la blancheur de tes doigts.
L'air nocturne répand la poussière des mondes.

Pourtant je ne sais plus, au sein des nuits profondes,
Te contempler avec l'extase d'autrefois.

La lune t'effleura d'une lueur oblique . . .
Ce fut terrible autant qu'un éclair prophétique
Révélant la hideur au fond de ta beauté.

Je vis—comme l'on voit une fleur qui se fane—
Sur ta bouche, pareille aux aurores d'été,
Un sourire flétri de vieille courtisane.
("Sonnet," *Poèmes de Renée Vivien*)

27. Charles Bernheimer cites this excerpt from Edmond and Jules de Goncourt's *Journal* (vol. 1, 348) in *Figures of Ill-Repute: Representing Prostitution in Nineteenth-Century France* (102).

28. Et j'ignorerai la souillure et l'empreinte
Comme l'eau du fleuve et l'haleine du nord.
Je fuirai l'horreur sanglante de l'étreinte,
Du baiser qui mord.
("Je demeurerai . . . ," *Poèmes de Renée Vivien* 5–8)

29. "A une passante" is part of the "Parisian Scenes" section, which Baudelaire added to the 1861 edition of *Les Fleurs du mal.*

30. L'orgueil des lourds anneaux, la pompe des parures,
Mêlent l'éclat de l'art à ton charme pervers,
Et les gardénias qui parent les hivers
Se meurent dans tes mains aux caresses impures.

Ta bouche délicate aux fines ciselures
Excelle à moduler l'artifice des vers:
Sous les flots de satin savamment entr'ouverts,
Ton sein s'épanouit en de pâles luxures.

Le reflet des saphirs assombrit tes yeux bleus,
Et l'incertain remous de ton corps onduleux
Fait un sillage d'or au milieu des lumières.

Quand tu passes, gardent un sourire ténu,
Blond pastel surchargé de parfums et de pierres,
Je songe à la splendeur de ton corps libre et nu.
("Sonnet," *Poèmes de Renée Vivien*)

31. On prostitutes as women in revolt against society, see Baudelaire (*Painter of Modern Life* 37).

32. The entire poem reads as follows:

Sleep on the breast of your gentle mistress.

Sleep between the breasts of the conquered love. Rest,
Oh virgin in whose glance a brash adolescent gleams,

And let nuptial Hesperus lead you in your passionate quest
Toward happy dreams. ("Sleep between the breasts . . . ," *Muse*)
Dors sur le sein de ta tendre maîtresse.

Dors entre les seins de l'amante soumise,
O vierge au regard d'éphèbe valeureux,
Et que l'Hespérôs nuptial te conduise
Vers le rêve heureux!
("Dors entre les seins . . . ," *Poèmes de Renée Vivien*)

33. "Jamais vous ne pourrez assouvir votre rage,/Et votre châtiment naîtra de vos plaisirs" (Baudelaire, "Femmes damnées: Delphine et Hippolyte," *Les Fleurs du mal* 92).

34. Le ciel l'encadre ainsi que ferait une châsse,
Et je vivrais cent ans sans jamais la revoir.
Elle est soudaine: elle est le miracle du soir.
L'instant religieux brille et tinte. Elle passe . . .
("Elle passe," *Poèmes de Renée Vivien* 1–4)

35. O forme que les mains ne sauraient retenir!
Comme au ciel l'élusif arc-en-ciel s'évapore,
Ton sourire, en fuyant, laisse plus vide encore
Le cœur endolori d'un trop doux souvenir.
("Sonnet," *Poèmes de Renée Vivien* 1–4)

36. Vivien, "Qu'une vague l'emporte . . . ," *Poèmes de Renée Vivien* 8.

37. Notre amour participe aux choses infinies,
Absolu comme sont la mort et la beauté . . .
Voici, nos cœurs sont joints et nos mains sont unies
Fermement dans l'espace et dans l'éternité.
("Union," *Poèmes de Renée Vivien* 17–20)

38. In Baudelaire's account, the figure of the modern artist is not an artist "pure and simple" but an amalgamation of artist, dandy, and flâneur-poet; above all, he is a "spiritual citizen of the universe." See Baudelaire (*Painter of Modern Life* 6–7, 9).

39. Ta forme est un éclair qui laisse les bras vides,
Ton sourire est l'instant que l'on ne peut saisir . . .
Tu fuis, lorsque l'appel de mes lèvres avides
T'implore, ô mon Désir!
("*Ta forme est un éclair . . .*" 1–4)

40. Vivien, "*Je demeurerai . . .* ," *Poèmes de Renée Vivien* 1.

41. For a discussion of discourses about lesbian elusiveness in postwar France, see Carolyn Dean's exploration of lesbian invisibility in *The Frail Social Body* (171–215).

42. Les remous de la mer miroitaient dans ta robe.
Ton corps semblait le flot traître qui se dérobe.
Tu m'attirais vers toi comme l'abîme et l'eau;
Tes souples mains avaient le charme du réseau,

Et tes vagues cheveux flottaient sur ta poitrine,
Fluides et subtils comme l'algue marine.
Cet attrait décevant qui pare le danger
Rendait encor plus doux ton sourire léger;
Ton front me rappelait les profondeurs sereines,
Et tes yeux me chantaient la chanson des sirènes.
("Naïade moderne," *Poèmes de Renée Vivien*)

43. Les jours ondoyants que la clarté nuance,
Les nuits de parfums viendront éterniser
Nos frémissements, notre ardente souffrance
Et notre baiser.
("Dans les lendemains . . . ," *Poèmes de Renée Vivien* [11–12])

CHAPTER 3

1. This quote is from a letter Hall wrote to her friend and supporter, Newman Flower, of Cassells's publishing house on April 16, 1928. Determined to secure a publisher who would "stand behind" her novel, Hall wrote to Flower a few days prior to sending him the completed manuscript of *The Well of Loneliness* (Dickson 141). In the letter, she sought to inform him of the "nature" of the book and to state up front that she "could not consent to one word being modified or changed" (Cline 234). Hall continues:

> In a word, I have written a long and very serious novel entirely upon the subject of sexual inversion. So far as I know, nothing of the kind has ever been attempted before in fiction. Hitherto the subject has either been treated as pornography, or introduced as an episode as in *Dusty Answer*, or veiled as in *A Regiment of Women*. I have treated it as a fact in nature—a simple, though at present tragic, fact. I have written the life of a woman who is a born invert, and have done so with what I believe to be sincerity and truth; and while I have refused to camouflage in any way, I think I have avoided all unnecessary coarseness. (Dickson 140)

Despite her prior connection with Cassells and Flower's considerable admiration for her work, Hall was soon informed by Flower that Cassells was not an appropriate house for *The Well*.

2. The controversy surrounding the publication of *The Well* and its subsequent trial for obscenity in 1928 has been well documented. For accounts of *The Well*'s publication history and trial, as well as biographical information on Hall, see Baker; Cline; Dickson; Souhami. Una Troubridge, Hall's life partner, gives a firsthand account of these events in her biography, *The Life and Death of Radclyffe Hall*. For discussions of *The Well*'s trial in relation to the aesthetics of modernism and female modernist literary circles, see Benstock, *Women of the Left Bank*; Marcus, "Sapphistory"; Parkes; Scott.

3. For lesbian, feminist, and lesbian-feminist interpretations of *The Well of Loneliness* see Cook, Faderman; Gilbert and Gubar; Marcus; Newton; Radford; Ruehl;

Rule; Smith-Rosenberg; Stimpson; Whitlock. Although she also views the novel as a depiction of lesbian subjectivity, Teresa de Lauretis diverges from such feminists readings in order to explain—rather than dismiss—"the lure of the mannish lesbian." She provides a complex theory of lesbianism as fetishistic desire in *The Practice of Love*. For queer interpretations of *The Well* see Dollimore; Castle; Glasgow. For the most part, however, queer theorists and critics have steered clear of Hall's novel, as evidenced by its striking omission from the recent anthology, *Novel Gazing: Queer Readings in Fiction* (Sedgwick, ed.).

4. Revealing the logical contradictions presented by the notion of the womanly, female invert, Newton's essay concludes with the assertion that "Mary's real story has yet to be told" (Newton 293). Loralee MacPike seeks, in part, to take up this project by presenting the character of Mary Llewellyn as "an excellent standpoint from which to begin deconstructing sexology's lesbian" (77).

5. Hall probably would have considered Mary Llewellyn to be bisexual, not inverted (Glasgow 10).

6. For the "woman-identified" lesbian-feminist of the 1970s, the figure of the mannish or butch lesbian was typically perceived as an embarrassing example of false consciousness. Because it challenges rather than reproduces lesbian feminism's devaluation of female masculinity, Newton's work represents a significant shift in feminist thinking about gender variance.

7. Gert Hekma, for example, notes the enormous influence of Krafft-Ebing's *Psychopathia sexualis* in promoting this theoretical intertwining of homosexual preference and gender inversion: "Although not everybody accepted his mixture of gender and sexual inversion, it has nevertheless distinctly influenced the discussion on homosexuality to this day" (Hekma 226).

8. Although Hall's investment in a reification of sexual and gender categories is clear, Stephen Gordon's transgressive desires and embodiment must be recognized as profound challenges to the coherence and integrity of gendered norms.

9. Valérie Seymour offers an example of another form that nostalgia takes in *The Well*. Although relentlessly pursuing beauty within the ugliness of modernity, Valérie explicitly longs for the authentic aesthetic and erotic plentitude of Sappho's Lesbos. Like Renée Vivien and Natalie Barney, her heart is buried in Sappho's city of Mytilène (Hall 269). Whereas Gordon is depicted as nostalgic and yet modern, the figure of the perverse lesbian that Valérie embodies becomes an undialectical emblem of a decidely prelapsarian past. Hall reveals this most explicitly when, during a conversation with Valérie, Stephen is struck with the following realization: "And as they talked on it dawned upon Stephen that here was no mere libertine in love's garden, but rather a creature born out of her epoch, a pagan chained to an age that was Christian, one who would surely say with Pierre Louÿs: 'Le monde moderne succombe sous un envahissement de laideur'('The modern world is dying beneath a seige of ugliness')"[*my translation*] (Hall 246).

10. Foucault's highly influential *History of Sexuality: Volume I* offers the classic formulation of this argument. As Foucault asserts, the operation of power in modern cul-

ture is contingent upon a "specification" of individuals that imbeds sex in bodies (42–44).

11. This is not surprising, since Hall was quite familiar with the decadent tradition's representation of lesbianism. In 1911, for example, Hall studied nineteenth- and early twentieth-century French literature, focusing on Sapphic eroticism in writers such as Emile Zola (Cline 64).

12. Joseph Bristow explores this shift in the cultural history of manhood and masculinity in his *Effeminate England.* See especially Bristow's work the implications of the Wildean dandy-aesthete for gay and lesbian history and homoerotic literature in "Wilde's fatal effeminacy."

CHAPTER 4

1. Illustrating the increasing link between dandyism and homosexual "vice," historian George Chauncey notes that

> Granville Dill, an activist in the National Association for the Advancement of Colored People and the business manager of its magazine, *The Crisis*, was widely known and admired in Harlem circles. He had a reputation as a dandy, who always wore a bright chrysanthemum in his buttonhole and was known to engage in flamboyant behavior in public. In 1928, he was arrested in a subway washroom. W. E. B. Du Bois, the editor of *The Crisis*, promptly fired him. (*Gay New York* 198)

2. For discussions of the opposition of queerness and blackness in black cultural studies, as well as African American criticism's amnesia about the erotic affinities of writers ranging from Langston Hughes to James Baldwin see Butler; Clarke; Edelman; Gates; Hammonds; Harper; McBride; Mercer; Mercer and Julien; Somerville; Thomas. Recent studies of the Harlem Renaissance have increasingly attended to the centrality of queer identities and desires for African American modernism. See, for example, Boone; Cobb; Holcomb; Knadler; Maiwald; Ponce; Schwarz; Silberman; Wirth. Monica L. Miller examines the black dandy's anti-essentialism as a visible and controversial sign of black modernism, but her readings do not engage with the queerness of the African American dandy figure.

3. Kenneth Kushner's *The Great Migration and After* explores the social, political, and economic impact of African Americans' resettlement in the North and the emergence of a new black urban culture.

4. Van Vetchen's commodification of the "exotic material" of Harlem life was, interestingly enough, far from universally condemned among Renaissance writers. Langston Hughes, Wallace Thurman, Nella Larsen, and James Weldon Johnson were among Van Vetchen's supporters.

5. For an overview of Harlem's black cabarets, see Huggins 288–90 and Lewis 164–65, 208–11, and 242.

6. Tyler Stovall argues that the crucial difference between French and American notions of blackness was that, in France, Parisian intellectuals took black culture seriously, unlike the white American intellectuals who frequented Harlem nightspots (32).

7. Moers discusses Barbey D'Aurevilly's work as a pivotal shift toward remaking the dandy into the figure of the bohemian artist (264). On the merging of dandyism and bohemianism, see also Williams 116. Gluck argues that the bohemian serves as our stereotype of the modern artist (373). For a classic study of the bohemian and this figure's relationship to the politics of modernism, see Benjamin's discussion of the *bohème* in *Charles Baudelaire: A Lyric Poet in the Era of High Capitalism* 11–34.

8. It is not my project to investigate the dandy's challenge to gender norms—ground that is well tilled by numerous other studies. It is worth noting, however, that—for all its investment in dandyism as ambiguity, contradiction, and so on—this gendered reading often neglects to recognize the dandy's hypermasculinity (and antifeminism) in order to privilege his effeminacy as a form of gender rebellion. See chapter 1 for a discussion of contemporary scholarship on European dandyism as it relates to queer identity formation in modern culture.

9. As I hope the preceding chapters have made clear, my understanding of the relation between desire and value relies on Marx's formulation in *Capital*, Vol. 1 and Baudrillard's theory of desire in exchange value. Of central importance here is the fetish character of commodities, which founds capitalism on a contradiction, mobilizing desire and promising a satisfaction that cannot be fulfilled. Lack and negativity are fundamental to the sphere of value because, as Baudrillard puts it, "desire is not fulfilled there in the phantasm of value" (*For a Critique* 207).

10. Challenging the Western separation of the spiritual and the corporeal, Paul calls his boldly erotic and unabashedly phallic designs "spirit portraits" (133).

11. I am thinking here of Beardsley's notoriously phallic drawings to illustrate Arisophanes's *Lysistrata*. Since Paul is widely known to be modeled on Richard Bruce Nugent, it is worth noting that "by the end of his teens Nugent had become an extravagant decadent, and he began to draw in the style of Aubrey Beardsley" (Watson, *Harlem Renaissance* 90). For an insightful study of Nugent's transformation of Wildean and Beardsleyan aesthetics in the context of his *Salomé* series, see Ellen McBreen. Thomas H. Wirth's definitive collection of Nugent's drawings, paintings, and writings also notes the influence of Beardsley, Huysmans, and Wilde on the artist.

12. In his study of the Harlem Renaissance, Hutchinson argues that the importance of American cultural nationalism to African American modernism has been "ignored or repressed" in the vast majority of accounts of the movement (14).

13. Although he emphasized black Americans' privileged relationship to their African "fatherland," Du Bois linked the experience and political goals of African Americans with the liberation of the world's people of color. On the role of pan-Africanism in Du Bois's art and politics, see Rampersad.

14. Hutchinson's study, which argues that interracial affiliations fundamentally shaped the Harlem arts movement, is an important exception.

15. In his persistent rebukes of the younger generation for their decline into decadence, Du Bois seems to refute Baudelaire's claim that modernity and decadence are fundamentally linked. Nevertheless, in his attacks on the increasing "decadence" of the Renaissance, Du Bois actually provides evidence for the Baudelairean theory he disputes.

16. For an examination of the stylistic structure and thematic concerns of African art, as well as the relationship between primitivism and modernism, see Baldwin et al. and Szalay.

17. Aubrey Beardsley's decadent aesthetic and the contradictions of the "Beardsley Period" are explored in Calloway's *Aubrey Beardsley*; Snodgrass; Wilson.

18. Debora Silverman locates the rococo model in the social and political context of art nouveau and the decorative arts movement (9).

19. In *The Souls of Black Folk*, Du Bois concludes his discussion of the "sorrow songs" with the declaration: "Here we have brought our three gifts and mingled them with yours: a gift of story and song—soft, stirring melody in an ill-harmonized and unmelodious land" (186). For a discussion of folk forms and African American modernism, see Nicholls.

20. My logic draws on Paul Gilroy's influential study of the institution and experience of slavery and its relationship to the construction of modernity. From the perspective of racist, colonialist ideology, what Gilroy calls "the black Atlantic" constitutes a counterculture of modernity.

21. Very much like Wilde's Dorian Gray, Paul's death is marked by an excess of color and a theatrical aestheticism.

CHAPTER 5

1. Burroughs embraced the word "queer" as early as 1952 (instead of the more clinical term "homosexual"). A gesture at once resistant and repressive, this strategic appropriation is always linked to Burroughs's tendency to privilege the supposedly strong, masculine "queer" over and against the weak, swishy "fag." I will discuss the implications of this masculinist gesture, as well as Burroughs's complex relationship to femininity, in detail.

2. The following abbreviations will be used in citations: J (*Junky*); Q (*Queer*); NL (*Naked Lunch*); YL (*Yage Letters*). Due to the complex publishing history of Burroughs's early work, I include here a brief summary of that history as it pertains to the preceding works. Writing under the pseudonym William Lee, Burroughs published *Junkie: Confessions of an Unredeemed Drug Addict* with pulp publisher Ace Books in 1953. He originally titled his book *Junk*, but this title was rejected by A. A. Wyn of Ace as well as Penguin, who republished the novel as *Junky* in 1977. Although written in 1952 at the same time as the author was working on the *Junk* manuscript, *Queer* was not published until 1985. *Naked Lunch* was first published by Maurice Girodias of Olympia Press in 1959; however, the novel was embroiled in a long censorship con-

troversy that was not resolved until 1966 when the Massachusetts Supreme Court ruled that the novel possessed "redeeming social value" and was therefore "not obscene." Finally, I will be referring primarily to the first section of *Yage Letters*, entitled "In Search of Yage," which was written in 1953. Although the piece is presented as letters written to Allen Ginsberg, Burroughs invented the majority of these "letters" using material drawn from his own travel notes (Harris 177). For a detailed, critical discussion of the literary history of these works, see Harris.

3. I am indebted to Corber's analysis of the ways in which Fordism's reorganization of masculinity prompted widespread anxiety about the penetration of male subjectivity by the commodity form (*Homosexuality in Cold War America* 14).

4. In *Junky* a different sort of nostalgia is also present in Burroughs's appreciation for a vanishing criminal underworld of "old time thieves" and pickpockets. As he states in a 1965 interview, these thieves were "show business" in their glory days but now are reduced to a "dying race" of old timers (*Burroughs Live* 72).

5. Describing his experience living in Tangier in the 1950s and 1960s, Burroughs claims that "the special attraction to Tangier can be put in one word: exemption. Exemption from interference, legal or otherwise. Your private life is your own, to act exactly as you please. . . . Tangier is one of the few places in the world where, so long as you don't proceed to robbery, violence or some form of crude, antisocial behavior, you can do exactly as you want. It is a sanctuary of noninterference" (*Word Virus* 128). For a biographical account of Burroughs's experience in Tangier, see Miles.

6. Kasturi Ray alerted me to this distinction between the solitary figure of the postwar heroin addict and the feminized and racialized sociality of opium dens.

7. To cite a few examples, see Ayers; Morelyle; Murphy; Savran. Murphy argues that the transformation of the individual into an "'addict agent' who is the mirror image of the controller" characterizes all of Burroughs's early work (4).

8. This line of thinking is reflected in a *New York Times* article by Robert C. Doty, "Narcotic Menace Held Nation-Wide," which appeared on June 18, 1951. Doty quotes various experts, including a criminologist, who posits that the "social disintegration" that characterizes urban life—including "poverty, alcoholism and racial prejudice"—caused the nationwide "epidemic" of juvenile addiction. Although certainly the intention here is to extend sympathy to these young addicts, the liberal logic of the piece nevertheless installs a pre-criminalized identity and status on the junkie.

9. Hereafter I will be using the now conventional spelling of the author's first novel, which is *Junky*.

10. For an example of a more typical pulp treatment of the theme of addiction, see Leroy Street's moralistic *I Was a Drug Addict*, which was published by Random House in 1953, the same year Burroughs's text appeared.

11. As Lee Server notes, the pulps were considered "depraved and dangerous reading" by some educators, psychologists, and religious and civic organizations (19). In 1952, a House Select Committee on Current Pornographic Materials investigated the threat of paperback novels. The chairman of the committee, Rep. E. C. Gathings,

declared that pocket-size books "have largely degenerated" into "artful appeals to sensuality, immorality, filth, perversion, and degeneracy."

12. For accounts of cold war homosexuality along these lines, see Corber's *Homosexuality in Cold War America*; D'Emilio's "The Homosexual Menace" and *Sexual Politics, Sexual Communities*; Edelman; Hauser; Johnson; Miller. Arguing that "homosexual difference produces the imperative to recognize and expose it," Edelman proposes that the era's contradictory representations of the gay male body are constitutive of homosexual identity itself ("Tearooms and Sympathy" 571, n. 23).

13. Corber develops this claim in *Homosexuality in Cold War America.*

14. See Berube; D'Emilio; D'Emilio and Freedman.

15. On lesbian identities, representations and communities in the 1940s and 1950s, see Corber's "Cold War Femme"; Faderman; Kennedy and Davis; and Nestle's classic essay, "Butch-Fem Relationships: Sexual Courage in the 1950s" in *A Restricted Country*.

16. For an examination of the implications of this move for a queer reading of Burroughs's fiction, see Russell.

17. It is worth noting that Burroughs's figuration of the queer junkie puts forward a radically shameless model of queer identification. As Burroughs asserts in *Naked Lunch*, "Junkies have no shame. . . . They are impervious to the repugnance of others" (NL 57).

18. Bronski discusses postwar wounded models of masculinity in the context of gay male pulp fiction.

CHAPTER 6

1. Andy Warhol, as quoted in Richard A. Ogar, "Warhol Mind Warp," *The Berkeley Barb*, 1–7 September 1968, n.p.; as cited by Benstock (11).

2. For an excellent study of Warhol's performance of naiveté and his transformation of the "historically and conceptually intertwined personae of the naif (or fool) and the trickster," see Cresap (5).

3. Truman Capote, as quoted in Jones (240).

4. In his *Time Capsules* (1974–1987), Warhol saved countless objects and materials that passed across his desk or through his hands on a given day (the capsules numbered over six hundred by the time of his death). In fact, as Pat Hackett notes in her introduction to *The Diary of Andy Warhol*, "less than one percent of all the items that he was constantly being sent or given did he keep for himself or give away. All the rest were 'for the box': things he considered 'interesting,' which to Andy, who was interested in everything, meant literally everything" (xv). Because newspaper and magazine articles are so frequently included, the Time Capsules contain many examples of the cool and vacant persona Warhol projected to the press. To cite one example, in 1971, when Andy visited Britain to advocate for an X certificate for the general release of his

film *Trash*, Geoffrey Matthews writes about the frustrating experience of "interviewing" the artist: "Mr. Warhol, you say respectfully, and pose a question. The reply is either 'Ahhh . . . yes' or 'Ahhhh . . . no.'" Later in the article, Matthews continues, "Paul Morrissey, the director of several Warhol films, said: 'Andy is a non-verbal type of person.' It sounded like the understatement of the year" (Matthews). On Warhol as an interviewer for his own magazine, *Interview*, see Bockris (370–71).

5. As an example, we may consider Richard Morphet's essay in the catalogue for the "Warhol" exhibition at the Tate Gallery in London in 1971. Morphet argues that, although Warhol's choices of images "inevitably constitute one picture of a late twentieth-century mass urban culture" (20), the primary significance of Warhol's work is the "new vitality" it has given to the material and process of artmaking (32). Although my project departs from the high-art standpoint of which Morphet is representative, I agree with Morphet's suggestion that the formal elements of Warhol's work—especially the inextricability of vision, image, material, and process—have been underemphasized.

6. Of course, Warhol himself invited this account of his work as an aesthetics of surface, famously asserting in a 1967 interview that "if you want to know all about Andy Warhol, just look at the surface of my paintings and films and me, and there I am. There's nothing behind it" (Berg 56).

7. The assumptions of the high-art position are echoed in various influential readings informed by poststructuralism and postmodernism. Critics as disparate as Jean Baudrillard and Fredric Jameson seem to agree that the "depthlessness" of Warhol's work makes it paradigmatic of "the postmodernist moment" (Jameson 9). Dubbed the "simulacral reading of Warholian pop" by Hal Foster, these accounts tend to locate in Warhol a critique of representation that dismisses any humanist nostalgia for individuality or affect; instead, works like the Marilyn pictures are said to reframe the real as a simulation without origin or objectivity—a mirror of images that represents nothing at all (Foster 128). Foster opposes the "simulacral" and "referential" readings of Warhol's work, arguing instead for a third, Lacanian-inflected model he calls "traumatic realism," in which repetition "serves to *screen* the real understood as traumatic" (132). See Crimp (1998) for an interesting discussion of Foster's analysis. Drawing on Meyer's work (1995), Crimp offers a queer reading of Warholian repetition, which he asserts invokes "the sex appeal of the same."

8. For example, regarding his painting, one thinks immediately of Warhol's selection and placement of the image, repetition of the image, use of color and paint, scale, and use of the silkscreen printing process.

9. John W. Smith, archivist, the Andy Warhol Museum. Personal conversation. September 10, 2003.

10. The mirror quote is Warhol's from *The Philosophy* (7).

11. I am not the first scholar to combine a focus on Warhol's sexuality with a sustained attention to the context of capitalism. In his insightful study of camp and queer cinema, Matthew Tinkcom presents camp as a critical philosophy of modernity that enables Warhol (and other queer men) to express sex/gender dissidence, forge their

own ways of consuming mass culture, and also—most crucially—articulate new forms of cultural production that attend to "the centrality of the commodity and labor in contemporary life" (75). In addition to Tinkcom's theory of Warholian camp as a form of "queer labor," see Doyle; Flatley; Suárez. Other queer scholarship has addressed the iconography of commodity culture in Warhol's work or interpreted such images in light of their sexual content: as evidence of a gay sensibility that violates gender prescriptions and delights in the feminized pleasures of consumer culture. See Berger; Cresap; Crimp; Doyle; Dyer; Fairbrother; Francis and King; Grundmann; Hailey; Jones; Katz; Koestenbaum; Meyer; Nochlin; Siegal.

12. "Pop dandyism" should not be confused with camp, a related but distinct sensibility I explore later in the chapter. It is worth noting that Pop dandyism possesses many of the characteristics of the flâneur. In a fascinating essay on Warhol discussing the figures of the flâneur and the dandy and their centrality to Baudelaire's account of modernity, Patrizia Lombardo uses these two figures to situate Warhol's opposing tendencies within "the constitutive tension of modernity, the interplay between love and scorn for the crowd, or, in other words, between mass and élite culture, between a movement of revolt and its framing within the very system it wants to denounce. The dandy and flâneur are two halves of the modern artist—and what probably makes Andy Warhol exemplary is that his artistic behavior is equally made up of both attitudes" (Lombardo 36).

13. Fordism, which had its heyday in the 1950s and 1960s, was characterized by intensive accumulation, high productivity, mass consumption, extension of wage labor, state regulation of the economy, automation, standardization, and the increasing penetration of capital into American society. See Amin; Gramsci; Harvey; Hefferen. In his classic study, "Americanism and Fordism," Gramsci argues that Fordism's rationalization of production and work requires "a new type of man" whose sexuality is also regulated and rationalized (282).

14. I am indebted to Richard Meyer's discussion of gay male aesthetic expression as "outlaw representation." My argument also draws on Robert Corber's analysis of the ways in which the emergence of a distinctly gay macho style—a theatrically masculine sensibility—functions as a rebellion against the reorganization of masculinity in the 1940s and 1950s in particular and the domesticated values of the white middle class in general.

15. In a fascinating "rethinking" of the concept of reification—usually understood as a category of domination in Marxist theory—Kevin Floyd argues that Marcuse fleshes out a qualitative and dialectical notion of reification that embraces its positive and liberatory possibilities. By, paradoxically, turning the body into an object, and thus "polymorphously re-eroticizing" it, the use of the body as an instrument for pleasure and the erotic has the potential to negate its reification by instrumental reason. This "erotics of reification" (Floyd, "Rethinking Reification" 104) is, I will argue, precisely the direction in which Warhol's queer aesthetics moves. For a queer Marxist examination of reification and totality, see Floyd's *The Reification of Desire*.

16. Following Harvey and Heffernan, I see Fordist modernity and postmodernist flexibility not as static or stable socioeconomic and cultural configurations but expressions of "the flux of internal relations within capitalism as a whole" (Harvey, *The Con-*

dition of Postmodernity 342). From this perspective, "Fordism" and "post-Fordism" can be understood as processes that articulate a problematic within the logic of capital; in other words, they "do not so much specify answers as map out broad fields of investigation and posit key questions for contestation and argument (Heffernan 214).

17. For a discussion of the philosophical questions raised by *Brillo Box*, see Danto.

18. Warhol as quoted in Katz (n.p.).

19. My reading here is indebted to Katz's analysis.

20. Warhol was a very successful, award-winning illustrator throughout the 1950s and continued to work in the commercial art world secretly in the early 1960s, when he was transforming himself into a Pop artist. See *Andy Warhol: Drawings and Illustrations of the 1950s* and De Salvo's *"Success Is a Job in New York . . .": The Early Art and Business of Andy Warhol.*

21. Buchloh makes a similar point about the ways in which Warhol's early art-making and collecting express a yearning for "noncommercial charm" (7).

22. It is worth noting Warhol's use of gold paper, since metallic surfaces are often associated with the appeal of the artificial and the seductions of commodity culture (a topic I will be exploring in the next section of this chapter). Warhol's gold-plated image of James Dean becomes a perfect emblem for the imbrication of the artificial and the authentic I wish to emphasize.

23. See Bronksi's *The Pleasure Principle* (160–70) on the role of pornography in shaping gay male self-definition from the 1950s to the 1980s.

24. *Body Beautiful: Studies in Masculine Art*, from *Time Capsule 44*—containing mostly magazines from the 1950s and 1960s—is a perfect example.

25. As Bronski points out, the image of the "wild one" or J.D. was closely linked with homosexuality in the culture of the 1950s: both juvenile delinquency and homosexuality were seen as social illnesses (91).

26. Here, Corber refers to the nostalgia of film noir.

27. Warhol himself argued that his films became unwatchable (Tinkcom 113).

28. Approaching Warhol's work dialectically, my argument is that the artist's "earnestness" and nostalgic yearning for authenticity can only be grasped in and through their connections with his embrace of camp artifice. For a quintessential example of Warholian artifice, we might consider the ways in which *The Exploding Plastic Inevitable*, Warhol's multimedia collaboration with the Velvet Underground, expresses the artist's celebration of a decadent aesthetic that rejects the earnest, hippie values of peace and love. Even the use of the word "plastic"—a buzzword for hollow, commerical culture of the 1950s and 1960s (Dyer 152–53)—suggests a Warholian affection for all that the counterculture considered fake and inauthentic. As Warhol puts it in *POPism*: "vacant, vacuous Hollywood was everything I ever wanted to mold my life into. Plastic. White-on-white . . . it looked like it would be so easy to just walk into a room the way those actors did and say those wonderful plastic lines" (40). On the EPI, see Bockris and Malanga; Warhol's *POPism*; Watson's *Factory Made.*

29. Despite Geldzahler's suggestion to the contrary, Aubrey Beardsley's aesthetic was not in fact "invented" by Wilde.

30. On camp as queer aesthetics and/or queer cultural practice see Bergman, *Camp Grounds* and "Strategic Camp"; Cleto; Newton, "Role Models"; Sontag; Tinkcom.

31. Warhol elaborates on his famous claim—"I like boring things"—in *POPism* (50).

32. Warhol comments on his swish performance in the context of the macho postwar art world: "You'd have to see the way all the Abstract Expressionist painters carried themselves and the kinds of images they cultivated, to understand how shocked people were to see a painter coming on swish. I certainly wasn't a butch kind of guy by nature, but I must admit, I went out of my way to play up the other extreme" (*POPism* 12–13).

33. Cresap makes a similar point in his study, which critiques what he sees as an oversimplified treatment of the "real" and "fake" Warhols in Colacello's biography (54).

34. See Bratby; Hughes.

35. The source for this quote is a personal conversation I had with Terrence E. Dempsey, director of the Museum of Contemporary Religious Art (MOCRA), St. Louis University, St. Louis, Missouri, January 2002.

36. The artist did a television interview during this time in which he stated, "You open a window and let them float away and that's one less object." Warhol's presentation of the clouds as disposable art, however, did not help sales according to Bourdon (*Warhol* 230).

37. One of my favorite examples of this strategy is when—shortly after graduating from art school and moving to New York in 1950—Warhol met Greta Garbo and gave her a drawing of a butterfly, which she then crumpled up and threw away. He reclaimed the drawing and retitled it *Crumpled Butterfly by Greta Garbo.*

38. As many critics have pointed out, Warhol opposed his "swish" sensibility to the macho Abstract Expressionist tradition, which "went along with their agonized, anguished art" (*POPism* 12–13).

AFTERWORD

1. Rebecca Voight, "A New Dandyism Takes Shape," *International Herald Tribune*, January 18, 2005.

2. Mari Davis, "Les Hommes Menswear Spring 2007: A New Perspective of Dandyism," *Fashion Windows*, June 27, 2006.

3. Roberta Smith, "That Imperial Punk," *New York Times*, May 5, 2006.

4. For example, journalist Linda Immediato declared a "West Coast–East Coast" fight between LA dandies such as Christian M. Chensvold and Michael Mattis and East Coast dandies such as Lord Whimsy. Chensvold and Mattis, the creators of

Dandyism.net, separate their own hypermasculinist, James Bond-inspired vision of dandyism from what they see as East Coast bohemianism. "Gentleman's Disagreement," *LA Weekly*, November 1, 2006.

5. For discussions of the the role of the gay market, commodity culture, and the politics of visibility in gay/queer politics and theory, see Chasin; Hennessy; Sender; Walters.

BIBLIOGRAPHY

Abelove, Henry, Michèle Aina Barale, and David M. Halperin, eds. *The Lesbian and Gay Studies Reader*. New York: Routledge, 1993.

Abraham, Julie. *Are Girls Necessary?: Lesbian Writing and Modern Histories*. New York: Routledge, 1996.

Adams, James Eli. *Dandies and Desert Saints: Styles of Victorian Masculinity*. Ithaca: Cornell University Press, 1995.

Adorno, Theodor. *Prisms*. Trans. Samuel and Shierry Weber. Cambridge: MIT Press, 1981.

Adorno, Theodor, and Max Horkheimer. *Dialectic of Enlightenment*. London: Verso, 1979.

Algren, Nelson. *The Man with the Golden Arm: A Novel*. Garden City, NY: Doubleday, 1949.

Allen, Carolyn. *Following Djuna: Women Lovers and the Erotics of Loss*. Bloomington: Indiana University Press, 1996.

Althusser, Louis, and Étienne Balibar. *Reading "Capital."* Trans. Ben Brewster. London: NLB, 1970.

Amin, Ash, ed. *Post-Fordism: A Reader*. Oxford: Blackwell, 1994.

Auslander, Leora. "The Gendering of Consumer Practices in Nineteenth-Century France." *The Sex of Things: Gender and Consumption in Historical Perspective*. Ed. Victoria de Grazia, with Ellen Furlough Berkeley: University of California Press, 1996. 79–112.

Ayers, David. "The Long Last Goodbye: Control and Resistance in the Work of William Burroughs." *Journal of American Studies* 27 (1993): 223–36.

Baker, Houston A. *Modernism and the Harlem Renaissance*. Chicago: University of Chicago Press, 1987.

Baker, Michael. *Our Three Selves: A Life of Radclyffe Hall.* London: GMP, 1985.

Baldwin, James, et al. *Perspectives: Angles on African Art.* New York: Center for African Art; Harry N. Abrams, Inc., 1987.

Barnes, Djuna. *Collected Stories.* Ed. Phillip Herring. Los Angeles: Sun and Moon, 1996.

———. *Ladies Almanack.* Normal, IL: Dalkey Archive, 1992.

———. *Nightwood.* New York: New Directions, 1961.

Barney, Natalie Clifford. *Adventures of the Mind.* Trans. John Spalding Gatton. 1929. New York: New York University Press, 1992.

Barthes, Roland. *The Language of Fashion.* Trans. Andy Stafford; Eds. Andy Stafford and Michael Carter. Oxford: Berg, 2006.

Battcock, Gregory. "The Andy Warhol Generation." *Other Scenes* 4.9 (1970): n.p. *Time Capsule 7.* Archives of the Andy Warhol Museum, Pittsburgh.

Baudelaire, Charles. *Artificial Paradises.* 1860. Trans. Stacy Diamond. Reprint, New York: Citadel-Carol, 1996.

———. *The Flowers of Evil.* Trans. James McGowan. 1861. Oxford: Oxford University Press, 1993.

———. *My Heart Laid Bare and Other Prose Writings.* Trans. Norman Cameron. New York: Vanguard, 1951.

———. *The Painter of Modern Life and Other Essays.* Trans. Jonathan Mayne. 2nd ed. London: Phaidon, 1995.

Baudrillard, Jean. *For a Critique of the Political Economy of the Sign.* Trans. Charles Levin. St. Louis: Telos, 1981.

———. *Selected Writings.* Ed. Mark Poster. Stanford: Stanford University Press, 1988.

Bech, Henning. *When Men Meet: Homosexuality and Modernity.* Trans. Teresa Mesquit and Tim Davies. Chicago: University of Chicago Press, 1997.

Benjamin, Walter. *The Arcades Project.* Trans. Howard Eiland and Kevin McLaughlin. Cambridge: Harvard University Press, 1999.

———. *Charles Baudelaire: A Lyric Poet in the Era of High Capitalism.* Trans. Harry Zohn. London: Verso, 1983.

———. *Illuminations.* Trans. Harry Zohn. Ed. Hannah Arendt. New York: Schocken, 1969.

———. *Reflections.* Trans. Edmund Jephcott. New York: Schocken, 1986.

Benstock, Shari. "Expatriate Sapphic Modernism: Entering Literary History." *Lesbian Text and Contexts: Radical Revisions.* Ed. Karla Jay and Joanne Glasgow. New York: New York University Press, 1990. 183–203.

———. "Paris Lesbianism and the Politics of Reaction, 1900–1940." *Hidden from History: Reclaiming the Gay and Lesbian Past.* Ed. Martin Duberman, Martha Vicinus, and George Jr. Chauncey. New York: Meridian, 1990. 332–46.

———. *Women of the Left Bank: Paris, 1900–1940.* Austin: University of Texas Press, 1986.

Berg, Gretchen. "Andy Warhol: My True Story." *The East Village Other* 1 Nov. 1966. Rpt. in *I'll Be Your Mirror: The Selected Andy Warhol Interviews*. Ed. Kenneth Goldsmith. New York: Carroll and Graf, 2004. 85–96.

Bergman, David, ed. *Camp Grounds: Style and Homosexuality*. Amherst: University of Massachusetts Press, 1993.

———. "Strategic Camp: The Art of Gay Rhetoric." *Camp Grounds: Style and Homosexuality*. Ed. David Bergman. Amherst: University of Massachusetts Press, 1993. 92–190.

Bernheimer, Charles. *Figures of Ill-Repute: Representing Prostitution in Nineteenth-Century France*. Cambridge: Harvard University Press, 1989.

Berube, Alan. *Coming Out Under Fire: The History of Gay Men and Women in World War Two*. New York: Free Press, 1990.

Birken, Lawrence. *Consuming Desire: Sexual Science and the Emergence of a Culture of Abundance, 1871–1914*. Ithaca, Cornell University Press, 1988.

Blackmore, David. "'Something . . . Too Preposterous and Complex to Be Recognized or Considered': Same-Sex Desire and Race in *Infants of the Spring*." *Soundings* 80.4 (1997): 519–29.

Blankley, Elyse. "Return to Mytilène: Renée Vivien and the City of Women." *Women Writers and the City: Essays in Feminist Literary Criticism*. Ed. Susan Merrill Squier. Knoxville: University of Tennessee Press, 1984.

Blessing, Jennifer. "Claude Cahun, Dandy Provocateuse." *Dandies: Fashion and Finesse in Art and Culture*. Ed. Susan Fillin-Yeh. New York: New York University Press, 2001. 185–203.

Bockris, Victor. *Warhol: The Biography*. Cambridge: Da Capo Press, 2003.

——— and Gerard Malanga. *Up-Tight. The Story of the Velvet Underground*. London: Omnibus Press, 1996.

Bongie, Chris. "Exotic Nostalgia: Conrad and the New Imperialism." *Macropolitics of Nineteenth-Century Literature*. Ed. Jonathan Arac and Harriet Ritvo. Durham: Duke University Press, 1995. 268–85.

Boone, Joseph Allen. *Libidinal Currents: Sexuality and the Shaping of Modernism*. Chicago: University of Chicago Press, 1998.

Bourdieu, Pierre. *Distinction: A Social Critique of the Judgement of Taste*. Trans. Richard Nice. Cambridge: Harvard University Press, 1984.

Bourdon, David. "Andy's Dish." *Raid the Icebox I (with Andy Warhol): An Exhibition Selected from the Storage Vaults of the Museum of Art, Rhode Island School of Design*. Providence: Museum of Art, Rhode Island School of Design, 1969.

———. *Warhol*. New York: Abrams, 1989.

Bratby, John. "Bratby v Warhol, the Egocentric Non-Plastic Souperstar." *The Sunday Times* [London] 21 February 1971: n.p. *Time Capsule 7*. Archives of the Andy Warhol Museum, Pittsburgh.

Bristow, Joseph. *Effeminate England: Homoerotic Writing After 1885*. New York: Columbia University Press, 1995.

———. "Wilde, *Dorian Gray* and Gross Indecency." *Sexual Sameness: Textual Differences in Lesbian and Gay Writing*. Ed. Joseph Bristow. London: Routledge, 1992. 44–63.

———. "'A Complex Multiform Creature': Wilde's Sexual Identities." *The Cambridge Companion to Oscar Wilde*. Ed. Peter Raby. Cambridge: Cambridge University Press, 1997. 195–218.

Bronski, Michael. *Cultural Clash: The Making of Gay Sensibility*. Boston: South End, 1984.

———. *The Pleasure Principle: Sex, Backlash, and the Struggle for Gay Freedom*. New York: St. Martin's, 1998.

———, ed. *Pulp Friction: Uncovering the Golden Age of Gay Male Pulps*. New York: St. Martin's, 2003.

Buchloh, Benjamin H. D. "Andy Warhol's One-Dimensional Art: 1956–1966." *Andy Warhol*. Ed. Annette Michelson. Cambridge: MIT Press, 2001. 1–46.

Buck-Morss, Susan. *The Dialectics of Seeing: Walter Benjamin and the Arcades Projects*. Cambridge: MIT Press, 1990.

Burroughs, William S. *The Adding Machine: Selected Essays*. New York: Arcade, 1986.

———. *Junky: The Definitive Text of "Junk."* 1953. Ed. Oliver Harris. Reprint, New York: Penguin, 2003.

———. *The Letters of William S. Burroughs 1945–1959*. Ed. Oliver Harris. London: Picador, 1993.

———. *Naked Lunch: The Restored Text*. 1959. Ed. James Grauerholz and Barry Miles. Reprint, New York, Grove, 2001.

———. *Queer*. New York, Viking-Penguin, 1985.

———. *Word Virus: The William S. Burroughs Reader*. Ed. James Grauerholz and Ira Silverberg. New York: Grove, 1998.

Burroughs, William S., and Allen Ginsberg. *The Yage Letters*. 1963. Reprint, San Francisco: City Lights, 1975.

Butler, Judith. "Against Proper Objects." *differences: A Journal of Feminist Literary Studies* 6.2–3 (1994): 1–26.

———. *Bodies That Matter: On the Discursive Limits of Sex*. New York: Routledge, 1993.

———. *Gender Trouble: Feminism and the Subversion of Identity*. New York: Routledge, 1990.

Calinescu, Matei. *Five Faces of Modernity: Modernism, Avant-Garde, Decadence, Kitsch, Postmodernism*. Durham: Duke University Press, 1987.

Calloway, Stephen. *Aubrey Beardsley*. New York: Abrams, 1998.

———. "Wilde and the Dandyism of the Senses" *The Cambridge Companion to Oscar Wilde*. Ed. Peter Raby. Cambridge: Cambridge University Press, 1997. 34–54.

Cartwright, David T. *Dark Paradise: A History of Opiate Addiction in America*. Cambridge: Harvard University Press, 2001.

Castle, Terry. *Noël Coward and Radclyffe Hall: Kindred Spirits*. New York: Columbia University Press, 1996.

Chalon, Jean. *Portrait of a Seductress: The World of Natalie Barney*. Trans. Carol Barko. New York: Crown, 1979.

Chasin, Alexandra. *Selling Out: The Gay and Lesbian Movement Goes to Market*. New York: St. Martin's, 2000.

Chauncey, George. "From Sexual Inversion to Homosexuality: Medicine and the Changing Conceptualization of Female Deviancy." *Salmagundi* 58/59 (Fall–Winter 1983): 114–46.

———. *Gay New York: Gender, Urban Culture and the Making of the Gay World, 1890–1940*. New York: Basic Books, 1994.

Cicolini, Alice. *The New English Dandy*. New York: Assouline, 2005.

Clarke, Cheryl. "The Failure to Transform: Homophobia in the Black Community." *Homegirls: A Black Feminist Anthology*. Ed. Barbara Smith. New York: Kitchen Table-Women of Color Press, 1983. 197–208.

Clarke, David B., Marcus A. Doel, and Kate M. L. Housiaux, eds. *The Consumption Reader*. London: Routledge, 2003.

Clarke, Eric O. *Virtuous Vice: Homoeroticism and the Public Sphere*. Durham: Duke University Press, 2000.

Cleaver, Eldridge. *Soul on Ice*. New York: Bantam, 1992.

Cleto, Fabio, ed. *Camp: Queer Aesthetics and the Performing Subject*. Ann Arbor: University of Michigan Press, 1999.

Cline, Sally. *Radclyffe Hall: A Woman Called John*. Woodstock, NY: Overlook Press, 1998.

Cobb, Michael L. "Insolent Racing, Rough Narrative: The Harlem Renaissance's Impolite Queers." *Callaloo* 23.1 (2000): 328–51.

Cohen, Ed. *Talk on the Wilde Side: Toward a Genealogy of a Discourse on Male Sexualities*. New York: Routledge, 1993.

Colacello, Bob. *Holy Terror: Andy Warhol Close Up*. New York: HarperCollins, 1990.

Colette, Sidonie Gabrielle. *The Pure and the Impure*. Trans. Herma Briffault. 1932. New York: Farrar, Straus and Giroux, 1966.

Cook, Blanche Wiesen. "'Women Alone Stir My Imagination': Lesbianism and the Cultural Tradition." *Signs: Journal of Women in Culture and Society* 4.4 (Summer 1979): 718–39.

Corber, Robert J. "Cold War Femme: Lesbian Visibility in Joseph L. Mankiewicz's *All About Eve.*" *GLQ: A Journal of Lesbian and Gay Studies* 11.1 (2004): 1–22.

———. *Homosexuality in Cold War America: Resistance and the Crisis of Masculinity.* Durham: Duke University Press, 1997.

Corbin, Alain. *Women for Hire: Prostitution and Sexuality in France After 1850.* Trans. Alan Sheridan. Cambridge: Harvard University Press, 1990.

Cornforth, Maurice. *Materialism and the Dialctical Method.* Vol. 1. New York: International, 1971.

Cosindas, Marie. "The Dandies of Marie Cosindas." *Camera* 9 (September 1967): n.p. *Time Capsule 14.* Archives of the Andy Warhol Museum, Pittsburgh.

Courtwright, David T. *Dark Paradise: A History of Opiate Addiction in America.* Cambridge: Harvard University Press, 2001.

Cresap, Kelly M. *Pop Trickster Fool: Warhol Performs Naivete.* Urbana: University of Illinois Press, 2004.

Crimp, Douglas. "Face Value: Andy Warhol's Blow Job." *UKS-Forum for Samtidskunst.* 3–4 (1999): 9 pp. 12 March 2005 <http://www.uks.no/uksforum/arkiv/3499/html/ D.Crimp_ WarholBlowJob.html>.

———. "Getting the Warhol We Deserve: Cultural Studies and Queer Culture." *Invisible Culture: An Electronic Journal for Visual Studies* 1 (Winter 1998): 25 pp. 12 March 2005 <http://www.rochester.edu/in_visible_culture/issue1/crimp/crimp.html>.

Cullen, Countee. *Color.* New York: Harper, 1925.

Cuordileone, K. A. *Manhood and American Political Culture in the Cold War.* New York: Routledge, 2005.

Danto, Arthur C. *Beyond the Brillo Box: The Visual Arts in Post-Historical Perspective.* New York: Farrar, Straus and Giroux, 1992.

D'Aurevilly, Jules Barbey. *Dandyism.* Trans. Doublas Ainslie. New York: PAJ, 1988.

Davidson, Michael. *Guys Like Us: Citing Masculinity in Cold War Poetics.* Chicago: University of Chicago Press, 2004.

Dean, Carolyn. *The Frail Social Body: Pornography, Homosexuality and Other Fantasies in Interwar France.* Berkeley: University of California Press, 2000.

———. *Sexuality and Modern Western Culture.* New York: Twayne, 1996.

Debord, Guy. *The Society of the Spectacle.* Trans. Donald Nicholson-Smith. New York: Zone, 1994.

de Grazia, Victoria, with Ellen Furlough, eds. *The Sex of Things: Gender and Consumption in Historical Perspective.* Berkeley: University of California Press, 1996.

de Lauretis, Teresa. *The Practice of Love: Lesbian Sexuality and Perverse Desire.* Bloomington: Indiana University Press, 1994.

Deleuze, Gilles, and Félix Guattari. *A Thousand Plateaus: Capitalism and Schizophrenia.* Trans. Brian Massumi. Minneapolis: University of Minnesota Press, 1987.

D'Emilio, John. "Capitalism and Gay Identity." *Powers of Desire: The Politics of Sexuality.* Ed. Ann Snitow, Christine Stansell, and Sharon Thompson. New York: Monthly Review, 1983. 100–13.

———. "The Homosexual Menace: The Politics of Sexuality in Cold War America." *Passion and Power: Sexuality in History.* Ed. Kathy Peiss and Christina Simmons with Robert A. Padgug. Philadelphia: Temple University Press, 1989. 226–40.

———. *Sexual Politics, Sexual Communities: The Making of a Homosexual Minority in the United States, 1940–1970.* Chicago: Chicago University Press, 1983.

D'Emilio, John, and Estelle B. Freedman. *Intimate Matters: A History of Sexuality in America.* New York: Harper and Row, 1988.

DeJean, Joan. *Fictions of Sappho: 1546–1937.* Chicago: University of Chicago Press, 1989.

De Salvo, Donna M., ed. *"Success Is a Job in New York . . .": The Early Art and Business of Andy Warhol.* New York and Pittsburgh: Grey Art Gallery and the Carnegie Museum of Art, 1989.

Dickson, Lovat. *Radclyffe Hall at the Well of Loneliness: A Sapphic Chronicle.* New York: Charles Scribner's Sons, 1975.

Doan, Laura. *Fashioning Sapphism: The Origins of a Modern English Lesbian Culture.* New York: Columbia University Press, 2001.

———. "Passing Fashions: Reading Female Masculinities in the 1920s. "*Feminist Studies* 24.3 (1998): 663–700.

Dollimore, Jonathan. *Sexual Dissidence: Augustine to Wilde, Freud to Foucault.* Oxford: Clarendon Press, 1991.

Doolittle, Hilda (H.D.). *Notes on Thought and Vision and the Wise Sappho.* San Francisco: City Lights, 1982.

Douglas, Ann. "Punching a Hole in the Big Lie: The Achievement of William S. Burroughs." Introduction to *Word Virus: The William S. Burroughs Reader.* xv–xxix.

Dowling, Linda. *Language and Decadence in the Victorian Fin de Siècle.* Princeton: Princeton University Press, 1986.

———. *The Vulgarization of Art: The Victorians and Aesthetic Democracy.* Charlottesville: University Press of Virginia, 1996.

Doyle, Jennifer. "Tricks of the Trade: Pop Art/ Pop Sex." *Pop Out: Queer Warhol.* Eds. Jennifer Doyle, Jonathan Flatley, and José Esteban Muñoz. Durham: Duke University Press, 1996. 191–209.

Doyle, Jennifer, Jonathan Flatley, and José Esteban Muñoz, eds. *Pop Out: Queer Warhol.* Durham: Duke University Press, 1996.

Du Bois, W. E. B. *The Souls of Black Folks.* New York: Bantam, 1989.

Duggan, Lisa. "Making It Perfectly Queer." *Socialist Review* 22.1 (1992): 11–31.

Du Plesis, Michael. "Blatantly Bisexual; Or, Unthinking Queer Theory." *Representing Bisexualities: Subjects and Cultures of Fluid Desire.* Ed. Donald Hall and Maria Pramaggorie. New York: New York University Press, 1996. 19–54.

Dyer, Richard, with Julianne Pidduck. *Now You See It: Studies in Lesbian and Gay Film.* 2nd ed. London: Routledge, 2003.

Eagleton, Terry. "Capitalism, Modernism and Postmodernism." *New Left Review* I/152 (July–August 1985): 60–73.

Ebert, Teresa L. *Ludic Feminism and After: Postmodernism, Desire, and Labor in Late Capitalism.* Ann Arbor: University of Michigan Press, 1996.

Edelman, Lee. *Homographesis: Essays in Gay Literary and Cultural Theory.* New York: Routledge, 1994.

———. "Tearooms and Sympathy, or, The Epistemology of the Water Closet." *The Lesbian and Gay Studies Reader.* Ed. Abelove, Henry, Michele Aina Barale, and David M. Halperin. New York: Routledge, 1993. 553–74.

Engelking, Tama Lea. "Renee Vivien and the Ladies of the Lake." *Nineteenth Century French Studies* 30.3 & 4 (2002): 363–80.

Elliot, Bridget, and Jo-Ann Wallace. "Fleurs du Mal or Second-Hand Roses?: Natalie Barney, Romaine Brooks, and the 'Originality of the Avant-Garde.'" *Feminist Review.* 40 (Spring 1992): 6–30.

Ellis, Havelock. *Sexual Inversion.* Vol. 2 of *Studies in the Psychology of Sex.* New York: Random House, 1936.

Faderman, Lillian, ed. *Chloe Plus Olivia: An Anthology of Lesbian Literature from the Seventeenth Century to the Present.* New York: Penguin, 1994.

———. *Odd Girls and Twilight Lovers: A History of Lesbian Life in Twentieth-Century America.* New York: Penguin, 1992.

———. *Surpassing the Love of Men: Romantic Friendship and Love Between Women from the Renaissance to the Present.* New York: William Morrow, 1981.

Fairbrother, Trevor. "Tomorrow's Man." De Salvo. 54–74.

Fiedler, Leslie. *The Collected Essays of Leslie Feidler, Volume One.* New York: Stein and Day, 1971.

———. *The Collected Essays of Leslie Feidler, Volume Two.* New York: Stein and Day, 1971.

Feldman, Jessica. *Gender on the Divide: The Dandy in Modernist Literature.* Ithaca: Cornell University Press, 1993.

Felski, Rita. *The Gender of Modernity.* Cambridge: Harvard University Press, 1995.

Field, Nicola. *Over the Rainbow: Money, Class and Homophobia.* London: Pluto Press, 1995.

Flanner, Janet. *Paris Was Yesterday: 1925–1939.* Ed. Irving Drutman. San Diego: Harcourt Brace Jovanovich, 1988.

Flatley, Jonathan. "Warhol Gives Good Face: Publicity and the Politics of Prosopopoeia." *Pop Out: Queer Warhol*. Eds. Jennifer Doyle, Jonathan Flatley, and José Esteban Muñoz. Durham: Duke University Press, 1996. 101–33.

Floyd, Kevin. "Rethinking Reification: Marcuse, Psychoanalysis, and Gay Liberation." *Social Text* 19.1 (2001): 103–28.

———. *The Reification of Desire: Toward a Queer Marxism*. Minneapolis: University of Minnesota Press, 2009.

Foster, Hal. *The Return of the Real: The Avant-Garde at the End of the Century*. Cambridge: MIT Press, 1996.

Foster, Jeannette H. *Sex Variant Women in Literature*. Tallahassee, FL: Naiad, 1985.

Foucault, Michel. *The History of Sexuality: Volume 1: An Introduction*. Trans. Robert Hurley. New York: Vintage, 1990.

Francis, Mark, and Margery King, eds. *The Warhol Look: Glamour, Style, Fashion*. Exhibition catalogue. The Andy Warhol Museum. Boston: Little, Brown, 1997.

Fraser, Nancy. "Rethinking the Public Sphere: A Contribution to the Critique of Actually Existing Democracy." *Habermas and the Public Sphere*. Ed. Craig Calhoun. Cambridge: MIT Press, 1997. 109–42.

Freud, Sigmund. *Three Essays on the Theory of Sexuality*. Ed. and Trans. James Strachey. Revised. New York: Basic Books, 1975.

Frisby, David. *Fragments of Modernity: Theories of Modernity in the Work of Simmel, Kracauer and Benjamin*. Cambridge: MIT Press, 1986.

Fuss, Diana. *Essentially Speaking: Feminism, Nature and Difference*. New York: Routledge, 1989.

Fuss, Diana, ed. *Inside/Out: Lesbian Theories, Gay Theories*. New York: Routledge, 1991.

Gagnier, Regenia. *Idylls of the Marketplace: Oscar Wilde and the Victorian Public*. Stanford: Stanford University Press, 1986.

———. "Is Market Society the *Fin* of History." *Cultural Politics at the Fin de Siècle*. Ed. Sally Ledger and Scott McCracken. Cambridge: Cambridge University Press, 1995. 290–310.

Garber, Marjorie. *Vested Interests: Cross-Dressing and Cultural Anxiety*. New York: Routledge, 1992.

Garelick, Rhonda. *Rising Star: Dandyism, Gender and Performance in the Fin de Siècle*. Princeton: Princeton University Press, 1998.

Gates, Henry Louis. "The Black Man's Burden." *Fear of a Queer Planet: Queer Politics and Social Theory*. Ed. Michael Warner. Minneapolis: University of Minnesota Press, 1993. 230–38.

Geldzahler, Henry. *Making It New: Essays, Interviews, and Talks*. San Diego: Harcourt Brace, 1996.

Geras, Norman. *Literature of Revolution: Essays on Marxism*. London: Verso, 1986.

Giddens, Anthony. *The Consequences of Modernity*. Stanford: Stanford University Press, 1990.

Gilbert, Sandra M., and Susan Gubar. "No Man's Land: The Place of the Woman Writer in the Twentieth Century." *Sexchanges*. New Haven: Yale University Press, 1989.

Gilroy, Paul. *The Black Atlantic*. Cambridge: Harvard University Press, 1993.

Ginsberg, Allen. *Deliberate Prose: Selected Essays, 1952–1995*. New York: HarperCollins, 2000.

———. *Journals: Early Fifties, Early Sixties*. 1977. Ed. Grover Ball. Reprint, New York: Grove, 1994.

Glasgow, Joanne, ed. *Your John: The Love Letters of Radclyffe Hall*. New York: New York University Press, 1997.

Gluck, Mary. "Theorizing the Cultural Roots of the Bohemian Artist." *Modernism/Modernity* 7.3 (September 2000): 351–78.

Gramsci, Antonio. *The Antonio Gramsci Reader: Selected Writings 1916–1935*. Ed. David Forgacs. New York: New York University Press, 2000.

Gregroy, Eileen. *H.D. and Hellenism: Classic Lines*. Cambridge: Cambridge University Press, 1997.

Grundmann, Roy. *Andy Warhol's Blow Job*. Philadelphia: Temple University Press, 2003.

Gubar, Susan. *Racechanges: White Skin, Black Face in American Culture*. New York: Oxford University Press, 1997.

Habermas, Jürgen. "Modernity—An Incomplete Project." *The Anti-Aesthetic: Essays on Postmodern Culture*. Ed. Hal Foster. New York: New Press, 1999. 3–15.

———. *The Structural Transformation of the Public Sphere: An Inquiry Into a Category of Bourgeois Society*. Trans. Thomas Burger and Frederick Lawrence. Cambridge: MIT Press, 1989.

Hailey, Bruce. "Urine Sample." *Andy Warhol: Piss and Sex Paintings and Drawings*. Exhibition catalogue. New York: Gagosian Gallery, 2002. 5–9.

Halberstam, Judith. *Female Masculinity*. Durham: Duke University Press, 1998.

———. *Skin Shows: Gothic Horror and the Technology of Monsters*. Durham: Duke University Press, 1995.

Hall, Radclyffe. *The Well of Loneliness*. 1928. New York: Doubleday, 1990.

Hammonds, Evelyn. "Black (W)Holes and the Geometry of Black Male Sexuality." *differences: A Journal of Feminist Literary Studies* 6 (Summer–Fall 1994): 126–45.

Harper, Phillip Brian. *Are We Not Men?: Masculine Anxiety and the Problem of African American Identity*. New York: Oxford University Press, 1996.

Harris, Oliver. *Willam Burroughs and the Secret of Fascination*. Carbondale and Edwardsville: Southern Illinois University Press, 2003.

Harvey, David. *A Brief History of Neoliberalism*. Oxford: Oxford University Press, 2007.

———. *The Condition of Postmodernity: An Enquiry Into the Origins of Cultural Change*. Cambridge: Blackwell, 1990.

Haug, Wolfgang Fritz. *Commodity Aesthetics, Ideology and Culture*. New York: International General, 1987.

Hauser, Katherine. "George Tooker, Surveillance, and Cold War Sexual Politics." *GLQ: A Journal of Lesbian and Gay Studies* 11.3 (2005): 391–425.

Heffernan, Nick. *Capital, Class and Technology in Contemporary American Culture: Projecting Post-Fordism*. London: Pluto Press, 2000.

Hekma, Gert. "'A Female Soul in a Male Body': Sexual Inversion as Gender Inversion in Nineteenth-Century Sexology." *Third Sex, Third Gender: Beyond Sexual Dimorphism in Culture*. Ed. Gilbert Herdt. New York: Zone, 1994. 213–39.

Helming, Steve. "Constellation and Critique: Adorno's 'Constellation,' Benjamin's 'Dialectical Image.'" *Postmodern Culture*. 14.1 (September 2003).

Hennessy, Rosemary. *Profit and Pleasure: Sexual Identities in Late Capitalism*. New York: Routledge, 2000.

Henson, Leslie J. "'Articulate Silence[s]': Femme Subjectivity and Class Relations in *The Well of Loneliness*." *Fem(Me): Feminists, Lesbians, and Bad Girls*. Ed. Laura Harris and Liz Crocker. New York: Routledge, 1997. 61–67.

Herrmann, Anne. *Queering the Moderns*. New York: Palgrave, 2000.

Holcomb, Gary E. "Diaspora Cruises: Queer Black Proletarianism in Claude McKay's *A Long Way from Home*." *Modern Fiction Studies* 49.4 (2003): 714–45.

Holland, Sharon Patricia. *Raising the Dead: Readings of Death and (Black) Subjectivity*. Durham: Duke University Press, 2000.

Holleran, Andrew. *The Beauty of Men*. New York: Plume-Penguin, 1997.

Huggins, Nathan Irvin. *Harlem Renaissance*. London: Oxford University Press, 1971.

Hughes, Robert. "Man for the Machine." *Time* 17 May 1971: 80–83. *Time Capsule 7*. Archives of the Andy Warhol Museum, Pittsburgh.

Hunt, Lynn. *The Family Romance of the French Revolution*. Berkeley: University of California Press, 1992.

———. "Pornography and the French Revolution." *The Invention of Pornography: Obscenity and the Origins of Modernity, 1500–1800*. Ed. Lynn Hunt. New York: Zone, 1993. 301–39.

———. "The Unstable Boundaries of the French Revolution." *A History of Private Life*. Ed. Michelle Perrot. Vol. 4. Cambridge: Harvard University Press; Belknap Press, 1987. 13–46.

Hutchinson, George. *The Harlem Renaissance in Black and White*. Cambridge: Harvard University Press, 1995.

Huxley, Aldous. *Brave New World*. 1932. New York: HarperCollins, 1998.

Huysmans, J. K. *Against Nature.* Trans. Robert Baldick. 1884. Baltimore: Penguin, 1959.

Jagose, Annamarie. *Queer Theory: An Introduction.* New York: New York University Press, 1996.

Jameson, Frederic. *Th e Political Unconscious: Narrative as a Socially Symbolic Act.* Ithaca, NY: Cornell University Press, 1981.

———. *Postmodernism, or, the Cultural Logic of Late Capitalism.* Durham: Duke University Press, 1991.

Jay, Karla. *The Amazon and the Page: Natalie Clifford Barney and Renée Vivien.* Bloomington: Indiana University Press, 1988.

Jay, Martin. *The Dialectical Imagination: A History of the Frankfurt School and the Institute of Social Research, 1923–1950.* Berkeley: University of California Press, 1996.

Jennings, Michael W. *Dialectical Images: Walter Benjamin's Theory of Literary Criticism.* Ithaca, NY: Cornell University Press, 1987.

Johnson, Charles S., ed. *Ebony and Topaz: A Collectanea.* Freeport, NY: Books for Librairies Press, 1971.

Johnson, David K. *The Lavender Scare: The Cold War Persecution of Gays and Lesbians in the Federal Government.* Chicago: University of Chicago Press, 2004.

Jones, Caroline A. *Machine in the Studio: Constructing the Postwar American Artist.* Chicago: University of Chicago Press, 1996.

Katz, Jonathan. *Andy Warhol.* New York: Rizzoli, 1993.

Katz, Jonathan Ned. *The Invention of Heterosexuality.* New York: Dutton, 1995.

Kelley, James. "Blossoming in Strange New Forms: Male Homosexuality and the Harlem Renaissance." *Soundings* 80.4 (1997): 498–517.

Kennedy, Elizabeth Lapovsky, and Madeline D. Davis. *Boots of Leather, Slippers of Gold: The History of a Lesbian Community.* New York: Routledge, 1993.

Kerouac, Jack. *Tristessa.* 1960. Reprint, New York: Penguin, 1992.

Knadler, Steven. "Sweetback Style: Wallace Thurman and a Queer Harlem Renaissance." *Modern Fiction Studies* 48.4 (2002): 899–936.

Koch, Stephen. *Stargazer: Andy Warhol's World and His Films.* New York: Marion Boyars, 1985.

Koestenbaum, Wayne. *Andy Warhol.* New York: Penguin, 2001.

Kushner, Kenneth L., ed. *The Great Migration and After, 1917–1930.* Vol. 5 of *Black Communities and Urban Development in America, 1720–1990.* Ed. Kenneth L. Kushner. New York: Garland, 1991.

Lacan, Jacques. *The Four Fundamental Concepts of Psycho-Analysis.* Trans. Alan Sheridan. New York: W.W. Norton, 1981.

Ladenson, Elisabeth. "Colette for Export Only." *Yale French Studies* 90 (1996): 25–46.

Lafargue, Paul. *The Right to Be Lazy and Other Studies.* New York: Gordon Press, 1973.

Laity, Cassandra. "H. D. and A. C. Swinburne: Decadence and Sapphic Modernism." *Lesbian Texts and Contexts: Radical Revisions*. Eds. Karla Jay and Joanne Glasgow. New York: New York University Press, 1990.

Larrain, Jorge. *The Concept of Ideology*. Athens: University of Georgia Press, 1979.

———. *Marxism and Ideology*. London: Macmillan, 1983.

Larsen, Nella. *Quicksand and Passing*. Ed. Deborah E. McDowell. 1928;1929. New Brunswick: Rutgers University Press, 1986.

Lea, John. *Crime and Modernity: Continuities in Left Realist Criminology*. London: Sage, 2002.

Leach, William. *Land of Desire: Merchants, Power, and the Rise of a New American Culture*. New York: Pantheon, 1993.

Lefebvre, Henri. *Introduction to Modernity: Twelve Preludes, September 1959–May 1961*. Trans. John Moore. London: Verso, 1995.

Lemke, Sieglinde. *Primitivist Modernism: Black Culture and the Origins of Transatlantic Modernism*. Oxford: Oxford University Press, 1998.

Lewis, David Levering. *When Harlem Was in Vogue*. New York: Penguin, 1997.

Lippard, Lucy R. "Eros Presumptive." *Minimal Art: A Critical Anthology*. Ed. Gregory Battcock. Berkeley: University of California Press, 1995. 209–21.

Locke, Alain. "Introduction." *The New Negro*. 3–16.

———. "The Negro Spirituals." *The New Negro*. 199–213.

———, ed. *The New Negro: Voices of the Harlem Renaissance*. 1925. New York: Touchstone, 1997.

Lombardo, Patrizia. "Warhol as Dandy and Flâneur." MacCabe, Francis, and Wollen 33–40.

Lorenz, Paul. *Sapho 1900: Renée Vivien*. Paris: Julliard, 1977.

Lotringer, Sylvère, ed. *Burroughs Live: The Collected Interviews of William S. Burroughs, 1960–1997*. Los Angeles: Semiotext(e); Cambridge: MIT Press, 2001.

Lott, Eric. *Love and Theft: Blackface Minstrelsy and the American Working Class*. New York: Oxford University Press, 1993.

Lovell, Terry. *Consuming Fiction*. London: Verso, 1987.

Lucchesi, Joe. "The Dandy in Me: Romaine Brooks's 1923 Portraits." *Dandies: Fashion and Finesse in Art and Culture*. Ed. Susan Fillin-Yeh. New York: New York University Press, 2001. 153–84.

Lukács, Georg. *History and Class Consciousness: Studies in Marxist Dialectics*. Trans. Rodney Livingstone. Cambridge: MIT Press, 1971.

MacCabe, Colin, with Mark Francis and Peter Wollen, eds. *Who Is Andy Warhol?* London: British Film Institute; Pittsburgh: Andy Warhol Museum, 1997.

MacPike, Loralee. "Is Mary Llewellyn an Invert? The Modernist Supertext of *The Well of Loneliness*." *Unmanning Modernism: Gendered Re-Readings*. Ed. Elizabeth Jane Harrison and Shirley Peterson. Knoxville: University of Tennessee Press, 1997. 73–89.

Maiwald, Michael. "Race, Capitalism, and the Third-Sex Ideal: Claude McKay's *Home to Harlem* and the Legacy of Edward Carpenter." *Modern Fiction Studies* 48.4 (2002): 825–57.

Marcus, Jane. "Liberty, Sorority, Misogyny." *The Representation of Women in Fiction*. Ed. Carolyn G. Heilbrun and Margaret R. Higgonet. Baltimore: Johns Hopkins University Press, 1983. 60–97.

———. "Sapphistory: The Woolf and the Well." *Lesbian Texts and Contexts: Radical Revisions*. Ed. Karla Jay and Joanne Glasgow. New York: New York University Press, 1990. 164–79.

Marcuse, Herbert. *Eros and Civilization: A Philosophical Inquiry into Freud*. Boston: Beacon, 1966.

———. "Liberation from the Affluent Society." *Critical Theory and Society: A Reader*. Ed. Stephen Eric Bronner and Douglas MacKay Kellner. New York: Routledge, 1989. 276–87.

———. *Negations: Essays in Critical Theory*. Trans. Jeremy J. Shapiro. Boston: Beacon, 1968.

———. *One-Dimensional Man: Studies in the Ideology of Advanced Industrial Society*. Boston: Beacon, 1966.

Marks, Elaine. "Lesbian Intertextuality." *Homosexualities and French Literature: Cultural Contexts/Critical Texts*. Ed. George Stambolian and Elaine Marks. Ithaca, NY: Cornell University Press, 1979. 353–77.

Marler, Regina, ed. *Queer Beats: How the Beats Turned America On to Sex*. San Francisco: Cleis, 2004.

Martin, Biddy. "Sexualities Without Genders and Other Queer Utopias." *Diacritics* 24.2–3 (1994): 104–21.

Martinez, Manuel Luis. *Countering the Counterculture: Rereading Postwar American Dissent from Jack Kerouac to Tomás Rivera*. Madison: University of Wisconsin Press, 2003.

Marx, Karl. *Capital: A Critique of Political Economy: Volume One*. Trans. Ben Fowkes. London: Penguin; New Left Review, 1990.

———. *Early Writings*. Trans. Rodney Livingstone and Gregor Benton. London: Penguin; New Left Review, 1992. 211–41.

———. *Grundrisse: Foundations of the Critique of Political Economy*. Trans. Martin Nicolaus. New York: Random House, 1973.

———. "On the Jewish Question." Trans. Rodney Livingstone and Gregor Benton. *Early Writings*. London: Penguin; New Left Review, 1992. 211–41.

Marx, Karl, and Frederick Engels. *The Communist Manifesto: A Modern Edition*. London: Verso, 1998.

Matthews, Geoffrey. "Laughing All the Way to the Trash Can." *London Evening News*. 25 February 1971: 10. *Time Capsule 7*. Archives of the Andy Warhol Museum, Pittsburgh.

Maxwell, William J. *New Negro, Old Left: African American Writing and Communism Between the Wars*. New York: Columbia University Press, 1999.

McBreen, Ellen. "Biblical Gender Bending in Harlem: The Queer Performance of Nugent's *Salome*." 57.3 (1998): 22–28.

McBride, Dwight. "Can the Queen Speak? Racial Essentialism, Sexuality and the Problem of Authority." *Callaloo* 21.2 (1998): 363–79.

Mepham, John. "Theory of Ideology in Capital." *Issues in Marxist Philosophy: Epistemology, Science, Ideology*. Ed. John Mepham and David-Hillel Ruben. Vol. 3. Atlantic Highlands, NJ: Humanities, 1979. 141–73.

Mercer, Kobena. *Welcome to the Jungle: New Positions in Black Cultural Studies*. New York: Routledge, 1994.

Mercer, Kobena, and Isaac Julien. "Race, Sexual Politics and Black Masculinity: A Dossier." *Male Order: Unwrapping Masculinity*. Ed. Rowena Chapman and Jonathan Rutherford. London: Lawrence and Wishart, 1988. 97–165.

Merck, Mandy. *Perversions: Deviant Readings*. New York: Routledge, 1993.

Mészáros, István. "Lukács' Concept of the Dialectic." *Georg Lukács: The Man, His Work and His Ideas*. Ed. G. H. R. Parkinson. New York: Random House, 1970. 34–85.

Meyer, Richard. *Outlaw Representation: Censorship and Homosexuality in Twentieth-Century American Art*. Boston: Beacon, 2002.

———. "Warhol's Clones." *Negotiating Lesbian and Gay Subjects*. Eds. Monica Dorenkamp and Richard Henke. New York: Routledge, 1995. 92–122.

Miles, Barry. *William Burroughs: El Hombre Invisible*. London: Virgin, 1992.

Miller, D. A. *The Novel and the Police*. Berkeley: University of California Press, 1988.

Miller, Monica L. "The Black Dandy as Bad Modernist." *Bad Modernisms*. Ed. Douglas Mao and Rebecca L. Walkowitz. Durham: Duke University Press, 2006. 179–205.

———. "W.E.B. Du Bois and the Dandy as Diasporic Race Man." *Callaloo* 26.3 (2003): 738–65.

Miller, Neil. *Sex-Crime Panic: A Journey to the Parnoid Heart of the 1950s*. Los Angeles: Alyson, 2002.

Moers, Ellen. *The Dandy: Brummell to Beerbohm*. New York: Viking, 1960.

Morelyle, Jason. "Speculating Freedom: Addiction, Control and Rescriptive Subjectivity in the Work of William S. Burroughs." *Retaking the Universe: William S. Burroughs in the Age of Globalization*. Ed. Davis Schneiderman and Philip Walsh. London: Pluto, 2004. 74–86.

Morphet, Richard. "Andy Warhol." *Warhol.* Exhibition catalogue. London: Tate Gallery, 1971. 8–34. *Time Capsule 44*. Archives of the Andy Warhol Museum, Pittsburgh.

Morton, Donald, ed. *Marxism, Queer Theory, Gender Transformation—Marxist Boundary Work in Theory, Economics, Politics, and Culture.* Syracuse: Red Factory, 2001.

———, ed. *The Material Queer: A LesBiGay Cultural Studies Reader.* Boulder: Westview Press, 1996.

Mosse, George L. *The Image of Man: The Creation of Modern Masculinity.* New York: Oxford University Press, 1996.

Mullins, Greg A. *Colonial Affairs: Bowles, Burroughs and Chester Write Tangiers.* Madison: Univeristy of Wisconsin Press, 2002.

Murphy, Timothy S. *Wising Up the Marks: The AModern William Burroughs.* Berkeley: University of California Press, 1997.

Nadel, Alan. *Containment Culture: American Narratives, Postmodernism, and the Atomic Age.* Durham: Duke University Press, 1995.

Namaste, Ki. "Tragic Misreadings: Queer Theory's Erasure of Transgender Subjectivity." *Queer Studies: A Lesbian, Gay, Bisexual and Transgender Anthology.* Ed. Brett Beemyn and Mickey Eliason. New York: New York University Press, 1996. 183–203.

Nestle, Joan. *A Restricted Country.* Ithaca, NY: Firebrand, 1987.

Newton, Esther. "The Mythic Mannish Lesbian: Radclyffe Hall and the New Woman." *Hidden from History: Reclaiming the Gay and Lesbian Past.* Ed. Martin Duberman, Martha Vicinus, and George Chauncey, Jr. New York: Meridian, 1990. 281–93.

———. "Role Models." [Excerpt from *Mother Camp: Female Impersonators in America.* Englewood Cliffs: Prentice Hall, 1972] Cleto. 96–109.

Nicholls, David G. *Conjuring the Folk: Forms of Modernity in African America.* Ann Arbor: University of Michigan Press, 2000.

Nochlin, Linda. "'Sex Is So Abstract': The Nudes of Andy Warhol." *Andy Warhol Nudes.* Ed. John Cheim. New York: Robert Miller Gallery and Overlook Press, 1995. n.p.

Nugent, Richard Bruce. [Richard Bruce, pseud.]. "Smoke, Lilies and Jade." *FIRE!!.* I (November 1926): 33–39.

Nunokawa, Jeff. *Tame Passions of Wilde: The Styles of Manageable Desire.* Princeton: Princeton University Press, 2003.

Ollman, Bertell. *Dance of the Dialectic: Steps in Marx's Method.* Urbana and Chicago: University of Illinois Press, 2003.

———. *Dialectical Investigations.* New York: Routledge, 1993.

Parkes, Adam. *Modernism and the Theater of Censorship.* New York: Oxford University Press, 1996.

Perrin, Stephen. "Hero and Heroin: Opiate Use and Sexual Identity." *Dionysos: The Literature and Addiction Triquarterly* 4.3 (1993): 25–29.

Ponce, Martin Joseph. "Langston Hughes's Queer Blues." *Modern Language Quarterly* 66.4 (December 2005): 505–37.

Prins, Yopie. *Victorian Sappho.* Princeton: Princeton University Press, 1999.

Prosser, Jay. *Second Skins: The Body Narratives of Transsexuality.* New York: Columbia University Press, 1998.

———. "Transsexuals and Transsexologists: Inversion and the Emergence of Transsexual Subjectivity." *Sexology in Culture: Labelling Bodies and Desires.* Ed. Lucy Bland and Laura Doan. Chicago: University of Chicago Press, 1998. 116–31.

Raby, Peter, ed. *The Cambridge Companion to Oscar Wilde.* Cambridge: Cambridge University Press, 1997.

Radford, Jean. "An Inverted Romance: *The Well of Loneliness* and Sexual Ideology." *The Progress of Romance: The Politics of Popular Fiction.* Ed. Jean Radford. London: Routledge, 1986. 97–111.

Rampersad, Arnold. *The Art and Imagination of W.E.B. Du Bois.* New York: Schocken, 1990.

———. "Introduction." *The New Negro: Voices of the Harlem Renaissance.* Ed. Alain Locke, 1997. ix–xxiii.

Ratcliff, Carter. *Warhol.* New York: Abbeville Press, 1983.

Ray, Chelsea. "Decadent Heroines or Modernist Lovers: Natalie Clifford Barney's Unpublished *Feminine Lovers or the Third Woman.*" *South Central Review* 22.3 (2005): 32–61.

Reid, Norman. Forward. *Warhol.* Exhibition catalogue. London: Tate Gallery, 1971. 5. *Time Capsule 44.* Archives of the Andy Warhol Museum, Pittsburgh.

Rhodes, Chip. *Structures of the Jazz Age: Mass Culture, Progressive Education, and Racial Discourse in American Modernism.* London: Verso, 1998.

Richards, Thomas. *The Commodity Culture of Victorian England: Advertising and Spectacle, 1851–1914.* Stanford: Stanford University Press, 1990.

Roberts, Mary Louise. "Gender, Consumption, and Commodity Culture." *The American Historical Review.* 103.3 (June 1998): 817–44.

Roediger, David R. *The Wages of Whiteness: Race and the Making of the American Working Class.* London: Verso, 1991.

Rosaldo, Renato. "Imperialist Nostalgia." *Representations* 26 (1989): 107–22.

Ross, Andrew. "Uses of Camp." *Camp Grounds: Style and Homosexuality.* Ed. David Bergman. Amherst: University of Massachusetts Press, 1993. 54–77.

Ruehl, Sonja. "Inverts and Experts: Radclyffe Hall and the Lesbian Identity." *Feminism, Culture, and Politics.* Ed. Rosalind Brunt and Caroline Rowan. London: Lawrence, 1982. 15–36.

Rule, Jane. *Lesbian Images*. Garden City, NY: Doubleday, 1975.

Russell, Jamie. *Queer Burroughs*. New York: Palgrave, 2001.

Said, Edward. *Orientalism*. New York: Vintage, 1979.

Sappho. *Sappho: A Garland: The Poems and Fragments of Sappho*. Trans. Jim Powell. New York: Farrar, Straus, and Giroux, 1993.

Savran, David. *Taking It Like a Man: White Masculinity, Masochism and Contemporary American Culture*. Princeton: Princeton University Press, 1998.

Scalon, Jennifer, ed. *The Gender and Consumer Culture Reader*. New York: New York University Press, 2000.

Scott, Bonnie Kime. *Refiguring Modernism: The Women of 1928*. Bloomington: Indiana University Press, 1995.

Sedgwick, Eve Kosofsky. *Epistemology of the Closet*. Berkeley: University of California Press, 1990.

———, ed. *Novel Gazing: Queer Readings in Fiction*. Durham: Duke University Press, 1997.

Sender, Katherine. *Business, Not Politics: The Making of a Gay Market*. New York: Columbia University Press, 2004.

Server, Lee. *Over My Dead Body: The Sensational Age of the American Paperback, 1945–1955*. San Francisco: Chronicle, 1994.

Shaviro, Steven. "Warhol before the Mirror." MacCabe, Francis and Wollen 89–95.

Shore, Stephen [photographs] and Lynne Tillman [text]. *The Velvet Years: Warhol's Factory 1965–67*. New York: Thunder Mouth Press, 1995.

Showalter, Elaine. *Sexual Anarchy: Gender and Culture at the Fin de Siècle*. New York: Penguin, 1990.

Shwarz, A. B. Christa. *Gay Voices of the Harlem Renaissance*. Bloomington: Indiana University Press, 2003.

Siegal, Marc. "Doing It for Andy." *Art Journal* Spring 2003: 6–13.

Silberman, Seth Clark. "Lighting the Harlem Renaissance *AFire!!*: Embodying Richard Bruce Nugent's Bohemian Politic." *The Greatest Taboo: Homosexuality in Black Communities*. Ed. Delroy Constantine-Simms. Los Angeles: Alyson, 2000. 254–73.

Silverman, Debora L. *Art Nouveau in Fin-de-Siècle France: Politics, Psychology, and Style*. Berkeley: University of California Press, 1989.

Sinfield, Alan. *The Wilde Century: Effeminacy, Oscar Wilde and the Queer Moment*. New York: Columbia University Press, 1994.

Slater, Don. *Consumer Culture and Modernity*. Cambridge, UK: Polity, 1997.

Smith, Charles Michael. "Bruce Nugent: Bohemian of the Harlem Renaissance." *In the Life: A Black Gay Anthology*. Ed. Joseph Beam. Boston: Alyson, 1986. 209–20.

Smith, John W., ed. *Possession Obsession: Andy Warhol and Collecting*. Exhibition catalogue. Pittsburgh: The Andy Warhol Museum, 2002.

Smith-Rosenberg, Carroll. "Discourses in Sexuality and Subjectivity: The New Woman, 1870–1936." *Hidden from History: Reclaiming the Gay and Lesbian Past*. Ed. Martin Duberman, Martha Vicinus, and George Chauncey, Jr. New York: Meridian, 1990. 264–80.

Snodgrass, Chris. *Aubrey Beardsley, Dandy of the Grotesque*. New York: Oxford University Press, 1995.

Somerville, Siobhan B. *Queering the Color Line*. Durham: Duke University Press, 2000.

———. "Scientific Racism and the Invention of the Homosexual Body." *Sexology in Culture: Labelling Bodies and Desires*. Ed. Lucy Bland and Laura Doan. Chicago: University of Chicago Press, 1998. 60–76.

Sontag, Susan. *Against Interpretation and Other Essays*. New York: Farrar, Straus, and Giroux, 1967.

Souhami, Diana. *The Trials of Radclyffe Hall*. London: Weidenfeld & Nicolson, 1998.

Steiner, Wendy. *Venus in Exile: The Rejection of Beauty in Twentieth-Century Art*. New York: Free Press, 2001.

Stevenson, Robert Louis. *Dr. Jekyl and Mr. Hyde*. New York: Signet-Penguin, 1987.

Stewart, Susan. *On Longing: Narratives of the Miniature, the Gigantic, the Souvenir, the Collection*. Durham: Duke University Press, 1993.

Stimpson, Catherine R. "Zero Degree Deviancy: The Lesbian Novel in English." *Critical Inquiry* 8.2 (Winter 1981): 363–79.

Stovall, Tyler. *Paris Noir: African Americans in the City of the Light*. Boston: Houghton Mifflin, 1996.

Stryker, Susan. *Queer Pulp: Perverted Passions from the Golden Age of Pulp*. San Francisco: Chronicle Books, 2001.

Suárez, Juan A. *Bike Boys, Drag Queens, and Superstars: Avant-Garde, Mass Culture, and Gay Identities in the 1960s Underground Cinema*. Bloomington: Indiana University Press, 1996.

Szalay, Miklós, ed. *African Art from the Han Coray Collection*. Munich: Prestel, 1998.

Thomas, Kendall. "'Ain't Nothin' Like the Real Thing': Black Masculinity, Gay Sexuality, and the Jargon of Authenticity." *The House That Race Built: Black Americans, U.S. Terrain*. Ed. Wahneema Lubiano. New York: Pantheon Books, 1997. 116–35.

Thurman, Wallace. *Infants of the Spring*. 1932. Boston: Northeastern University Press, 1992.

Tinkcom, Matthew. *Working Like a Homosexual: Camp, Capital, Cinema*. Durham: Duke University Press, 1992.

Tomkins, Calvin. *Duchamp: A Biography*. New York: Henry Holt, 1996.

Troubridge, Una. *The Life and Death of Radclyffe Hall.* London: Hammond, 1961.

Twitchell, James. *The Living Dead: A Study of Vampire in Romantic Literature.* Durham: Duke University Press, 1981.

Tyler, Parker. "Dragtime and Drugtime; Or Film a la Warhol." 1967. *Andy Warhol Film Factory.* Ed. Michael O'Pray. London: British Film Institute, 1997.

Van Vetchen, Carl. *Nigger Heaven.* Champaign: University of Illinois Press, 2000.

Veblen, Thorstein. *The Theory of the Leisure Class.* New York: Sentry, 1965.

Vicinus, Martha. "'They Wonder to Which Sex I Belong': The Historical Roots of the Modern Lesbian Identity." *The Lesbian and Gay Studies Reader.* Ed. Henry Abelove, Michèle Aina Barale, and David M. Halperin. New York: Routledge, 1993. 432–52.

Vivien, Renée. *At the Sweet Hour of Hand in Hand.* Trans. Sandia Belgrade. 1906. Tallahassee, FL: Naiad, 1979.

———. *The Muse of Violets.* Trans. Margaret Porter and Catherine Kroger. Bates City, MO: Naiad, 1977.

———. *Poèmes de Renée Vivien.* New York: Arno, 1975.

———. *A Woman Appeared to Me.* Trans. Jeannette Foster. 1904. Tallahassee, FL: Naiad, 1982.

———. *The Woman of the Wolf and Other Stories.* Trans. Karla Jay and Yvonne M. Klein. New York: Gay Presses of New York, 1983.

Wagner, Peter. "Modernity, Capitalism and Critique." *Thesis Eleven* 66 (August 2001):1–31.

Waldrep, Shelton. *The Aesthetics of Self-Invention: Oscar Wilde to David Bowie.* Minneapolis: University of Minnesota Press, 2004.

Walters, Suzanna Danuta. *All the Rage: The Story of Gay Visibility in America.* Chicago: University of Chicago Press, 2001.

Warhol, Andy. *Andy Warhol: Drawings and Illustrations of the 1950s.* Ed. Ivan Vartanian. New York and Tokyo: Distributed Art Publishers and Goliga Books, 2000.

——— [with Pat Hackett]. *The Andy Warhol Diaries.* Ed. Pat Hackett. New York: Warner Books, 1989.

——— [with Pat Hackett]. *The Philosophy of Andy Warhol (From A to B and Back Again).* New York: Harcourt Brace, 1977.

Warhol, Andy, and Pat Hackett. *POPism: The Warhol Sixties.* New York: Harper and Row, 1983.

Warner, Michael, ed. *Fear of a Queer Planet: Queer Politics and Social Theory.* Minneapolis: University of Minnesota Press, 1993.

Watson, Steven. *The Birth of the Beat Generation: Visionaries, Rebels, and Hipsters, 1944–1960.* New York: Pantheon, 1995.

———. *Factory Made: Warhol and the Sixties*. New York: Pantheon, 2003.

———. *The Harlem Renaissance: Hub of African American Culture, 1920–1930*. New York: Pantheon, 1995.

Waugh, Thomas. "Cockteaser." Doyle et al. 51–77.

Webb, Barbara. "The Black Dandyism of George Walker: A Case Study in Geneological Method." *Drama Review* 45.4 (2001): 7–24.

Weed, Elizabeth. "The More Things Change." *differences: A Journal of Feminist Literary Studies* 6.2–3 (1994): 249–73.

Weeks, Jeffrey. *Sex, Politics and Society: The Regulation of Sexuality Since 1800*. 2nd ed. London: Longman, 1989.

Weir, David. *Decadence and the Making of Modernism*. Amherst: University of Massachusetts Press, 1995.

Weiss, Andrea. *Paris Was a Woman: Portraits from the Left Bank*. San Francisco: Harper San Francisco, 1995.

Whimsy, Lord Breaulove Swells. *The Affected Provincial's Companion, Volume I*. New York: Bloomsbury, 2006.

———. "Men of the Cloth," *Swindle* 8 (2006): 145–52.

Whitlock, Gillian. "'Everything Is Out of Place': Radclyffe Hall and the Lesbian Literary Tradition." *Feminist Studies* 13.3 (Fall 1987): 555–82.

Wickes, George. *The Amazon Letters: The Life and Loves of Natalie Barney*. London: Allen, 1977.

Wilde, Oscar. *The Complete Works of Oscar Wilde*. New York: Barnes and Noble, 1994.

———. *The Picture of Dorian Gray and Other Writings*. New York: Bantam, 1982.

Williams, Rosalind H. *Dream Worlds: Mass Consumption in Late Nineteenth-Century France*. Berkeley: University of California Press, 1982.

Wilson, Elizabeth. "Forbidden Love." *Feminist Studies*. 10.2 (Summer 1984): 213–326.

Wilson, Simon. *Beardsley*. New York: E. P. Dutton, 1976.

Wilson, William. "'Prince of Boredom': The Repetitions and Passivities of Andy Warhol." *Art and Artists*. March 1968: 13–15. *Time Capsule 15*. Archives of the Andy Warhol Museum, Pittsburgh.

Wintz, Cary D. *Black Culture and the Harlem Renaissance*. Houston: Rice University Press, 1988.

Wirth, Thomas H., ed. *Gay Rebel of the Harlem Renaissance: Selections from the Work of Richard Bruce Nugent*. Durham: Duke University Press, 2002.

Wolff, Janet. *The Social Production of Art*. 2nd ed. New York: New York University Press, 1993.

Wollen, Peter. *Raiding the Icebox: Reflections on Twentieth-Century Culture*. Bloomington: Indiana University Press, 1993.

Wood, Ellen Meiksins. *The Origins of Capitalism: A Longer View.* London: Verso, 2002.

Zola, Emile. *Nana.* Trans. George Holden. 1880. Harmondsworth: Penguin, 1972.

FILM SOURCES

Warhol, dir. *Blow Job.* Black-and-white, silent, 41 minutes at 16fps, 1964.

———, dir. *Couch.* Black-and-white, silent, 58 minutes at 16fps, 1964.

———, dir. *Sleep.* Black-and-white, silent, 5 hours, 21 minutes at 16fps, 1963.

ARCHIVAL SOURCES

Archives of the Andy Warhol Museum, Pittsburgh. Time Capsules; commercial drawings from the 1940s and 1950s; private drawings from the 1950s; source materials.

INDEX

Note: Page numbers with an "f" indicate figures.